# The Soviet View of War, Peace and Neutrality

**P. H. Vigor**

*Soviet Studies Centre,*
*Royal Military Academy Sandhurst*

Routledge & Kegan Paul
London and Boston

*First published in 1975*
*by Routledge & Kegan Paul Ltd*
*Broadway House, 68-74 Carter Lane,*
*London EC4V 5EL and*
*9 Park Street,*
*Boston, Mass. 02108, USA*
*Set in Monotype Plantin*
*and printed in Great Britain by*
*John Sherratt & Son*
*St Ann's Press, Park Road, Altrincham,*
*Cheshire WA14 5QQ*

*ISBN 0 7100 8143 X*

# Contents

# Acknowledgments

I am extremely grateful to Professor John Erickson, of the University of Edinburgh, who has read the whole of the typescript. Also to Professor Michael MccGwire, of Dalhousie University, Nova Scotia and to Mr Richard Luckett, of St Catharine's College, Cambridge, both of whom read the second chapter. Mr Luckett also read the chapter on 'Peace'. The comments and suggestions put forward by these three distinguished people have, for the most part, been incorporated into this book; and where I have failed to do so, I have only myself to blame.

I must also thank the staff of the Central Library, RMA Sandhurst; of St Antony's College, Oxford; and of the library at Chatham House for their unfailing patience and courtesy to me while I was writing this book. Without their help it would certainly never have got written.

# I  Whose View?

The present population of the Soviet Union is approximately 250,000,000. It is obvious that I have not been able to ask the view of each one of this vast number for his personal opinion of the subjects discussed in this book; so that, when I entitle it The Soviet View of War, Peace and Neutrality, the view I describe must necessarily be selective.

It is, in fact, an *extremely* selective view; for it is that of no more than the twenty or thirty people who are today the rulers of the Soviet Union, and of those who have been its rulers in years gone by.

However, although I may have concentrated my attention upon a mere handful of the teeming millions who make up the population of the Soviet Union, nevertheless, in doing so, I have not thereby completely ignored the feelings and opinions of the latter. For the views of that handful of men who make up the Politburo have themselves inevitably been influenced (and frequently sharply influenced) by those of their fellow-citizens. It is often said of Khrushchev that he had a peasant mentality; but this, if true, must have been largely due to the fact that he was born into a peasant household, was reared by peasants, grew up with peasants, and, in so far as he had any primary schooling, he got it at a peasant school. No man is an island. It is true that a man who makes his career in the Soviet Communist Party does tend more and more to isolate himself from the 'lay' public opinion of the USSR; but he cannot possibly isolate himself completely.

Indeed, it is almost certainly true that many of the changes which have occurred in Soviet thinking in recent years have *not* originated with the leadership at the top, but have been suggested by subordinates from below—perhaps sometimes by people who were not even members of the Communist Party. Nevertheless this, which I believe to be true, does not at all invalidate the conception of this book; for, in the Soviet Union, no suggestions of any importance are implemented unless they have first been approved by the men at the top. It may not have been the Politburo, for instance, who originated the doctrine of 'peaceful coexistence'; but until the Politburo had approved it, Lenin's old thesis of the inevitability of war between capitalism and communism was the basic premiss on which Soviet foreign policy was largely based.

A*

It is the purpose of this book to examine such basic premisses.

But if one is going to concern oneself with the reasons for a set of decisions, one must clearly also concern oneself with the decision makers. By a great stroke of luck for the student of the USSR, these latter are not only readily identifiable, but they also subscribe to a common philosophical doctrine. They may (and no doubt do) disagree on questions of tactics; but on questions of strategy they show a remarkable cohesion. And this cohesion is due to the fact that they have all accepted, and devoted their lives to the service of, a strict, rigidly defined set of philosophical beliefs which derive from Marx and Lenin and their successors.

This set of beliefs is all-embracing; there is no sector of human thought and activity which is not covered by it. Thus there is, for example, a communist theory of war. War, that is to say, has been analysed by the Party; its nature has been dissected, its uses explained; and the appropriate Soviet reference books will tell you what sort of wars are acceptable to the Party leadership, and what are not. They will also tell you in what circumstances the acceptable wars are thought to be likely to be beneficial to the communist cause, and precisely what those benefits are likely to be. Similar guidelines exist for the other concepts and the other factors which have so much influence upon Soviet foreign policy.[1]

I therefore felt that it was not only possible, but also well worth while, to attempt to set before the ordinary Western reader the general outline of these various Soviet analyses; so that he would have in his mind at least the basic principles which lie behind the approach of the communist leaders to such concepts as war, peace and neutrality.

Of course, I would not be so foolish as to maintain that everything that the USSR has done in the field of international affairs (or in domestic affairs, for that matter) has been done in complete accord with the theories of Leninism. No man, and no set of men, has ever succeeded in making his every action square with his professed principles. Saints have erred; princes of the Church have sinned; and Soviet Party leaders, who have on their shoulders the enormous and complex task of running a vast country, have failed to reconcile their own particular principles with their own practice as often as anyone else. But just as no student of the history of Western Europe who did not also possess at least some knowledge of the teachings of the Christian religion could have much more than a narrow unreal idea of his subject, so no student of the politics of the USSR, or of its economics, can really have much idea of what lies behind them, unless he is also aware of the Leninist doctrines on those particular aspects he is considering.

The proof of the pudding is in the eating. The Soviet attitude towards China in the period between the wars was very largely determined by ideological considerations. No one can have more than an extremely superficial understanding of why Stalin behaved in the way that he did towards Chiang Kai-Shek and Mao Tse-tung respectively, unless that person has grasped the basic principles of the Marxist-Leninist theory of 'the National Liberation Movement' (a theory which, incidentally, I would like to discuss in detail in another book).

Nor is this just one isolated instance, drawn from foreign policy. In the realm of domestic policy, the enormous delays and difficulties which have recently been experienced in trying to improve the functioning of the Soviet economy have been at least partly due to ideological objections to the Liberman reforms. That the reforms have nevertheless been implemented at least to some extent is undoubtedly a proof that, when the need is great enough, ideology can be overruled; but the strength of Soviet ideology can be shown precisely in this, that the reforms have not really been implemented in the way which the reformers desired. Their key proposal smacked too much of the market mechanism: such a mechanism is repugnant to Marxist-Leninism; and the result is that only an emasculated version of it has been allowed to be put into practice.

But if this is true, where are these Marxist-Leninist doctrines to be found? Luckily again, there is no difficulty in finding them. The Communist Party of the Soviet Union, like any other tightly disciplined body, finds it essential, in order to rebut heresy, to define clearly the Party's attitude towards everything under the sun; to publish those definitions; and to make those publications readily available. In this respect, the Catholic Church acts in the same way; and so does the British Army. As a result, there are not only the works of the founders of Marxism-Leninism and their successors which can be consulted, but also a whole series of specialized 'dictionaries', 'programmes' and encyclopaedias, whose main object is to inform the Party membership and any potential proselyte of what is—and what is not—the correct view about any subject that you care to mention.

These publications are an essential tool for the student of the USSR. Not that by this I mean to imply that everything to be found in them is correct. On the contrary, many of the statements that they contain are doubtful, to say the least. For instance, *A Dictionary of Philosophy* declares that the reason why the rulers of the Roman Empire were interested in Christianity was because it did not affect the class foundations of their society, but did give divine sanction to the existing oppression.[2] This assertion, however, can hardly be regarded as an unchallengeable truth. Nevertheless, true or not, this was in 1967 the Party's approved view of the matter; and this was the view that the rest of the Soviet population was expected either to have, or at least to profess to have, on the particular subject in question.

Of course, it is true that, even in the Soviet Communist Party, opinions change. What was heresy yesterday is orthodoxy today. But in the USSR, when today comes, and the old heresy is the new orthodoxy, the Party takes care to make the position plain. It may teach at one moment that war between capitalism and communism is inevitable; and, at another, that it is not; but *at any one moment* it teaches the *same thing* throughout the length and breadth of the Soviet Union.

This latter point is often insufficiently appreciated in the West. For instance, the appearance of Solzhenitsyn's novel, *A Day in the Life of Ivan Denisovich*, was hailed by many Westerners as evidence that Russia was getting more liberal. But whether Russia was getting more liberal or not, the fact that Solzhenitsyn's novel was allowed to appear in print had nothing whatever to do with the matter. The Soviet leadership was engaged in de-Stalinization; *A Day in the Life of Ivan Denisovich* is an attack on Stalinism; the novel therefore was perfectly suited to the needs of the Party at that moment, and so was allowed to appear. The only valid evidence for the liberalization of Russia at that moment would have been the permission to publish *at that moment* a novel lauding Stalin to the skies.[3]

But of course there was no real liberalization of Russia, whether at that moment or subsequently. The *same* view of any political question continued to be propagated throughout the country; and the view that was propagated was, naturally enough, the view that was held by the Party.

But the Party is not merely a propagator of views; it is also the ruler of the country. As a result, it is the Party's views which determine the country's policies. The policies of the Soviet Union which seem to me to be of the greatest concern to the ordinary Western reader are those which relate to the fundamental questions of war, peace and neutrality; it is on these policies, therefore, that I want to concentrate. But in order to understand them, one has first got to understand the views and premisses that led to their formulation. As we have seen, these, in the case of the USSR, are the views and premisses of the Communist Party. So it is upon the Soviet Communist Party's views and premisses with regard to war, peace and neutrality (or, to be more accurate, the views and premisses of the Politburo) that I have concentrated in this book.

Hence the name of Trotsky is scarcely mentioned in it. For, most of Trotsky's contributions to the *theory* of war have been rejected by the Soviet Communist Party; and those that have not, have been unobtrusively assimilated into present Party doctrine by the simple process of ascribing them to Frunze or some other acceptable foster-parent. Trotsky's contributions to the *practice* of war have suffered a similar fate.

# 2    The Soviet View of War

## An introductory summary of the Soviet attitude to war

Many strands of the Marxist theory of war, and of the Soviet practice of that theory, are very strange to the ordinary Western reader. He tends to regard war nowadays as a terrible disaster which bursts upon men as a kind of act of God, erupting for no known reason and conducted for purposes which are never implemented when the fighting has finally stopped. The First World War, for instance, is generally portrayed by Western historians as coming about almost irrespective of the governments of the future combatants, as a result of a fatal mixture of human folly, the conflicting interests of the major European powers, and the peculiarities of the railway train as a vehicle for mass mobilization.[1] (This view, it should be added, was never that of Lenin.)[2]

Moreover, it is generally agreed nowadays by Western historians that the Treaty of Versailles, which ended that war, did not settle anything, a view which Lenin was vigorously propagating more than forty years ago;[3] and the West in consequence tends to believe that the Second World War was caused by a fatal mixture of the varied consequences of the Treaty of Versailles, the state of the German economy in the early 1930s, and the paranoia of Hitler. Soviet historians concur with this analysis only in respect of the consequences of the Treaty of Versailles; in other respects their view of the origins of the Second World War differs sharply from the Western.[4]

It is because of this considerable divergence between the communist and the Western attitudes towards the subject of war, and also of peace and neutrality, that the present work, before proceeding to a detailed discussion, begins with a synopsis of the way in which the Soviet Politburo looks at war, peace and neutrality today, and under what circumstances it indulges in them or refrains from indulging in them; for an understanding of the basic tenets is essential for a proper appreciation of the detailed arguments that follow. Here, then, is the synopsis.

Fundamentally, the concept of war is alien to a Marxist-Leninist. War is the result (almost the automatic result) of the existence of classes in society: war is therefore a servile thing, a feudal thing, a capitalist thing; it is not a communist thing. When communism has been established throughout the world, war will inevitably vanish; so, from the point of view of a Soviet statesman, war is 'them' and what 'they' do; it has little to do with 'us'.

Nevertheless, despite the theory, it does have something to do with the Soviet Union. Communism has not yet been established even in the USSR: the society that is to be found there is officially described as 'socialist'. A socialist state is a one-class state, ruled by the 'proletariat' (though the USSR is nowadays said to be a state 'of the whole people', and therefore presumably ruled by 'the whole people'). In either case, there exists a ruling class which, just like any non-Marxist ruling class, can make use of war to further its own class interests. According to the first edition of the *Bol'shaya Sovietskaya Entsiklopediya*, this was exactly what the Soviet Government did in the course of the war with Poland in 1920, and again in Georgia in 1921.[5]

But two things are obviously necessary if a ruling class is in fact going to further its interests by starting a war. The first is that war should be the most expedient instrument in furthering that class's interests in the particular circumstances of the time. To indulge in war when peaceful negotiation or threats or bribery or even substantial concessions might attain the same end at less overall cost would be, in Marxist eyes, the height of political irresponsibility. In this, their attitude contrasts sharply with that inbred in generation after generation of Europeans: that war is basically the proper occupation of a gentleman (indeed, in the days of chivalry, the *major* occupation of a gentleman); and this sentiment has been so strongly implanted that not even the horrors of two world wars and the threat of a still more terrible one has quite succeeded in rooting out that sentiment.

The second essential pre-requisite is that victory should be assured— if one loses a war, one fails to secure one's objectives. Consequently, the Soviet Union has never willingly engaged in war except under conditions where victory could be regarded as certain. A glance through Soviet history will show that, on those occasions where the USSR has initiated the use of force, in each case she could be absolutely confident of winning.

War, then, is a tool to be picked up and used for a particular purpose; and by the same token it is to be laid aside, so soon as that purpose has been accomplished. In 1929, when the Chinese Government unilaterally announced that the Soviet rights to the management of the Chinese Eastern Railway were thenceforth to be regarded as being solely the property of China, Russian forces crossed the frontier, seized Manchuli, and proceeded to advance upon Harbin. Chinese attempts at resistance proved wholly futile; and very soon the Chinese Government was glad to come to terms with the Russian Government, and acknowledge the Russian *status quo* on the railway.[6] So soon as this had been done, and so soon therefore as the Russians had attained their purpose, they stopped the war.

Soviet war aims, admittedly, are not always so neatly formulated or so precise as this example perhaps might seem to indicate. In the Winter War against Finland in 1939–40, the demands varied according to the circumstances of the time (according, that is, to the degree of difficulty that faced the Russians at any particular moment). Their initial demands were comparatively limited, for instance, because then the Soviet Government was not quite sure what help the Finns might get from foreign governments. But those enshrined in the Treaty of Moscow which ended the war were a great deal more severe; for by that time Finnish resistance was obviously nearly ended, and it was also clear that no foreign government was coming to Finland's aid.[7] Nevertheless, *both* sets of demands were within a logical band of the defence spectrum ranging from the minimum requirements necessary for Leningrad's safety to something a bit more comfortable; nevertheless, despite Zhdanov's subsequent expression of regret for missed opportunities,[8] no attempt was made to seize and occupy the whole of Finland.

This does not mean that Soviet war aims must necessarily be *limited* war aims. In 1921, she went to war with the Menshevik Republic of Georgia for the avowed purpose of 'bolshevizing' the whole of the country. In this case, therefore, it was not until the *whole* of the country was in Bolshevik hands that Russia stopped the war.

This particular example, however, might in some sense be regarded as an example of a limited war aim, because Georgia is a very small country. There is good reason to believe however that, in the event of another world war occurring, the war aim of the Soviet Union would be the very reverse of limited; for it would then consist of the total destruction of the 'imperialist' societies opposed to it, and of post-war reconstruction of those societies on a Marxist-Leninist basis. (This point is discussed in detail on pp. 112–26.)

The above theses must not lead the reader to imagine that, in every case where the Russians see profitable openings and where, even according to their cautious mode of reckoning, victory can be seen to be certain, they will therefore make use of force to achieve their goals. Even successful wars bring a price to be paid for victory; and Soviet history has shown that the Kremlin leaders are well aware of this fact. Besides, the USSR has never been in a position of overwhelming military strength *vis-à-vis* the rest of the world; and this point alone has induced caution. In other words, although the Soviet armed forces are obviously capable of winning a swift and convincing victory over, for example, Afghanistan, the repercussions in the rest of the world would be such as to more than counteract the kinds of gain that, in the foreseeable future, the USSR might win from such an invasion. True, the repercussions would be political rather than military; but war itself is a political act, and the Russian leaders know it.

Yet although the Russians may know it, the West does not. It is hard to find an ordinary Western citizen who really believes that war is a political act; and it is of course perfectly possible that his view may be correct. Correct or not, one thing is certain: unless he bears in mind the Soviet view of the matter, which *does* view war as a political act, he will not understand the Soviet approach to war, peace and neutrality.

Lenin, of course, never expected the ordinary Western 'bourgeois' to understand it. As he said himself, to such people peace has always been a fundamentally distinct concept, something quite *different* from war; and they do not realize that 'war is the continuation of the policies of peace; and peace, the continuation of the policies of war'.[9] In other words, according to Lenin, the underlying *policy* of a given government remains unchanged: it pursues the same aims in wartime as in peacetime, in peacetime as in wartime. Peace and war (and, to a limited extent, neutrality) are three of the tools available to it to further its pursuit of those aims. But they are *tools*, and, in the eyes of the Soviet Politburo, they are little else. War will therefore be declared or not be declared, peace will be made or not be made, according to whether it is the instrument best adapted *in the particular circumstances of the time* for furthering Soviet interests.

As Raymond Garthoff has written: 'War is not the goal of Soviet (political) strategy; the Soviets prefer to gain their objectives by pacific means—by forcing appeasement on the enemy. This consideration holds a significant place in Soviet strategy, which judges the long-term trends and possibilities in determining what risks are worth taking in the short run.'[10] But, as Garthoff also shows clearly, the Soviet leaders pursue their objectives relentlessly; and in suitable circumstances war will be used, in other circumstances peace will be used, in yet others again neutrality will be used, as the tool best suited in the particular circumstances for attaining Soviet objectives. The reader must therefore think of the Soviet Politburo as a master carpenter looking at his saw, his chisel, his hammer and his screwdriver, and selecting the one he thinks will be best for the job in hand. 'War is the *tool* of policy', said Clausewitz; and Lenin wholeheartedly agreed with him.[11]

This attitude to war and peace, to say nothing of neutrality, is only viable if it is master-minded by a coherent and enduring *Weltanschauung*. Bismarck, who had such a *Weltanschauung*, adopted towards these concepts an attitude much like the communists; and Marx and Engels, though they loathed his policies, admired the way he did so. Marx even went so far as to say that he showed 'greatness' in the field of international politics.[12]

We in the West nowadays have no particular *Weltanschauung*: each man has his own, which is probably not his neighbour's; and the result is a confusion of aims and ideals which irradiates Western society, and which makes it difficult for a Western government to operate from an agreed consensus. This makes impossible the adoption by any Western government today of that attitude of Realpolitik towards war, peace and neutrality which was once Bismarck's and is now the Soviet Union's.

Not that the Soviet Union has any real affection for Bismarck; the Marxist *Weltanschauung* is far removed from his. But the possession by Bismarck and by the communists of a solid, comprehensive philosophy of life is an important reason why their *modi operandi* in the field of international politics show very strong similarities.

## The relative expertise of Marx and Engels in matters concerning war

It was Engels, as everyone knows, who was the partnership's great expert in military matters: Marx himself acknowledged this, and Lenin said so repeatedly. Moreover, it is Engels, not Marx, who is regarded by the Soviet Union today as the founder of communist military science and communist military doctrine.[13] If, therefore, in the pages that follow, Engels' name predominates, this is because he had more to say than Marx on the subject of war.

On the other hand, this does not mean that Marx differed from Engels over military matters: on the contrary, so far as can be seen, their viewpoints coincided. Indeed, Marx learnt a great deal about war from Engels, and frequently asked his advice about weapons and tactics;[14] so that a lot of Marx's own views on the subject were originally Engels' views.

However, it is really not possible to unravel the woof from the warp of Marxism-Engelsism, in so far as that doctrine relates to the subject of war. Nor is it very profitable. On all important points concerning that subject, Marx and Engels were agreed; and the essential thing for us is to know what they were agreed upon.

On the other hand, the aspects of war which chiefly interested Marx were the political aspects; whereas Engels far preferred the military technicalities. The former never fought in a campaign; and his concern with war was mainly directed to considering the extent to which it served as a fermenting-vat for revolutionary viruses. By contrast, Engels was extremely interested in the techniques of waging war. He had served as adjutant to Colonel Willich in the fighting in 1849; he had worked as a war correspondent; and he had therefore acquired considerable personal experience of a soldier's calling. So it is no accident that his writings are full of references to types of equipment and questions of strategy, as well as to the effects that the economic basis of each country has upon the weapons that it commands. A favourite theme of his was the influence exerted upon strategy and tactics by the invention of new weapons.[15]

Thus, one may sum up by saying that Marx was more concerned with the political aspects of war; Engels, with the technical. Therefore the views of the two men largely complement each other; and the writings of both must be read in order to arrive at a fair assessment of what classical Marxism has to say about the subject of this chapter.

## Lenin's expertise in the matter of war

Up to the outbreak of the First World War, Lenin paid little attention to war as such: he was greatly interested in revolution and insurgency, but little in war. This, no doubt, was because he had not been old enough to take any serious interest in such things as war and politics before about 1886; and, in the years between then and 1914, few wars occurred to attract his attention. Moreover, whenever they did, he seems chiefly to have been concerned (naturally enough) with those that impinged on his own revolutionary interests. Thus, he has plenty to say on the Russo-Japanese War, quite a lot on the Balkan Wars, but almost nothing on the Boer War.

Furthermore, as it so happened, he never saw actual fighting in a proper war, prior to the Russian Civil War of 1918–20; for he was too young to fight in the Russo-Turkish War of 1877, and during the Russo-Japanese War he was abroad.[16] He was also abroad during the First World War up to the time that the Tsar abdicated, and was thus never conscripted into the Tsarist army. Since he possessed no natural interest in the technicalities of military affairs (strategy, tactics, weapons, equipment, etc.), and since he was not compelled by force of circumstance to acquaint himself with these matters prior to the outbreak of the Civil War, it is natural enough that, before that time, he should have had very little to say about them; and that his interest in war should have lain principally in its effects on revolutionary politics, and in war itself considered as a social phenomenon.

The above is true, however, only if placed in the context of what might be termed a 'proper' war (i.e. a war between independent sovereign states). For, at the time of the 1905 revolution in Russia, he became much concerned with other wars, that is to say, with such things as armed uprisings and civil wars; because it was by their means that he then expected the revolution to be successfully accomplished, and the Tsar toppled from his throne.

However, by 1909 or so, the prospect of an immediate revolution, reached by means of an armed 'proletarian' uprising, had receded into the distance; and Lenin therefore concentrated his attention upon other, more pressing problems. These were mostly political. His interest in war was consequently not revived until the outbreak of the First World War compelled him to revive it; and in the case of that war (a war between sovereign states) a knowledge of military *minutiae* was of no practical use to him, because he was not concerned with the waging of it. He therefore dropped the subject, and concentrated instead upon the political aspects of the struggle, and upon war as a social phenomenon. Indeed, it was not until the outbreak of the civil war in the summer of 1918 that he became really concerned with specifically military problems; because it was not until then that he had a war on his hands for whose conduct he was largely responsible. Even then, however, the raising, the training, and the deployment of the Red Armies were largely in the hands of others; while Lenin himself was chiefly occupied with problems of equipment and supply.

Thus it is that Lenin's writings on war, *taken as a whole*, are chiefly concerned with what one might term the political aspects of the subject, as distinct from the technical, despite his enforced involvement in the technical aspects in the years between 1918 and 1920. It is true that the Soviet Communist Party in recent years has gone to great lengths to try to prove to the world that not only was Lenin a genius in all other directions, but also in that of strategy and tactics, of the supply, design and development of equipment, and of the training and the deployment of armies. It has therefore made much of Lenin's views on the import-ance of good morale in a fighting army, the necessity for that army to be provided with first-class weapons, and to be constantly and liberally supplied. Such considerations as these, which have been the stock-in-trade of every writer on military affairs since men first took to setting pen to paper, are now seized upon by the Soviet authorities, and exhibited to their captive readership as pearls of the greatest price from Lenin's oyster, that inexhaustible bivalve. Lenin himself, however, was much more modest; and the wise reader will here accept Lenin's own self-assessment, the more so as it coincides with Frunze's assessment of him (*Lenin i RKKA*, January 1925).

The outbreak of the First World War, together with the fact that Russia was heavily involved in it, made Lenin realize that he must devote some study to war, a thing which, as we have seen above, he had felt little need to do previously. The main part of his study, so far as is known, consisted of a careful reading of Clausewitz's *On War*. He undertook this study at some time during 1915, and appears to have spent a considerable amount of time on it. It is therefore no accident that the first major work of Lenin on the subject of war, *Socialism and War*,[17] was not written until July and August of that year, nor that it was only subsequently that there appeared *The Junius Pamphlet* (1916), *The Military Programme of the Proletarian Revolution* (1916), *War and Revolution* (1917), and many others.

After the October Revolution, he produced no more full-dress academic studies on the subject of war; though naturally, being at the head of the Bolshevik Government during the Civil War and during the Russo-Polish War of 1920, he could not help occasionally speaking about it. These comments, however, are mostly concerned with war in relation to domestic and international politics, rather than with the more military aspects of war. The most important of his works on the subject during this period are *The Proletarian Revolution and the Renegade Kautsky* (1918); *On Fertile Soil* (1918); his speech at the Eighth Party Congress (1918); and his speech at the First All-Russia Congress on Adult Education (1919).

In addition to this, the Treaty of Brest-Litovsk caused him to set down on paper his views on a very important aspect of war, which he had previously scarcely examined. This aspect was the question of when to choose war and when to choose peace. His views on this aspect are well illustrated in his *On the History of the Question of the Unfortunate Peace* (prior to 11/24 February 1918); *The Revolutionary Phrase* (8/21 February 1918); *Strange and Monstrous* (15/28 February 1918 and 26 February/1 March 1918); *A Painful but Necessary Lesson* (12/25 February 1918); and his three speeches to the Party's Central Committee of 24 January, 1 February and 18 February 1918. (Alternative dates, when given, are the result of the Soviet Government's reform of the calendar.)

Finally, I should mention that, despite the fact that I tended to dismiss his interest in war prior to 1914, no one can claim to be well acquainted with Lenin's attitude towards this subject, who has not read his major writings at the time of the Russo-Japanese War and the 1905 uprising. In particular, *The Fall of Port Arthur* (1905), *Revolutionary War and Revolutionary Government* (1905), *From Defence to the Attack* (1905) and *Lessons of the Moscow Uprising* (1906) are essential reading.

It will be clear from the above that the October Revolution formed a watershed in the development of the Soviet communists' attitude towards war, peace and neutrality (but especially war).

Before that date, it was mostly philosophical theorizing, and was concerned in particular with trying to discover to what extent a given war, which by the nature of things had necessarily been started by others, would help or harm the cause of the revolution. Neither Marx nor Engels was ever in command of an army; and Lenin had no troops at his disposition before the winter of 1917. Any wars that happened to afflict our planet prior to the winter of 1917 were therefore bound to be the affair of people who, unlike the founders of communism, *were* in command of armies, or else who, being at the head of governments, had armies at their command.

After that date, things were very different and one can therefore say that for all practical purposes there was an enormous difference between Marx, Engels and the younger Lenin on the one hand, and the Lenin who in November 1917 became in fact, if not in name, the head of the new Soviet state. For this older Lenin, being in control of a state, by that very fact became possessed of control over the state's apparatus, which included an army.

Lenin therefore, unlike Marx and Engels, could start a war if he judged it expedient to do so, as he did in the case of Georgia (see pp. 77–8), and as he wanted to do in the case of Finland and Hungary, though militarily too weak to do it (see pp. 56–7). Furthermore, the state he ruled was also open to being attacked by others; and other countries did indeed attack it.

As a result, Lenin and his fellow Bolsheviks acquired a considerable amount of military experience which naturally subsequently affected the Soviet view of war. Generally speaking, this experience was of a certain type of warfare which was not at all typical of the kind of warfare that the Western Europeans had experienced. The war which schooled the budding Red Army generals was the civil war and its concomitants, such as the Russo-Polish War of 1920; and these wars were fought over enormous distances with quantities of troops which, though considerable, must be rated small in relation to the distances involved.

As a result, the civil war and its concomitant wars were all wars of manoeuvre, as modern Soviet writing is fond of emphasizing.[18] This in turn exerted a powerful influence on Soviet strategical thinking; because this kind of war demanded speed and mobility, and made static defence a virtual impossibility. When, therefore, the Red Army was being re-created in the late 1920s and early 1930s, it was natural enough that mechanization, that great aid to mobility, was much in vogue in Soviet military circles. So, too, were the aeroplane and the parachute; and so, too, was cavalry.

By an historical accident, the war that enveloped the USSR in 1941 was launched by a man who also believed in the virtues of speed and mobility, and the fighting took place in the kind of terrain which had nurtured Soviet strategy. This is not the moment at which to discuss the implications of these circumstances; but the point should be noted. So, too, should the further point that the Soviet Army, having very largely contributed to the defeat of Hitler, became convinced by virtue of its successes that its strategy and tactics were sound. As a result, it has continued to believe in them; and if we discount those aspects of them that relate to nuclear weapons, their basic 'line' has remained very largely unchanged right up to the present day.[19]

This book, however, is more about war as a socio-political pheno- menon and as a continuation of policy and a tool of policy than about its strategy and tactics. And in this regard, too, the Bolsheviks' attitude to it changed very little as a result of their first-hand, practical experience of waging it. The views of Marx and Engels and the younger Lenin continued to be accepted by the older Lenin, and also by his successors, almost without modification. War continued to be regarded, as Marx and Engels had regarded it, as the product of a 'class' society; and it continued to be valued as a revolutionizing solvent of the fabric of a 'class' society in just the way that the Founding Fathers had valued it. War as a continuation of policy and a tool of policy was a contribution of Lenin, following upon his study of Clausewitz; but it was the younger Lenin who studied him and absorbed his most appealing doctrines. The elder Lenin was seemingly content with the formulations of his earlier years; because, even after his practical experience of warfare, he made no change in the formulae.

Despite all this, however, it must be stressed that in one respect at least the October Revolution marked a real turning-point in the history of war on this planet. Before that event, no communist state existed anywhere in the world; so that no war was possible between a capitalist and a communist country. After that date, this was no longer true; and armed clashes between capitalism and communism became possible, and indeed occurred. In particular, it was now possible for capitalist governments to organize crusades in order to strangle com- munism; and for the Soviet Government forcibly to 'bolshevize' other countries by means of 'revolutionary war'. Prior to 1917, none of this was possible; and the way in which successive Soviet governments faced up to these possibilities is a main theme of this book.

## The origin of war

In Marx's view, war is essentially an evil; and therefore under com- munism, which was the name he gave to his perfect form of society, war would cease to exist. But in order to be able to eradicate war, one must first discover the causes of it; and, in Marx's opinion, the sole cause of war was the existence of the 'class' system.

The expression 'the class system' is to be understood, of course, in the sense in which Marxists always understand the word 'class' and the cognate expressions derived from it: in other words, it denotes a form of society in which there are to be found both an 'exploiting' class and an 'exploited' class. The former actually owns the means of production, but depends for its ability to work them upon the labour supplied by the latter. However, because of its control of the means of production, the 'exploiting' class is inevitably the ruling class; and, being the ruling class (and therefore, by definition, in control of the state apparatus), it will make use of that apparatus to further its own interests.

One such use that it will make of it will be the waging of war, whenever that occupation seems likely to be economically profitable; though the actual aims for which the wars will be fought will naturally vary according to the circumstances of the time. In a slave-owning society, for instance, the object of a war is the capture of more slaves; in a feudal society, it is the seizure of more land; while in a capitalist society, the aim pursued by the ruling 'class' when it engages in war has traditionally (according to Marxist tradition, that is) been the acquisition of larger markets for its industries, or access to cheap labour and raw materials.

In addition to the directly economic benefits which war provides for the ruling 'classes' (according to Marxist doctrine), the latter also derive considerable benefits from the mere existence of the actual phenomenon of war. For, so long as war exists, armies must be kept in being (at any rate in embryo), in order to defend their country against foreign attack. But when no such attack is being mounted, and the country in question is at peace, the army can then be employed by the ruling 'class' for keeping its own workers in subjection; and this can be done either obviously and outrageously, in defiance of normal convention, or else it can be done more subtly under the guise of 'maintaining law and order' or 'aid to the Civil Power'.

In 1926 for instance, during the General Strike, the British Government employed troops for a variety of purposes, none of which was concerned with the defence of the United Kingdom from foreign attack. The troops were used to escort food convoys or to guard vital installations; and they were also used for unloading ships at the docks. From the 'bourgeois' point of view, all such uses were concerned with 'maintaining law and order'; but from the Marxist point of view, the *effect*, if not the intention, of such uses was to strengthen the position of those opposing the strike, thereby weakening the strike, and thereby, in the long run, enabling the capitalist bosses to win.

It is, of course, a matter of historical fact that the capitalist bosses did win, and that, in the case of the coalfields for instance, they made use of their victory to compel the beaten miners to return to work on very onerous terms. During the General Strike, therefore, the employers undoubtedly profited by the existence of a Regular British Army, while the strikers, just as undoubtedly, were the losers by it; and since the Army would not have been in existence if the world had never known of the phenomenon of war, it is possible to say (as Marxists always do say) that here is another way in which the 'bourgeois' reap an advantage, albeit at one remove, from the continued existence of the actual phenomenon of war.

Now if the root cause of war really does lie in the existence of a 'class' system, as the Marxists say that it does, then clearly it can only be eradicated when 'class' is eradicated too. In other words, a Marxist believes that the only way to eradicate war is to abolish capitalism and all other 'class' societies, and to set up communism in their stead, since communism, according to Marx, is wholly 'classless'—and is, moreover, in Marxist eyes, the only form of 'classless' society which can possibly exist. Furthermore, if war is really to be abolished, this communism must be set up, not in just one country, but over the whole globe; for otherwise there would be countries which would not be communist, and would therefore be ruled by 'exploiting classes'; and these 'exploiting classes', of course, would still be capable of indulging in war whenever they thought it would serve their own interests to do so.

In Soviet opinion, the truth of the above proposition was abundantly demonstrated by what took place between the end of the First World War and the beginning of the Second. For during that period there was in existence only one 'proletarian' state (the USSR), while the rest of the world was either capitalist or else under capitalist domination; and, twenty years after the First World War had ended, the Second World War began. By communist reckoning, the sole real cause of the outbreak of the second conflict was the continued existence of capitalist states on this planet; and furthermore, as the communists see things, the fact that the war undoubtedly did break out is decisive proof of the correctness of their opinion.

This view of war, and of the remedy for war, is the reason why Marx, Engels, Lenin and their disciples have always regarded pacifists with contempt. For it is clear enough that those who preach pacificism, or who propound any solution to the problem of war other than that of the world-wide establishment of communism, are (in communist eyes) distracting attention from the task of making the revolution, and are thus in fact not helping to abolish war, but, however unwittingly, are serving to perpetuate it. Furthermore, pacifists oppose *all* wars; whereas Marxism-Leninism condemns some wars as being 'unjust' wars, but approves others as being 'just'. (The distinction made by the communists between 'just' and 'unjust' wars will be explained later in this chapter.) Pacifists therefore are *not* held in high esteem by Marxist-Leninists; though the latter are willing to make use of them for their own purposes.

### The value of war as a tool of revolution

If war can be eliminated only by the complete victory of communism, it follows that, until that victory has actually been achieved, war will continue to exist. Since this will be so whether we like it or not, the only sensible thing to do is to recognize the fact, and to derive from it such benefits as may be possible.

In Marx's, Engels' and Lenin's opinion, the chief of the benefits that can be derived from war is the speeding-up of the revolutionary process. Indeed in certain circumstances this speeding-up may attain such a high tempo that it brings about the achievement of the revolution itself.

The 'revolutionary process' is a concept of Marx and his followers which is based upon their conviction that all human societies are destined to become communist; and that this destiny is to be welcomed. However, Marx was also convinced that, before they could attain communism, they had first to pass through a series of evolutionary stages which, in the classic Marxist formulation, ran through the slave state, feudalism and capitalism; and only after a nation had first become capitalist was it at all possible for it to evolve further, and become communist. (Lenin, it is true, modified this scheme a little; but his modifications do not materially affect the course of our present argument.)

When a human society passes from one of these stages to another, a revolution can be said to have occurred. This revolution may be brought about by an actual revolution (i.e. an armed uprising), or it may come about peacefully, or it may take place as a result of the waging of war. This is because war imposes great strains on the fabric of society, even in those instances where the society in question is victorious. Thus, Britain was ultimately victorious in both the First and the Second World Wars; yet none can deny the strains they imposed upon the fabric of her society, nor the great social changes which these strains produced.

But in the case of the combatant who is defeated, the strains imposed will be enormously greater, and very far-reaching changes may be expected as a consequence. Thus, the defeats suffered by Russia at the hands of Germany during the course of the First World War were a prime cause of the subsequent revolution. This is the most obvious recent example of an actual revolution occurring as the result of defeat in war; but although the American failure to achieve victory in the Vietnam War has not, after years of fighting, led to a revolution in the United States, it has given rise none the less to tremendous social pressures, and begotten great changes in the structure of American society.

Marx summed up the notion in 1855, when he observed: 'War puts nations to the test. Just as mummies fall to pieces, the moment that they are exposed to the air, so war pronounces its sentence of death on

those social institutions which have become ossified.'[20] The occasion of
his remarks was the conduct of the Royal Navy in its operations before
Sevastopol; but his words clearly have, or can be made to have, an
almost universal application.

Lenin continued to write in the same tradition. In *The Collapse of
the Second International*, written in 1915, he said, 'It has long been
recognized that war, for all the horror and misery it brings, brings a
greater or lesser benefit, unmasking and destroying a lot of what was
dead and decaying in human institutions.' Later that year, he repeated
this assertion in slightly different language: 'Some wars in history, for
all their beastliness, have helped the development of mankind, have
destroyed harmful and reactionary institutions such as absolutism or
feudalism.'[21] Three years later, at the Seventh Party Congress, Lenin
expressed it as follows: 'For Engels realized that, for all the horrors of
war, and even though one cannot guarantee that a particular war will
bring the victory of socialism, nevertheless he said that that victory
would come.'

In this exposition of the value that communists ascribe to war as a tool
of revolution, I have confined myself so far to war in its usual sense, that
is to say, to war between independent sovereign states. But Marxist
theory also takes account of civil wars, of 'wars of national liberation',
and of 'revolutionary wars'; and these too are seen in the Marxist
*Weltanschauung* as being valuable tools for furthering the revolutionary
cause. A detailed examination of what Marxists mean by these three
types of war will be found in a later section; here I am concerned only
with their effect in speeding up the revolutionary process.

And the effect of civil war in this particular context is believed by
Marxist theory to be very great. Lenin asserted in his *Prophetic Words*
(1918) that without civil war 'no great revolution has yet come to pass
and without it no serious Marxist has ever imagined the transition from
capitalism to socialism'. Around ten years later, an authoritative Soviet
publication declared that civil war is the accompaniment to every
revolution; and it cited as examples the English Revolution of the
seventeenth century, the French Revolution of the eighteenth century,
the Paris Commune, and the October Revolution in Russia.[22] Similar
sentiments are expressed today in modern Soviet writing.[23]

'Wars of national liberation' are seen by Marxists as having a twofold
revolutionary effect. First, they are a strain on the economy of the
colonial or occupying power; because that power has to maintain troops
in the field in order to suppress the liberators, and this is an expensive
business. Thus, the 'war of national liberation' conducted by the
Spaniards against the French at the beginning of the nineteenth century
(which British historians generally call 'the Peninsular War') put a

great strain in terms of both men and money upon the economy of the French invaders. Similarly, that 'war of national liberation' which the English generally refer to as 'the Indian Mutiny' was also extremely costly to the British Raj. Moreover, even when the Mutiny itself had ultimately been suppressed, the need to prevent a subsequent repetition necessitated the maintenance in India of a powerful military establishment, which was a great drain upon the imperial economy.

The second revolutionary effect exerted by 'wars of national liberation' occurs when they are successful. For, in the first place, this is supposed to weaken the imperial power by depriving it of part of its possessions. The loss of India, for instance, was seen by communists as a serious blow to the economy of Britain herself. But, in the second place, victory in a 'war of national liberation' bestows independence upon the former colony or protectorate; and, in the Marxist *Weltanschauung*, such independence is an absolutely essential pre-requisite for that colony's further progress towards communism. According to this reckoning, the winning of its independence by a former colony is thus necessarily a speeding-up of the revolutionary process; for it is only then that the revolution proper has any hope of succeeding. For instance, as long as North Vietnam was a French colony, it was quite impossible for her to experience a 'proletarian' revolution, for the simple reason that the French Government would never allow it to happen. Such a revolution could only come after the country had been freed from French control; and it is an undoubted fact that, the moment the French were compelled to withdraw from the country, a communist government took over in North Vietnam.

One may sum up, therefore, this second revolutionizing effect of a 'war of national liberation' by saying that it is a double one: it weakens imperialism by depriving it of its colonies; and at the same time it strengthens socialism by creating a new independent state which is capable of passing immediately into the 'camp of socialism', and ultimately will inevitably do so.

The revolutionary influence exerted by 'revolutionary wars' is bound to be considerable, almost by definition. For a 'revolutionary war' is a war waged for a revolutionary purpose; and however you may define that term, it can hardly fail to be concerned with speeding the revolutionary process. (The phrase 'revolutionary war' is explained on pp. 52–6.)

The most famous example in history of such a war is certainly that of the wars of the French Revolution, which were specifically termed 'revolutionary wars' by Marx, Engels and Lenin. The reason why they gave this name to them was that, after Valmy, the soldiers of Revolutionary France marched across Europe to put an end to feudalism by force. Since, according to Marxist theory, the change from a feudal aristocracy to a 'bourgeois' system is one of the main stages along the road of a society to communism, this action of the French armies is bound to be regarded by all communists as having had a revolutionary effect; and Marx, Engels and Lenin did so regard it.

Similarly, the operations in Georgia in 1921 by units of the Red Army destroyed the non-communist government of that country, and replaced it with one that was communist. Those operations therefore produced a profoundly revolutionary effect; and they have accordingly been termed 'revolutionary war' by authoritative Soviet sources.[24]

Not only, therefore, are 'ordinary' wars (wars between independent sovereign states) regarded by Marxist theory as valuable tools for bringing about, or at least for hastening, the 'proletarian' revolution, but also civil wars, 'wars of national liberation' and 'revolutionary wars' are regarded in this way too.

Furthermore, it should be noted as an important corollary of the foregoing that these latter types of war are just as much wars as 'ordinary' wars, according to Marxism-Leninism. As Lenin put it: 'Civil wars are also wars';[25] and he laid down rules for the waging of civil wars in the same spirit as Clausewitz laid down rules for the waging of 'ordinary' wars.[26] From which it follows that the Kremlin rulers will regard these wars in just the same light as 'ordinary' wars, and will use or refrain from using them on account of exactly the same kind of considerations as motivate them with regard to 'ordinary' wars between independent sovereign states.

## Marx's, Engels' and Lenin's views on the evils of war

This chapter began by asserting that, in Marx's, Engels' and Lenin's view, war was essentially an evil; but much of what follows has been devoted to showing the advantages which they detected in it.

Nevertheless, the words which appeared at the beginning of this chapter are true; and it is for this reason that there is such a profound ambivalence in the Marxist attitude to war. For, despite the advantages that wars bring to the cause of the 'proletariat' as a whole, they also bring the most dreadful misery and suffering to thousands of individual 'proletarians'. Moreover, it is precisely upon the 'proletariat', together with the peasantry, that the misery and suffering caused by war is bound to fall most heavily; for it is they who are conscripted in the greatest numbers into the armies of the various combatants; and it is they, therefore, who do the bulk of the actual fighting. Moreover, it is upon these people that the greatest material damage is likely to fall; because it is their little farms and their hovels which will be the most frequent victims of the bombardment, if only because they are so much more numerous than the splendid mansions of the rich.

Nor do the workers and the peasants receive any comparable recompense for the wounds and the losses that they suffer. For the chosen few, a medal, perhaps, or a gracious acknowledgment from their king or president that they have deserved well of their country. But for the rest—wounds, death, three-halfpence a day while serving; and nothing at all when the loss of a limb or an eye compels their discharge from the Army and their return to civilian life.[27]

Moreover, it was realized, particularly by Engels, that the enormous improvements in military technology, which had started in the middle of the nineteenth century, would make future wars many times more bloody and more terrible than previous wars had been. Thus, Engels, writing to Sigmund Borkheim in 1877, asserted roundly that: 'The next war will be a World War of a force unknown hitherto. Eight or nine million men will cut each other's throats and will devastate Europe as locusts have never done.' And he made the same point in his Introduction to Marx's *The Class Struggle in France* (March 1895) when he said that a war on the continent of Europe between the major powers would be 'a World War of unheard-of cruelty'. This view, incidentally, was not peculiar to Marx and Engels; it was endorsed by other Marxist writers and also by the Second International: it was a view, moreover, which was shared by many who had no connection at all with revolutionary socialism.

It is by no means true that, with regard to a given question, the view of the intellectuals will always be the right one: they have had, as a group, their fair share of failure as well as their share of success. On the question of the change in the nature of war, however, there is no doubt that they were in the right of it; though it took some time for the correctness of their opinion to be accepted by the man-in-the-street.

My Uncle Arthur, for instance, went off to the Boer War in command of a battery of field artillery, and thoroughly enjoyed himself. One or two of his pals got killed, it is true, but that was just bad luck; and in any case it was possible to reflect that they had died for Queen and Country. As for the rather greater number who got wounded, their wounds were, as a rule, simple and clean, being made by nothing more messy than a rifle bullet; and consequently, they usually healed. There was nothing there to daunt a right-thinking man.

Therefore when, in 1914, the bugles blew again, my Uncle Arthur responded to the sound much as the war horse did in the Book of Job. Nor was he alone in his response. Incredible as it must seem to many today, large numbers of people in all the countries of Europe answered the call to arms with whoops of joy. It was not until about the end of the first year's fighting that it slowly dawned on the ordinary man-in-the-street that this war was somehow different. My Uncle Arthur, who had embarked his battery at Dover in festive mood, acquired a very unfestive view of the war as a result of the First Battle of Ypres.

The final evil of war, in the opinion of Marx and Engels, was that most wars contained within themselves the seeds of another war. This was because the side which was defeated in the original conflict would sooner or later start another in an attempt to put things right. This, thought Marx and Engels, was particularly true of those wars which were ended by the kind of peace treaty that demands of the conquered nation the payment of tribute or the cession of territory.

The best illustration of their views on this particular question is to be found in their writings on the Franco-Prussian War of 1871; and, in particular, on the Prussian demand that Alsace-Lorraine should be ceded to Prussia by France. In his *The Civil War in France*, for example, Marx has this to say:

*If limits are to be fixed by military interests, there will be no end to claims, because every military line is necessarily faulty, and may be improved by annexing some outlying territory, and moreover they can never be fixed finally and fairly, because they always must be imposed by the conqueror upon the conquered, and consequently carry within them the seed of fresh wars* (Marx and Engels: *Selected Works* (FLPH, Moscow, 1951), vol. 1, p. 448).

But if war is indeed a evil, how is it then that we find Marx and Engels approving of it so often, and even revelling in it?[28] And under what circumstances does it become lawful for a Marxist to employ this evil for the furtherance of his own designs?

The answer to the first question is quite simple; and indeed we have already answered it at the very beginning of this chapter. By Marx's own theories, it will be remembered, it was only possible to eradicate war by the world-wide triumph of communism; and there was no chance whatever of this happening during Marx's and Engels' lifetimes. Consequently, the two men were confronted by a phenomenon which, although admittedly evil, was beyond their power to eradicate, and by which, therefore, they thought it would be only sensible to profit, if ever they could. Moreover, this latter consideration was rendered all the more cogent in their eyes because the chief profit that they would derive from war, whenever they should be able to make use of it, would be the bringing nearer, by however small a degree, of that total triumph of communism which, apart from its other virtues, was seen by Marx as at one and the same time the precondition, and also the sufficient cause, of the complete abolition of war. To use war to further the cause of communism was therefore, from the Marxian point of view, to do a little evil in order that much good might come; it was, indeed, a plain, straightforward example of the end justifying the means.

The answer to the second question is equally simple: Given that war was an inescapable ingredient of the society in which they lived, Marx and Engels thought it right to resort to it whenever, by so doing, they could hope to promote the revolutionary cause. This statement applies to 'normal' war (i.e. a war between sovereign states), and also to civil war, 'revolutionary war' and 'wars of national liberation'. Indeed, it applies to violence in all its forms since war, in Engels' famous phrase, is only 'organized violence'.

Moreover, not only did Marx and Engels think it right to profit by all kinds of wars, when these should happen to have been started by other people; but they also thought it right to start them themselves, whenever it seemed to them that the good of their cause demanded it. This statement may be received with incredulity by some people; so, a little later on, this book includes a whole section devoted to an analysis of Marx's and Engels' views on starting a war (see pp. 64–70). Meanwhile, it is necessary to repeat that the two men approved of war, whenever they thought that the good of their cause demanded it.[29]

## Lenin's doctrine of the inevitability of war between capitalism and communism, and its so-called 'refutation'

In the nineteenth century, when no communist countries were in existence, the only wars that could be waged by 'bourgeois' rulers were either colonial wars or else wars against other 'bourgeois' rulers (civil wars and 'wars of national liberation' are not relevant in this present context). Both types of war could be extremely profitable to a 'bourgeois' ruling class, provided that they were successful; for the former could provide the victors with sources of cheap labour and raw materials, while the latter could be used to damage the trading position of a rival or acquire some territory from him.

However, after the First World War, there appeared on this planet something which Marx and Engels had never known. From the ashes of Tsarist Russia there arose the world's first 'proletarian' state. Thenceforth a third type of war became possible for the 'bourgeois' countries; because they could now fight not only colonial wars and wars against other 'bourgeois', but also wars against communists.

However, if the ruling class of a 'class' society only engages in war when it is to its economic advantage to do so, what economic advantage could the 'bourgeois' see in waging war on communism?

The answer, said Lenin, is simple. Once a Workers' and Peasants' State was actually in existence, the workers and peasants living in the 'bourgeois' countries would be mightily enheartened, and would work the more actively to promote their own revolution. Their efforts, if successful, would topple the 'bourgeois' rulers, and oust them from their lucrative positions; and these efforts would receive as much help from the Bolsheviks as the latter could possibly give them. By this argument, it is therefore very clearly to the economic advantage of the 'bourgeois' to march upon the Soviet Union and put an end to the communist government; for this will improve their chances of survival, and thus of retaining their privileges. Moreover, so long as Soviet Russia was weak, it was easy for the 'bourgeois' to do this.

It was for this reason, said Lenin, that war between capitalism and communism was to be considered inevitable.

But, much as the capitalists might dislike the communists and long for their destruction, they would only actually attack them if they thought they would be successful. And this would happen only if the communists were weak.

The Bolshevik leaders had no doubt that, right from the October Revolution to the outbreak of the Second World War, the USSR was extremely weak compared with the forces of capitalism taken as a whole. By the middle 1950s, however, they thought the situation had changed.

For, by the middle 1950s, the USSR had not only acquired a most formidable conventional army, but she had also got nuclear weapons. She was therefore able to make things extremely uncomfortable for any country that might wish to launch an attack on her. Should an attack be launched, the aggressor might even be victorious in the ensuing war (though the Russians thought not); but it was beyond doubt that he would suffer terribly for it.

In other words, by the middle 1950s an attack on Russia could not possibly be profitable for the aggressor. It might just conceivably satisfy his hatred of the communists; it could not be advantageous economically. In which case, the principal motive for a ruling 'class' to engage in war would be lacking; and all that would be left to impel the would-be aggressor would be his emotional hatred of communism. It was the view of the Soviet leaders of the time that this might well not be sufficient; and that the bulk of the ruling 'class' of the capitalist nations would realize that, much as they hated communism, it would not pay them to indulge that hatred and attack it. In other words, war between capitalism and communism could no longer be considered inevitable; and this modification to Leninist doctrine was given to the world by Khrushchev at the Twentieth Party Congress.

However, the modification must not be interpreted as meaning that the Russians have said that Lenin had got things wrong. On the contrary, it is their belief that, given the circumstances of the time when he launched his doctrine (the advantage to the capitalists if communism could be destroyed, together with the communists' military weakness), his view was abundantly justified. It was only because the circumstances had changed, they said, that the doctrine based upon them had lost its validity; and the cause of the change in the circumstances was the new-found military strength of the USSR.

But this change of circumstance has produced no change in the basic nature of capitalism, which, according to Marxism-Leninism, remains bellicose. The 'bourgeoisie' will continue to indulge in war, whenever they see an economic advantage in doing so. Not against the Soviet Union, of course, since that would not be profitable; but against other, weaker countries that may excite their greed, or their political or economic enmity. The basic Marxist doctrine remains in force that wars are inevitable so long as capitalism persists; and though these wars may not manifest themselves in the shape of wars between capitalism and communism, they will still arise in the shape of wars between capitalism and anyone else (including two sets of capitalists).

For instance, in 1920 Lenin expected war to break out between America and Japan (see, for instance, his speech at the Eighth All-Russian Congress of Soviets, December 1920); in 1928, Stalin believed that America and Britain would soon be fighting each other.[30] As if to prove their point, in 1939 Britain, France and Germany were indeed fighting one another; and in 1941 Japan attacked America. Nor did the doctrine seem to need revision after the end of the Second World War. Khrushchev, for instance, declared to an audience in Moscow that wars between two sets of capitalist countries must still be considered probable.[31] Brezhnev and Kosygin have not yet contradicted him.

As for wars between capitalist countries and underdeveloped countries, the 'bourgeoisie' have initiated them and waged them (as communist leaders see things) in Malaya, Kenya, Cyprus, Algeria, Jordan, Lebanon, Suez, Vietnam and half a score of other places in the course of the last two decades. From the Soviet viewpoint, basic Marxist doctrine is not short of evidence to support its continuing validity.

## The different kinds of war in Marxist reckoning and the attitude of communists towards them

There are two obvious ways in which a man can classify wars. He can group them according to whether he approves them or condemns them; and he can also group them according to their type (e.g. 'civil wars', 'colonial wars', 'imperialist wars' and so on).

Marx, Engels and Lenin habitually classified wars by *both* these two different methods; and a great deal of their writing must necessarily remain unclear, so long as the terms they used, and the criteria by which they applied them, are not understood of the reader. A thorough

B

analysis of these terms and of these criteria must accordingly form the next part of our discussion.

If we turn from the question of classification to that of whether a given war should be approved or condemned by communists, it must be borne in mind that their sole criterion is whether it furthers or hinders the revolutionary cause; and that this criterion was invariably used by Marx, Engels and Lenin.

The reader must also continually remember that it takes two to make a quarrel—that is to say, that in every war there are at least two sets of combatants. Therefore, no one can say, when confronted by a particular war, 'I support this war'; he can only say, 'I support this particular combatant'. (The converse, however, is not true. A man can say 'I condemn this war', because it is perfectly possible to condemn *both* sets of combatants.) Consequently, when in the course of this discussion we say, as we *shall* say, that Marx supported that 'war of national liberation' which is known to British historians as 'the Indian Mutiny', what we mean by this is that Marx supported the sepoys and condemned the British.

## GROUP A: 'GOOD' AND 'BAD' WARS

It is often said that communists divide wars into two categories: 'just' and 'unjust'; and that 'just' wars are, in the words of a well-known Soviet textbook, 'non-predatory, liberating wars, which have as their aim either the defence of a people from external aggression and attempts to enslave it, or the freeing of a people from capitalist enslavement, or finally, the freeing of a colony or dependent country from the oppression of the Imperialists'.[32] 'Unjust' wars, on the other hand, are 'predatory wars, having as their aim the seizure and enslavement of other countries and other peoples'.[33] This classification, however, belongs to Stalin's time; Marx, Engels and Lenin were not nearly so tidy.

To begin with, the latter three men seldom actually spoke of wars as being either 'just' or 'unjust'. That may have been the meaning that they intended; it was rarely the word they used. Lenin, for instance, generally called those wars of which he approved *zakonniye* (legitimate) or *progressivniye* (progressive) or *revolutsionniye* (revolutionary); while those which he condemned he most often termed *reaktsionniye* (reactionary) or *grabitel'skiye* (predatory) or *zakhvatnicheskiye* (rapacious or grasping).

Sometimes, instead of an adjective, he used a phrase; and wars of which he approved became 'wars of the progressive class'[34] or 'wars to get rid of class oppression'[35] or 'wars serving the interests of democracy and the proletariat'.[36] By contrast, the phrases applied by Lenin to wars he condemned were 'wars profiting the exploiting classes',[37] 'wars which satisfy the appetites of the predatory gang',[38] 'wars which serve to increase class oppression'[39] etc., etc.

The above are the specific epithets employed by Lenin: those employed by Marx and Engels are similar; though, as their mother tongue was German and not Russian, they are obviously not wholly identical. Nevertheless, the differences are not of much importance for our present purposes; for one thing, we are here concerned with the *Soviet* attitude towards war, and the Soviet attitude is (and always has been) more deeply influenced by Lenin than by Marx and Engels. Second, though there may have been differences in the actual verbiage employed by these three men, there were none in the basic reasoning that lay behind it.

For it really is a matter of little moment that Marx terms a particular war 'unjust', that Engels calls it 'illegitimate', while Lenin prefers to label it 'reactionary' (or the other way round). These things are the merest name-tags. The point is that Marx and Engels and Lenin are all agreed that the particular war in question is to be condemned; and they have merely rummaged in the Marxist stock of adjectives of condemnation, and brought out the one they fancied. They rummage again, this time among the adjectives of praise and approval, when they want to support a war.

From this it follows that we may write down a list of epithets which Marx, Engels and Lenin employed in order to approve a war, and another list of those they used for wars that they wanted to condemn. (For our present purposes it does not matter that not all the adjectives to be found in the following list were used by each of the men; that Marx, for instance, so far as I know, did not use the term 'non-predatory'. The important point is that the following epithets are to be found in the works of one or another of the three, or else in Stalin's writings; and that these, taken together, form a corpus of adjectives of approval and condemnation which has traditionally been the stock-in-trade of Soviet political writers in the past, and which is still that of Soviet writers today.)

The most common of the epithets of approval are: *just, legitimate, progressive* and *revolutionary*. The most common of the adjectives of condemnation are: *unjust, illegitimate, reactionary, predatory* and *rapacious.*

It follows from the above that any particular kind of war of which Marx, Engels and Lenin definitely approved (e.g. a 'war of national liberation') may be called by them 'progressive' at one moment, 'legitimate' at another, and 'revolutionary' at a third, without any real change of meaning being intended by the change of epithet. The same thing is true, *mutatis mutandis,* of those wars of which they disapprove.

It seems to me, therefore, that in view of this loose and somewhat haphazard nomenclature, Stalin and his successors were surely sensible to have reduced to two the epithets to be applied to 'good' wars, and to a further two those to be applied to 'bad'. In respect of 'good' wars, the two epithets are 'progressive' and 'just'; while in respect of 'bad' wars, they are 'reactionary' and 'unjust'.[40] These four adjectives are the four stock epithets which are still those most frequently used by Soviet writers today; and the truth of the above remark is not contraverted by asserting that Soviet writers also employ the opprobrious term 'imperialist' war.

To be sure, they do. But to say that a war is an 'imperialist' war is to employ the second of the two modes of classification which we have adumbrated above. In other words, an 'imperialist' war is a *kind* of war, like a 'civil war' or a 'war of national liberation'. It is true that Soviet political thinking regards all 'imperialist' wars as damnable wars; but it does not regard all damnable wars as 'imperialist' wars. To take a case in point, the wars waged by Napoleon Bonaparte after he had been proclaimed Emperor are always condemned by communists. However, since Lenin's time, they could never correctly describe them as 'imperialist' wars; because France was not then an 'imperialist' country in the Leninist meaning of the term. (See pp. 34-8) We therefore return to our previous statement that, ever since Stalin's time, there have been two stock epithets for praising wars ('progressive' and 'just') and two more for condemning them ('reactionary' and 'unjust').

But not all wars can be labelled unequivocally 'good' or 'bad', or given such other synonym for these two adjectives as may be acceptable to Leninist vocabulary. Some wars bear a dual character, being considered to be partly 'good' by Marxism-Leninism, and at the same time partly 'bad'.

An admirable example of such a war is the one that is known to British historians as 'the Peninsular War'. To Marx and Engels, it was a 'war of national liberation' on the part of the Spanish people against Napoleon; and in that respect they gave it their fervent support. At the same time, however, it was clear to them that the *result* of the expulsion of the French from the Iberian Peninsula would be to allow the ruling classes of Spain and Portugal to relapse into semi-feudalism, and to undo the political, social and other reforms which the French had introduced. Consequently, in this respect they disapproved of the war most strongly.[41]

GROUP B: CIVIL WARS, WARS OF NATIONAL LIBERATION,
IMPERIALIST WARS, ETC.

We turn now to the second of the two ways of classifying wars that I mentioned at the beginning of this section: grouping them according to their *kind*. In the following pages are listed and defined the most common kinds of war that the communists recognize; but though all the most important kinds are here, it is not claimed that the list is in any way exhaustive.

(a) *Wars of territorial aggrandizement, of plunder, or of dynastic ambition*
Wars between independent sovereign states, although classed here as category (b), may easily be wars of this type; because it is independent sovereign states that have most frequently indulged in them. The same war, therefore, can belong to two different categories at once. The Napoleonic Wars, for instance, were obviously wars between independent sovereign states; they were also wars for territorial aggrandizement, plunder and dynastic ambition. (It is correct to say in this case '*and* dynastic ambition', because in this case Napoleon did have dynastic ambitions for his family.)

The Marxist attitude to such wars is to oppose them; because they do not believe that an indulgence in territorial aggrandizement, plunder, or dynastic ambition by a slave-owning, feudal or capitalist ruling 'class' will further the cause of communism, as a general rule. Every rule, however, has its exceptions; and there have been occasions where the *effect* of a war of this kind has been thought to have been 'progressive' by Marxist theory. Thus, the aim of the Goths and Visigoths, when they marched on Rome, was obviously plunder and territorial aggrandizement; yet Marxists approve the long-term effect of their action, which was to put an end to the slavery of the Roman Empire, and to prepare the way for feudalism.

Moreover, the case of Eastern Europe today is a constant reminder that occasions can arise when communist leaders (Soviet communist leaders, at any rate) are prepared to regard a war of territorial aggrandizement as the best means of furthering the cause of communism in the particular circumstances of the time. The fate of the Baltic States in 1940 bears eloquent witness to this.

It goes without saying that the Soviet communists themselves do not accept that the forcible 'bolshevization' in 1940 of the three Baltic States was a 'war of territorial aggrandizement'. Their own description of the incident is to say that they sent 'brotherly help' to the Latvian, Estonian and Lithuanian communists in their struggle against their capitalists and landlords.[42] Nevertheless it is indisputable that, as a result of the operations conducted by the Red Army, the territory of the Soviet Union was considerably enlarged ('territorial aggrandizement'); and that the whole campaign must have been judged beneficial to the cause of communism, otherwise it would not have been embarked upon. Moreover, not merely must it have been judged beneficial at the time, but it must also be judged to be still beneficial today. Otherwise, the

Soviet authorities of the post-Stalinist era could easily have taken steps to have undone this error of Stalin, if they had really believed that in this particular instance Stalin had erred.

But of course they do not believe that Stalin did. The incorporation of the Baltic States as an integral part of the USSR was largely due to a wish to improve the strategic position of the Red Army *vis-à-vis* the Germans. To make such an improvement is, in the Soviet view, to benefit the cause of communism; and Stalin accordingly made it, and was praised for it.

This means, of course, that many Soviet actions are made from motives of national self-preservation as much as from ideological ones. Or, much more likely, from a mixture of the two. The point is of importance, and must be borne in mind while studying the theory of the matter; but since it is a point which will be discussed in detail later, there is no need to say more about it here (see pp. 130-5).

(b) *Wars between independent sovereign states [NB A war in which one or more communist states is a participant is not included in this category]*
These wars are what a non-communist would probably regard as constituting the 'normal' kind of war. According to Marx, Engels and Lenin, they are the inevitable product of the mere existence of a 'class' society, and are fought for the benefit of that society's ruling 'class'.

The expression 'war between independent sovereign states' is not a communist one; but it is used here because it is well understood of Westerners. Moreover, it is used here in the widest possible sense. That is to say that, although the Persia of Cambyses was not an 'independent sovereign state' in the strict sense of that term, nevertheless such campaigns as those he waged against Egypt and Ethiopia are grouped within the framework of this sub-heading.

In order to determine their attitude towards individual wars of this kind, Marx, Engels and Lenin first enquired as to whether the war in question was likely, in their judgment, to promote or hinder the cause of the revolution. If they thought it likely to promote it, they longed for its declaration; if they thought it would probably hinder it, they yearned for a continuance of peace. And once a war had actually erupted, they supported the combatant, or group of combatants, whose victory would, in their view, do most for the revolutionary cause. The USSR has continued to use this criterion; and the Soviet attitude towards such wars is therefore determined by it.

Since all wars in which a communist country is a participant have been excluded from the present category, it is self-evident that, seen from the communist viewpoint, no wars in this category will have a desirable *aim*. This is because, by communist definition, wars of this kind are undertaken to further the interests of the combatants' ruling 'classes'; and no communist is going to approve such a purpose.

On the other hand, the *effect* of these wars may well be very desirable from the communist viewpoint. For instance, the wars of Louis XIV undoubtedly weakened the fabric of French society, and must thus rate as an important cause of the subsequent French Revolution. The effect of the First World War upon the fabric of Russian society was likewise extremely damaging; and no one doubts that it greatly hastened the advent of the Russian Revolution. Since both these revolutions are highly approved by communists, it follows that they will approve equally highly the *effect* of the wars that led to them.[43]

In any event, wars of this kind happen, irrespective of whether the communists want them to happen or not. Imperial Germany did not seek Lenin's approval before invading Belgium in 1914; nor did Napoleon III ask leave of Marx and Engels before declaring war on Bismarck's Prussia. Japan attacked in Manchuria in 1931 without obtaining prior permission from Stalin; while Israel's offensive against Egypt in 1967 did not depend upon first getting clearance from the Kremlin. Faced with what is an unalterable fact of life, Marx, Engels and Lenin (and subsequently the Soviet Union) always sensibly decided that, when a war of this sort actually confronted them, the best thing to do was to support that combatant, or group of combatants, whose victory they judged most likely to further the revolutionary cause.

But by what criterion is one to know which that will be? In certain cases, of course, the answer is easy. When the French Revolutionary armies were fighting the allied monarchs of Europe, it was plain to all revolutionaries that it was the French who were to be supported; and Marx, Engels and Lenin consistently approved their cause. But what happened when the two sides were in much the same stage of the Marxian evolutionary scheme, when both, let us say, were 'bourgeois' states of the middle of the nineteenth century? For in such a case, neither protagonist was particularly revolutionary; and this made it very much harder to see whose victory would do most for communism.

There was, it is true, a rule of thumb which Marx and Engels often applied in these circumstances; and this was, that in any such war the side to be supported was the *less* despotic of the two, on the ground that the greater despotism was the greater enemy of the workers.

Moreover, as it so happened, right from the beginning of Marx's political career to the outbreak of the First World War, there was always at any one time one state in existence in Europe which was in Marxist eyes so indisputably the *most* despotic of the era that, in any war in which it became engaged, support was given automatically to its opponent. Up to 1848, this position was held by the Austria of Metternich; but after 1848, when Metternich resigned and Austria became more liberal, the most obnoxious country in Europe (in Marx's, Engels' and Lenin's opinion) was unquestionably Tsarist Russia.

As a result, whenever Imperial Russia happened to be engaged in war, the three men longed for a Tsarist defeat. In the case of the Crimean War, for instance, Marx was extremely desirous that the French and British should win; because he thought a Russian defeat would improve the chances of a revolution in Central and Eastern Europe; whereas, by contrast, a Russian victory would strengthen European reaction to such a degree that no further revolutionary progress would be at all possible for a very long time to come.[44]

When it came to the Russo-Turkish War of 1877–8, the matter was even simpler. For the Turks' victories over the Russians were such, in Marx's opinion, as to be likely to lead to the infliction of grave damage on the social fabric of Russia, and to increase considerably the chances of revolution in that country. As he himself put it in a letter to F. A. Sorge: 'The gallant Turks have hastened the explosion by years with the thrashing they have inflicted not merely to the Russian army and finances, but to the very persons of the dynasty commanding the army (the Tsar, the heir to the throne and six other Romanovs).'[45]

By 1904, when the Russo-Japanese War broke out, both Marx and Engels were dead; but Lenin's writings on that war observe the true Marxian principles. Thus, on the occasion of the frightful setback to Russian arms which occurred with the fall of Port Arthur, Lenin positively exulted in the Russian defeat. 'The proletariat has cause for rejoicing,' he wrote. 'The disaster that has overtaken our mortal enemy [the Tsar] not only signifies the approach of freedom in Russia, it also presages a new revolutionary upsurge of the European proletariat.'[46]

Occasionally, however, it became a matter of the most extreme complexity to decide precisely which side's victory would prove of the greater advantage to the cause of communism. When the Austro-Prussian War broke out, for instance, Marx was inclined at one time to favour Prussia, on the ground that a resounding victory for that country would place in mortal danger the throne of Napoleon III. He was also, however, inclined to support Austria; because he believed that if she defeated Prussia, it was likely to lead to a revolution in the latter country.[47]

In yet other instances, however, a decision was taken more easily. The Franco-Prussian War of 1870, for example, numbered among its protagonists neither Tsarist Russia nor the Austria of Metternich. But, although deprived of their comfortable rule of thumb, Marx and Engels were yet able to decide that it was Prussia who, in the first instance, should be accorded their support.

One reason for this was that it was France who was the aggressor. However, as will be shown in the next section, Marx, Engels and Lenin were generally little interested in who was the aggressor; and therefore this, though certainly a contributory reason in the case of the Franco-Prussian War, was by no means the only one.

A second reason is to be found in a letter of Engels. Writing to Marx on 15 August 1870, he declares:

*The case seems to me to be as follows: Germany has been driven by [Napoleon] into a war for her national existence. If [Napoleon] defeats her, Bonapartism will be strengthened for years and Germany broken for years, perhaps for generations. In that event there can be no more question of an independent German working-class movement either, the struggle to restore Germany's national existence will absorb everything, and at best the German workers will be dragged in the wake of the French. If Germany wins, French Bonapartism will at any rate be smashed, the endless row about the establishment of German unity will at last be got rid of, the German workers will be able to organize on a national scale quite different from that prevailing hitherto, and the French workers, whatever sort of government may succeed this one, are certain to have a freer field than under Bonapartism.*

That the above quotation may be fully understood, I should perhaps mention that Bismarck's efforts to unify Germany were strongly supported by Marxists, because they believed that small territorial units were both reactionary and inefficient, and consequently incapable of making progress towards the 'proletarian' revolution. A Prussian defeat would act as a check to this cause; a Prussian victory, on the other hand, would be bound to reinforce it. It is when both these reasons are taken together that one sees why Marx and Engels should have supported Prussia in the early stages of the war.

But if Marx, Engels and Lenin were little interested in the question of who was the aggressor, they were greatly troubled by wars of territorial aggrandizement. And once Wilhelm I had defeated Napoleon, he then, instead of offering an unfettered peace, insisted on demanding from his beaten enemy the cession of Alsace-Lorraine. This was territorial aggrandizement in its most naked form; and Marx and Engels thereupon switched their support from the Prussian king to the new-born French Republic.

For by now the second reason had ceased to operate. There was no possibility whatever of a Prussian defeat, so that Bismarck's plans for the unification of Germany were unlikely to receive a check. Furthermore, the regime of Napoleon III, which Marx and Engels so bitterly hated, had been utterly destroyed and a republic proclaimed in its stead. Since Marx had declared that the Prussians should invade France only to depose Napoleon and install a republic[48] (for all other purposes limiting themselves to purely defensive operations), he could obviously

B*

have no sympathy with a Prussian invasion when his two objectives had been attained already.

Similar considerations were applied by Marx and Engels to other wars of this kind, that is to say, to wars between sovereign states in which neither Tsarist Russia nor the Austria of Metternich was among the participants. Thus, Marx hoped that the war of 1859 between France, Austria and Italy would never actually break out; because he felt that its effects would be 'counter-revolutionary', at any rate in the short term.[49] Engels' chief worry about the Serbo-Bulgarian War of 1885 was that it might lead to a general conflict in Europe. This he did not want, because he thought that things were going nicely enough for the Marxist cause as it was. If, however, a European war did come, it might lead (he thought) to a 'proletarian' revolution in Paris.[50] Other conflicts were adjudged in the same spirit.

The Franco-Prussian War was the last great war in Europe prior to the First World War; and both Marx and Engels were dead when the latter broke out. Lenin, however, was there to observe and evaluate it; but this, in his opinion, was a totally new kind of war, which he called an 'imperialist' war; and therefore he said it could not be adjudged on the lines set out above.

A description of Lenin's concept of an 'imperialist' war, and of his attitudes towards it, accordingly form the subject of the next section.

### (c) 'Imperialist' wars

When capitalism reaches the peak of its development, it cannot (by definition) be capable of further progress; and, from this stage on, it can only be expected to decline. The stage in question is known to communists as 'imperialism'; and, in Lenin's opinion, all the major industrial countries had reached it by the early twentieth century.

There is no need here to go into all the details of the concept of 'imperialism', in Lenin's understanding of that term. They can be found in his own work, *Imperialism, the Highest Stage of Capitalism* (1916); or they can be had, authoritatively summarized, in the Soviet publication, *The Fundamentals of Marxism-Leninism*.[51] Here we are concerned with only two aspects of the concept—first, that when capitalism has reached the stage of 'imperialism', it cannot make further progress, and hence none of its actions can be considered to be 'progressive'; and, second, that an 'imperialist' country is ripe for the revolution.[52]

With regard to the first of these aspects, it is obvious that, since no action of an 'imperialist' country can possibly be 'progressive', such a country is wholly incapable of waging a 'progressive' war. But since the only wars that communists will support are those which are helping the world to progress towards the establishment of communism, it follows that they cannot support a war that is devoid of a 'progressive' element.

With regard to the second aspect, if a given country is ripe for the revolution, it is the obvious duty of every communist to do what he can to promote it. The two aspects, taken together, therefore lead to the conclusion that, when an 'imperialist' country wages a war of any kind, a communist is bound to condemn it; and that moreover he is also bound to take advantage of the strains imposed by the war effort upon the fabric of that country's society, in order to bring to maturity that revolution which he is convinced is steadily ripening within it.

The war that the Americans were fighting in Vietnam was invariably termed an 'imperialist' war by the communists. What was the policy of the American communists towards it? Was it not flat opposition to the American war effort, and a strenuous attempt to 'secure its speedy ending'? And was it not also to 'seek with all [their] might to exploit the economic and political crisis brought about by the war for the purpose of rousing the people, and thus hasten the destruction of the class rule of the capitalists'?

The words in inverted commas in the preceding paragraph come from the Manifesto of Basle.[53] They are part of the 'guiding principles' drawn up by the Second International, when it met in Basle in 1912 to consider its attitude to war. When in 1914 the war actually erupted, Lenin almost alone held fast to these guiding principles, despite the fact that other revolutionaries abandoned them (e.g. Kautsky). In other words, Lenin's attitude to the conflict was exactly that which has been adumbrated above: he opposed the war *in toto*, and he also did his utmost to exploit the crises which it caused, in order to rouse the people 'and thus hasten the destruction of the class rule of the capitalists'.[54] But, as we have just seen, these must have been his tactics, even if the Manifesto of Basle had never existed. From which it follows that the policies adopted by Lenin with regard to the First World War were not only in strict accordance with the Manifesto of Basle, they were also thoroughly Leninist in principle.

But how, it may be asked, could Lenin justify his policies when the war was being fought (we are assured) to make the world 'safe for democracy'? And, in any case, how could he deny to the French and Belgians the right to resist the invasion of the German armies? And what about 'gallant Serbia'?

His stance on all these questions is explained by him in detail in the course of the works that have just been listed in the note, and in other works written by him at the time; but since it is absolutely essential for the non-communist reader to grasp the communist view of the nature of 'imperialist' war, the next few paragraphs summarize Lenin's theses.

First, said Lenin, none of the combatants except Serbia could justly claim that it was acting in self-defence; because, by Marxist doctrine, the plea of self-defence could be invoked only in case of aggression committed for territorial aggrandizement or plunder or dynastic ambition. Ostensibly at least, none of the aggressors in 1914 were actuated by these motives; nor was it in fact to be expected that, if Germany and Austria won, they would proceed to colonize Britain or France or Russia.

Belgium, it might be thought, could legitimately claim to be fighting in self-defence, even by Marxist criteria; for there was no doubt but that the Germans had invaded and occupied her territory without any provocation on her part. Indeed, said Lenin, if this was all there was to the Belgian case, he would heartily agree with that argument; for no socialist could fail to desire the eviction of the Germans from Belgium.[55] But, he continued, it was not all. Belgium had colonies; and if she and her allies won, she would retain those colonies firmly in her own possession. The cause for which Belgium was therefore *really* fighting was to prevent her colonies being seized by the Germans and Austrians; and this was a war with which no socialist could possibly sympathize. Only if the Belgian Government granted immediate independence to its colonies could Marxist support be given to the cause of Belgium.[56]

As for the British claim to be fighting on behalf of Belgium, this was too obviously specious to be worth arguing about. The British were fighting to keep Germany from the Channel ports, and to prevent her from growing strong enough to swallow up the British Empire. She was also fighting to annex into her own empire the German colonies, if the latter should lose the war. What Great Britain therefore was really fighting for was territory; and the British cause was just as 'imperialist' as the rest of them. So was the cause of France.[57]

Serbia's cause undoubtedly was legitimate; but hers was such a tiny part of the vast web of hostilities that the war could not be considered to be a 'just' war simply on account of Serbia: the speck of yeast was too small to leaven the lump.[58] Nor could those countries' claims to righteousness be accepted, which asserted that the reason that they had entered the war was to help the Serbians recover their independence. Russia was the most important of such countries; but the Russians had entered the war principally (said Lenin) in order to get possession of Constantinople and the Dardanelles, not to protect Serbia.[59]

In Lenin's view, therefore, any plea to be fighting in self-defence, or to be supporting those who were fighting in self-defence, was utterly bogus except in the case of Serbia. But Serbia's war was so small a part of the whole, that the war as a whole must still be condemned by Marxists.

The second main point in determining Lenin's attitude was that, in his view, the victory of *neither* side would further the cause of communism—from which it followed that neither should be supported.[60] For what, asked Lenin, was the war really about? What would happen when one side or the other were victorious? Whichever side won, the only discernible result was that the colonies of the losers would be taken away from them—not, of course, in order that these colonies should be given their independence, but in order that they might be added as further colonies to the empires of the victors.

By this reckoning, the *real* aim of the combatants on *both* sides was to grab territory. In the case of Russia, the territory to which she was aspiring was Constantinople and the Dardanelles; in the case of the other combatants, it was territory in Africa or Asia. In Lenin's view, the war was consequently an 'imperialist' war in respect of *both* sets of combatants; and since it was a mandatory tenet of Leninism that all 'imperialist' wars must be condemned, it followed that, in the case of the First World War, both sets of combatants were damnable.

But, objected some Marxists, did not Marx and Engels, when confronted with a given war, sit down and choose from among the warring nations the one that they preferred? Certainly, replied Lenin; but, in the lifetimes of Marx and Engels, all warring nations were necessarily 'bourgeois'. As a result, the *real* choice that confronted them when a particular war broke out was not the choosing between the one set of 'bourgeois' combatants and the other set, but between doing nothing and choosing between 'bourgeois' combatants.

For, in the nineteenth century, the 'proletariat' was numerically extremely small; and, even in those capitalist countries which were the most advanced by the standards of the time, the urban working class did not exist in anything like sufficient numbers to make a 'proletarian' revolution seem even remotely possible.[61] In the nineteenth century, therefore (according to Lenin), it simply was not possible, when confronted by a war, to choose to support *neither* of the two sets of 'bourgeois' who were engaged in it: on the contrary, one was compelled to support either the one or the other, so as to advance the cause of communism by no matter how small a degree.

However, it was Lenin's belief that, by 1914, the whole situation had changed; and what had not been possible in the nineteenth century, was perfectly possible now.[62] Therefore, right from the outset of hostilities, he called upon all Marxists everywhere to carry out the provisions of the Manifesto of Basle and to oppose the war effort of all the combatants, to try to bring a speedy end to the fighting, and to exploit the economic and political crisis brought about by the war in order to hasten the destruction of the class rule of the capitalists, and bring the 'proletariat' to power.

We are thus left with the conclusion that, according to Leninist doctrine, under no circumstances can 'imperialist' wars receive the support of communists; and that this is so, whatever the war aims of the particular 'imperialist' combatants, and whatever the circumstances that caused the war to break out.

It is also obvious that 'imperialist' wars can often be wars between independent sovereign states as defined in this particular sub-section: this occurs, for instance, when one or more of the combatants is an 'imperialist' country, and none of the combatants is communist. On the other hand, when an 'imperialist' country is engaged in war with a communist country, this is not a 'war between independent sovereign states', in the meaning of category (b). Instead, it will be regarded by communists as an 'imperialist' war on the part of the 'imperialist' power; while the communist country's war effort will be described by them as a 'just' war, or a 'progressive' war, or a 'revolutionary war'. (The full meaning of the phrase 'revolutionary war' will be explained later.)

In this connection it should be noted that, when in 1939 the Second World War was confined to Nazi Germany, Poland, Britain and France (i.e. when no communist country was involved), the war was then called by the USSR an 'imperialist' war with respect to *all* the combatants; and no communist, whether British, French or Russian, would give it support. As soon as Hitler attacked Russia, however, this situation changed; and the war was then a 'war in defence of socialism'; and the anti-Hitlerite coalition was supported by all communists everywhere.

(d) *World wars (miroviye voiny)*

The main difference between the English and Russian expressions is that the latter regards a *mirovaya voina* as a global conflict between imperialism and socialism *which the imperialists have started*. Whereas Western writing on 'world war' admits the possibility of it being started by either side and also being started by accident, Soviet writing on *mirovaya voina* excludes the possibility of anything other than naked 'imperialist' aggression. Consequently, Soviet analysis of the nature of *mirovaya voina* must always be understood in this context: in other words, their literature discusses what might happen if the West should launch an attack on them; but it contains no reference to the way the Russians might launch an attack on the 'imperialists'. A great deal of Western theoretical writing omits to reckon with this point; and its conclusions must therefore be regarded with a certain amount of caution.

The same point is relevant in the context of Soviet foreign policy. Soviet statesmen take pains to assure the world that it is a prime task of

Soviet foreign policy to prevent a world war breaking out. Or so, at least, the English-speaking world is given to understand in the versions of their speeches that are delivered to it. In fact, however, the Soviet statesmen utter these phrases in Russian, not in English, so that, *in their own words*, the prime task of Soviet foreign policy is not 'the prevention of world war', but *predotvrashcheniye mirovoi voiny*.[63]

*Predotvrashcheniye* may fairly be translated as 'prevention';[64] but, as we have seen, *mirovaya voina* can only mean in modern Soviet Russian 'a war launched by the capitalists upon the socialist countries'. In which case the prime task of Soviet foreign policy consists of no more than preventing the imperialists from assailing the USSR. It may also consist of preventing the USSR from assailing the imperialists; but, if this is so, it does not actually say so.

Until quite recently, there was a second main difference between 'world war' and *mirovaya voina*. This was because the latter was regarded in the Soviet Union as being, if it occurred, the decisive encounter for the fate of capitalism or socialism. If Russia won, she would take care to extirpate capitalism completely; while if Russia lost, she expected that the victors would do away with the form of society at present operative in the territories of the USSR.[65] Hence, in the Soviet view, a *mirovaya voina* could not help but be nuclear. The most recent Soviet writing now suggests, however, that the USSR is prepared to consider the possibility that *miroviye voiny* need not nowadays inevitably be waged for such fundamental aims, and that they therefore need not necessarily be nuclear, though they probably will be. The Soviet Navy is a staunch proponent of this view.[66]

### (e) *Colonial wars*

The meaning is obvious. However, it should be noted that a similar distinction between aim and effect was sometimes made by Marx and Engels as was made by them in the case of wars of territorial aggrandizement, plunder and dynastic ambition.

Engels, for instance, saw a great deal to be said in favour of the wars waged by the Tsarist Government against the natives of Central Asia. To the unsophisticated 'bourgeois', these might seem to be as much 'colonial wars' (and therefore blameworthy) as any that the French and British have ever fought; but while Engels could see nothing good whatever in the whole history of the British occupation of India, he was full of praise for the action of the Tsarist officers who had, he said, played a civilizing role among the Asians, and also among the peoples of the areas around the Black Sea and the Caspian.[67]

So far as I know, however, Lenin *never* approved of colonial wars, whatever their aim or effect; and modern communist thinking agrees with Lenin.[68]

(f) *Wars of national liberation*

These are the wars (frequently termed 'rebellions' or 'insurgencies' by bourgeois writers), which are waged by countries that have been conquered by other countries, and that have subsequently resorted to violent means in order to recover their freedom. Such resorts to arms are termed by communists 'wars of national liberation', irrespective of whether the subjugated country is a colony, a dominion or a protectorate (e.g. Kenya or India prior to the Second World War); or whether it is regarded by the conqueror as an integral part of his metropolitan dominions (e.g. Piedmont under Metternich).

It should be noted that the terminology employed by communists to describe such wars is often completely the opposite to that employed by the West. In their view, for instance, the Indian Mutiny was not a 'mutiny', because the word implies a resistance to lawful authority, and Marxists regard the authority of the British in India as having been anything but lawful. For similar reasons, the Mau-Mau Rebellion in Kenya is never described as a 'rebellion' by Soviet writers. These see it as part of the Kenyan 'national liberation struggle'; and the fact that it was directed against a body (the colonial government) which claimed to be sovereign in Kenya is as completely and utterly irrelevant in their eyes as are the admittedly barbarous methods which the Mau-Mau used.

The communist insurgency in Malaya is another instance in point, all the more interesting because it is one that happened to fail. But the fact that it happened to fail means only, in Soviet eyes, that the Malayan 'national liberation struggle' has not yet been successfully concluded.

In the words of *Politicheskii Slovar'*, the British Army 'in June 1948 began military operations against the Malayan people, struggling for the genuine independence of their country'. (This 'genuine independence' must be distinguished from what the Russians see as the fictitious— because non-communist—independence which the British Government granted to Malaya in February of that same year.) The military operations continued until, in 1955, the 'National Liberation Army' was forced to agree to an armistice; but *Politicheskii Slovar'* states outright that the liberation struggle is still continuing under the aegis of 'the illegal Communist Party'.[69] By communist reckoning, it is obligatory for that struggle to continue until final victory is secured—a point which I shall discuss later in the chapter on 'Peace'.

Examples of 'wars of national liberation' therefore abound in the history of mankind; and, in addition to those that we have already mentioned, one may cite the Revolt of the Netherlands against the Spanish in the sixteenth century; the Italian Risorgimento; the guerrilla warfare of the Algerians against the French between 1954 and 1962; and the Polish uprising against the Russians in 1863.

The last example, however, must not be taken as implying that the

Hungarian uprising of 1956 or the Czech resistance to the Soviet invasion of 1968 would be regarded as 'wars of national liberation' by the Soviet Communist Party.

This is because the basic Soviet criterion for approving or condemning a war of whatever kind (which was also that of Marx, Engels and Lenin) is whether the war in question does, or does not, further the cause of communism. In Marxist terminology, the expression 'a war of national liberation' is invariably one of approval: therefore it is only possible to bestow it on those struggles for the freedom of subject peoples or communities which *do* further the cause.

But, in Marxist eyes, not every such struggle has done so. For one thing, communism was generally regarded as impossible of attainment except in a strong (and preferably large) centralized nation-State. This is why such a State was regarded by Marx and Engels as more desirable, more 'progressive', than a fragmented feudal one. Therefore Marx strongly supported the attempts of Bismarck to create a united Germany, and condemned those elements which tried to resist the process. This is despite the fact that such resistance might have been expected to have been viewed with sympathy by contemporary Marxist opinion, on the ground that what it was really resisting was the national domination of Prussia over the other Germans, and that hence what the latter were really waging was a 'national liberation struggle'.[70]

In modern times, it has also not seldom happened that a struggle for freedom on the part of a people or community has *not* been viewed with favour by the communists. This is because, once a particular people or community has achieved the revolution, and come under the leadership of the Communist Party, any attempt to secede from that community must obviously serve to *weaken* the cause of communism. Indeed, since such a secession can only be a form of protest against the achievements of the revolution, it must clearly be 'counter-revolutionary', the most heinous crime in the Communist Party's calendar.[71] Accordingly, all such efforts at 'counter-revolution' have been suppressed mercilessly, whether in the Ukraine, Hungary, Poland, Czechoslovakia, Latvia, Estonia, or elsewhere.

It should be pointed out, in addition, that the Soviet troops in Hungary and Czechoslovakia were not there to occupy and subjugate the country, in the view of the Moscow leadership: they were there to extend 'fraternal aid' to brother communists in trouble. The fact that large numbers of Czech and Hungarian communists did not want the 'fraternal aid' at any price was not, in the eyes of the Kremlin, any reason why it should not be given. On the contrary, it was a compelling reason for forcing it upon its recipients, because these were clearly in danger of falling victim to a most fearful heresy.

For the real reason that Soviet troops were used in Hungary in 1956 was because the Hungarian Government of the time wanted the country to leave the Warsaw Pact; and the real reason they were used in Czechoslovakia was that the Czech Government under Dubček was prepared to allow the existence of other political parties as well as the Communist Party. In the Kremlin's judgment, both these ambitions endangered the very existence of the 'proletarian revolution'. They were both, therefore, profoundly 'counter-revolutionary', and had to be suppressed.

One can sum up, then, by saying that movements directed against the rule of a communist party can never be regarded by communists as 'wars of national liberation'. In order to qualify for this title, a given war must be directed against a feudal or 'bourgeois' subjugator. But when it is indeed against such a subjugator that the war in question is directed, then *in modern times* (i.e. since the October Revolution) it is invariably termed a 'war of national liberation', and is given automatic approval by the Soviet Communist Party. As for the occasional inconsistencies that admittedly occurred in the days prior to the October Revolution, they have small practical significance for us now; and those interested are referred once more to Professor Carr's discussion (see note 70, p. 226).

### (g) *'National' wars*

This expression is to be met with chiefly in the classical Marxist literature. It denotes a war where a whole people is fighting for its existence, for its national independence. It is thus roughly equivalent to a 'war of national liberation'; and Lenin often treated it as synonymous with it (see, for instance, his *Krakh Vtorogo Internatsionala*).

In the Soviet period, its use seems to be confined to those cases where the author is describing the attitudes of Marx, Engels and Lenin towards the various wars of the past; and it usually comes in the form of a direct quotation. In the lists of the several types of war which are possible in our present epoch, and which are to be found in a number of authoritative Soviet publications, there is no mention anywhere of 'national' wars, though 'wars of national liberation' figure prominently.[72]

### (h) *Local wars (lokal'niye voiny)*

The phrase *lokal'niye voiny* was introduced into the Soviet vocabulary in order to provide a translation of the Western expression 'local wars'. The Western writers using this expression were discussing the problems of wars waged by a major power against a much smaller power or a guerrilla force in a confined area of the world. Their chief examples were those wars of this particular kind which had been waged in one part or another of the globe since 1945. As it so happened, in almost every one of these the major power was 'imperialist'; and it was therefore easy for Soviet writers to claim that *all* 'local wars' were 'imperialist' wars. In those cases where they were *not* (such as the Chinese invasion of Tibet, the Chinese attack upon India and the Soviet invasion of Czechoslovakia), satisfactory formulae were devised by the Soviet theoreticians to ensure that Soviet citizens were not compelled, for want of an alternative, to call these episodes *lokal'niye voiny*, which term remained reserved in *Soviet* writing for local wars in which the major power was 'imperialist'.

The point was well expounded in *Sovietskaya Voennaya Doktrina* published in Moscow in 1963. In this work the reader was told that *all lokal'niye voiny* were 'imperialist' wars; and he was expressly warned not to term a war a *lokal'naya voina* purely on the ground that it was being, or had been, fought within a small geographical area. If that were so, the book explained, 'wars of national liberation' and civil wars would have to be given this title; but since from the Soviet viewpoint these latter kinds of war are 'just', they could not be given an epithet which was reserved for wars that are 'unjust'.

A similar view was expressed in the first edition of Sokolovsky's *Military Strategy*, the Russian version of which appeared in 1962. Here *all* local wars are clearly designated 'imperialist' wars; and this view of things prevailed in Russia throughout the Khrushchev era.[73]

The Brezhnev era saw a remarkable change in the Soviet interpretation of 'local war'. The third edition of Sokolovsky carries a significant rephrasing of the statement referred to in the preceding paragraph: this new edition, which was published in 1968, roundly declares that civil wars and 'national liberation wars' are 'small, local wars', thus flatly contradicting what was said in the first edition.[74]

This apparent contradiction was resolved last year by the appearance of a textbook on military history designed for use in Soviet military colleges.[75] This work carries a whole section devoted to local wars, in which it summarizes the relevant argument as follows: 'Local wars' are aimed at suppressing the 'national liberation movement', at weakening the world socialist system and at strengthening the strategic position of the 'imperialists' in the most important regions of the world. [They thus clearly cannot be fought by the Soviet Union, which would not dream of indulging in any of these wicked activities.] Such wars are therefore invariably 'imperialist' in character. But those resisting 'imperialism' must necessarily also be fighting 'local wars', since the term nowadays relates purely to the limited geographical scale on which they are fought. However, by resisting the 'imperialists', they are also fighting 'national liberation wars', or even occasionally civil wars; and these two categories of war must consequently be included as types of 'local war'.

Nowadays, therefore, it is probably true to say that 'local wars' are neither expressions of praise nor condemnation: as the textbook says, the Vietnam War is a 'local war' which is 'just' with respect to the North Vietnamese, and 'unjust' with respect to the Americans.[76] On the other hand, the Encyclopaedia, the third edition of which was published in the same year as the textbook, seems to imply that only imperialists can wage 'local wars', and thus agrees with Sokolovsky.[77]

I would not have wearied the reader with all this pedantry, if something of practical value could not be deduced from it. That 'something', is that Soviet writing on the subject of 'local wars' focuses its attention on the way that the 'imperialists' wage it; and it may therefore have little to do with the way that the Russians would wage, not of course a 'local war' (for they would naturally never dream of waging any such wicked thing), but a war against a small power or a guerrilla force in a confined area of the world.

### (i) Limited wars (ogranichenniye voiny)

There is a profound difference in meaning between the Western and the Russian expressions. For many years, Western writing made no real distinction between 'limited wars' and 'local wars': the one was regarded as more or less a synonym of the other.[78] Subsequently the latter, as we have seen, came to be interpreted as meaning a 'war waged in a confined area of the world'; while the former came to be taken to signify 'a war waged solely with conventional weapons'.[79]

The Soviet Union understands perfectly that this is the Western view of the matter, but condemns that view as erroneous. For in the Russians' opinion it is tantamount to saying that, when the leaders of a country have found themselves driven to the regrettable necessity of waging war upon another country, they do not merely say to themselves, 'We will attack Ruritania tomorrow'; but they also say: 'And when we do, we will limit ourselves to conventional weapons, and will refrain from resorting to nuclear.'

But, in the Soviet view, it simply is not possible to make any such declaration; because in any war the strategy to be used is dictated by the political objectives for which the war is being fought. If it is being fought for fundamental objectives, one cannot possibly fight it with limited means, however much one may honestly wish to do so: one can only fight with limited means if the objectives themselves are limited. Furthermore, an objective which may be of comparatively small importance to the one side may be absolutely vital to the other. Britain would not have collapsed in utter chaos if she had failed to emerge the victor in the Zulu Wars; but the British triumph in those wars, though of marginal importance to Britain, was of decisive significance for the Zulu society of the time. While, therefore, Britain prosecuted the war without mobilizing anything like the full military resources of which the British Empire was capable, the Zulus, faced with an end to their independence, did all they could to preserve it (in other words, for the Zulu nation the war was 'fundamental'; and they mobilized for its prosecution their absolute maximum resources).

The sum total of the Zulus' resources was not, of course, sufficient to have any lasting effect on the course of the war; but then they were not in possession of nuclear weapons. If, however, they had been, or if they had had supporting them a Great Power which was in possession of them, and for whom the independence of the Zulus was also of *vital* concern, it is not hard to see how the aim of the British, which was to wage a minor war with minimal military effort, might easily have been frustrated; and how the United Kingdom might have found itself involved, *through no wish of its own*, in a major, totally *un*limited war, when it had hoped to fight merely a 'limited' one.

The point will be examined in greater detail when we come to consider the effect of policy on strategy (see pp. 89–96 below); there is no need to say more about it here. Here we shall merely content ourselves with repeating that the Russians believe that the Western notion of 'limited war' is erroneous; that, if put into practice, it carries with it the grave danger of escalation; and that a war can truly be said to be 'limited' only when the aims of *both* the combatants are limited.

On account of this difference between the Russian and the Western concepts, there is a tendency for Soviet writers to keep the expression *ogranichennaya voina* for translating the (erroneous) Western expression, while using *voina s ogranichennoi tsel'yu* ('war with a limited aim') to describe their own, a tendency which perhaps is becoming obsolete.

(j) *Coalition wars*

For Soviet Russia the phrase has an especial significance; because, as Soviet historians are never weary of telling us, it was upon Soviet Russia that there descended, soon after the October Revolution, an armed coalition of imperialist countries striving to extirpate communism in its seedbed before it had taken root. Furthermore, by an emotive historical coincidence that the Soviet historians are equally fond of recalling, a similar armed coalition of reactionary powers had advanced upon the infant French Revolution in an attempt to extirpate that.

Both the attempts failed; but the reasons for their failure must be sought, in the Russians' opinion, not so much in the inadequacies of the generals in charge of the invasions, but in the defects inherent in the nature of armed coalitions.

The chief of these is that a coalition, being merely a 'temporary combination for special ends between parties that retain distinctive principles',[80] is likely to be pursuing simultaneously a number of disparate objectives. In other words, the 'distinctive principles' tend to carry more weight with the members of an armed coalition than the 'special ends' for which they have come together. In the case of the Allied intervention of 1918-20, which is of especial significance for the way in which the Soviet view of 'coalition war' evolved, the main aim of the Americans in Siberia was to make a gesture of solidarity with their allies; that of the Japanese to 'build up their political and economic position on the Asiatic mainland' and, in particular, in the Soviet Far East; that of the French to overthrow the Soviet Government and recover as much as they could of their capital assets; while the British aim was to 'find a new channel of access to the Middle Eastern theatre of war'. The above is a summary of the motives of the various countries, as seen by George F. Kennan:[81] Lenin, while disagreeing somewhat with the details, concurs with Kennan in asserting that the four governments were inspired almost wholly by purely self-seeking considerations, and that the goals of each differed widely from those of the others. (See, for instance, his speech of 6 December 1920.)

If we now turn from the situation that faced the infant Soviet Republic to the one facing it today, there is an obvious historic parallel. The USSR is confronted by a Western alliance that, in its military embodiment of NATO, has all the hallmarks of a coalition. The defence policies of the member states are far from being perfectly coordinated; and it can scarcely be doubted that, in the event of a war with the Communist bloc, disagreements between the members concerning objectives would be likely to make themselves felt. The effect of such disagreements, as the Russians see things, will be similar to that produced by Allied disharmony in Siberia over half a century ago; it would, they think, be a powerful factor making for a Soviet victory.

If a Western critic should retort that the Warsaw Pact is also a coalition, the Russians would thoroughly agree with him: they are fond of saying that a third world war would be a 'coalition war' *on both sides*. But, they add, the members of the Warsaw Pact are all 'proletarian' countries, and are therefore linked by a single, unified 'class interest'. But since, according to Marxist-Leninist theory, it is 'class interest' that begets political objectives, it follows that the political objectives pursued by the members of the Warsaw Pact are bound to be identical. Hence there will be no disagreements among the Warsaw Pact coalition; and hence their capacity for waging war will be greater than that of NATO.

If my readers should feel that the above dogma is unreal, high-falutin' theorizing, there are two points that should be remembered which tend to give it more substance, though perhaps even then not much. The first is that the Russians have unquestionably much more influence over the other members of the Warsaw Pact than the Americans have over NATO; indeed, the Russians possess *at all times* a considerable amount of sheer physical, military domination over their allies which the Americans certainly do not possess in peacetime, and are unlikely to possess in war. *In this particular respect* therefore, and to the extent that this sort of political and military domination is not counter-productive, the Warsaw Pact may well be thought to have a greater military capacity than the NATO Alliance.

The second point is that the USSR's own theory is really only applicable to the situation where it is NATO that is the aggressor. All Soviet writing on the subject of 'coalition war' describes it in the context of a Western attack on the East. Now, it is not to be doubted that, in the unthinkable event of the NATO countries agreeing to launch an attack on the USSR, considerable divergencies of opinion, and indeed of strategy, would be likely to make themselves felt. But it is not in that context that the Western reader is accustomed to envisage a clash between East and West: the Western reader is accustomed to assuming that the outbreak of a third world war could only occur as the result of *Soviet* aggression; and it is the Soviet view of what would happen if the *USSR* were the aggressor that interests him. (He also believes that a third world war might come about by accident; but, by definition, the accidental is basically irrational, and so cannot form the object of rational analysis. I am therefore going to ignore it.)

This interest of the Western reader is most unlikely to be satisfied by any perusal of published Soviet material that bears directly on this question: overt Soviet sources are nowadays never willing even so much as to consider the possibility of the Russians starting a war.

If, however, we bypass the Soviet reticence on the subject, and ourselves proceed to consider it, we shall see at once that important consequences follow. For it must be obvious that a 'bourgeois' coalition which, when engaged in marauding enterprises, may reasonably be expected, like any band of robbers, to fall out over the spoils, is equally likely, when itself invaded, to sink its differences in its efforts to resist the invader. Those who would refer to past history in an effort to assert the contrary have probably missed the point. There have been many instances of members of a 'bourgeois' coalition (or of a feudal coalition in the context of a feudal era) who have willingly collaborated with 'bourgeois' invaders (or with feudal invaders, if we are talking about a feudal epoch); but in such instances, according to Marxist theory, they lose nothing vital by doing so. Dog does not eat dog; 'bourgeois' may gnaw at, but will not gollop up, 'bourgeois'; the 'bourgeois' conquerors will leave the 'bourgeois' vanquished at least some crumbs of comfort and may even actually improve their lot, if at the time of the invasion the latter were faced with formidable opposition from their workers.

But where the invaders are 'proletarians', this is not so. It is a major purpose of any 'proletarian' invasion to topple the reactionary ruling class of the invaded country (whether 'bourgeois' or feudal), and instal in its place a truly 'progressive' government. In such circumstances it is not merely true that the winner takes all; it is also true that the loser (or, to speak more accurately, the loser's ruling class) is deprived of all that he hath. Consequently we may reasonably expect, as Marx and Engels and Lenin always expected, that if a 'bourgeois' coalition is invaded by a revolutionary army, the 'bourgeoisie' of the countries of that coalition will resist the invaders to the utmost.

But what of their workers and peasants? A number of authoritative Soviet sources have provided an answer to this question; and it runs as follows: Although according to Marxist-Leninist theory the workers and peasants of a 'bourgeois' country should welcome that country's invasion by the troops of a 'proletarian' country, they are only likely to do so if what is termed a 'genuinely revolutionary situation' exists in their State. Even then the incursion of the 'proletarian' forces needs to be preceded by a period of intensive, carefully orientated propaganda aimed at persuading the workers of the invaded country that what is about to happen is no tawdry war of conquest, but the giving of aid ('fraternal aid') to help them topple the oppressive regime of their tyrannical 'bourgeois' masters.

Where there is no situation that can be considered sufficiently 'revolutionary', or where there has been no time to proclaim the fraternal message in sufficient depth, Soviet opinion accepts that the workers and peasants of the invaded country will take an 'incorrect' view of the attitude they should take towards the Red Army units, and will fight like hell to defeat them. Lenin ascribed the Red Army's failure to seize and bolshevize Poland in 1920 largely to this very cause.[82]

The fact, therefore, that a future world war ('world war' in the Western, not the Soviet, sense) is seen by the Soviet Union as being a 'coalition war' on both sides means that they expect, if the West starts it, to derive considerable advantages from that circumstance, for the reasons adduced above. If, however, the Russians start it, then we have good reason to assume that it is their belief that the characteristics of 'coalition war' would work somewhat to their disadvantage, except in the context of an obviously revolutionary situation in the countries of the Western Alliance.

It remains only to be said that the above unfavourable consideration is not regarded by Soviet military opinion as signifying an inevitable Soviet defeat in the event of a Russian attack on the NATO countries. On the contrary, there are factors making for victory which they believe outweigh it (see pp. 96–112). Furthermore, they may very well be right in their opinion. Nevertheless, it is bound to exert a certain degree of restraining influence upon their calculations.

(k) *Civil wars*

A civil war, if subjected to the analysis of Marxism, may be seen as being either a war waged within the confines of a given society between two factions of that society's 'exploiting' class (e.g. the Wars of the Roses in England) or else as one between a country's 'exploiting' class and its 'exploited' class (such as the war of Spartacus in ancient Rome or the Peasant War in sixteenth-century Germany). As seen by Marxism, the first of these two types of civil war is most unlikely to have a beneficial *purpose*, although it is quite possible that it may have a beneficial *effect*. For instance, every feudal society at one time or another was subject to internecine conflict between the barons; and, generally speaking, the objects for which the rival factions of the nobility were fighting were not such as to commend themselves to Marxists. However, in those cases where the exhaustion of the warring factions made possible the creation of a strong, centralized monarchy (and hence led subsequently to the creation of a nation-State), the war would be viewed by them as having a 'progressive' *effect*, despite the fact that the motives that prompted the fighting would be condemned by them.

The American Civil War is a quasi-exception to the above; for, although it was fought between two sections of the American 'exploiting' class, the Southern section based their 'exploitation' upon slave labour; and this, in communist eyes, was a 'mode of production' which had become obsolete by the middle of the nineteenth century. By contrast, the North was capitalist; and, according to Marxism, capitalism was still 'progressive' in the 1850s, especially when compared with slavery. In addition to this, it was the declared intention of the North to put an end to slavery in the South, if it should be victorious. Therefore, in the case of the American Civil War, not only did it have a 'progressive' *effect* (the end of slavery in the South and its replacement by capitalism) but also, so far as the North was concerned, it had a progressive *aim*.[83]

The second type of civil war according to Marxist analysis (the war between the 'exploiters' and the 'exploited' of a given country) is likely to have a beneficent aim, as well as a beneficent effect. For in such a war the aim of one of the combatants, the 'exploited', is bound to be the downfall of the 'exploiters'; and this aim is invariably approved by Marxists. For it is only when all 'exploiters' of every kind have been abolished that there can be any real hope of finally establishing communism.

Communists regard civil wars of this second kind as something almost inevitable in a capitalist society. Lenin, for instance, believed that it is almost always only as the result of a civil war of this kind that capitalism can be ended and the revolution achieved. In his *A Caricature of Marxism* and *On the Disarmament Slogan* (both of October 1916), he asserts this unequivocally; while nearly two years later he repeats this unequivocal assertion in *Prophetic Words*.

In a whole mass of his other writing, the assertion is not spelled out so literally, but is expressed in the form of a syllogism: The triumph of communism is inevitable; the necessary precondition for this triumph is revolution; a revolution cannot take place without the fiercest opposition from the 'bourgeois'; this opposition is bound to escalate into civil war: therefore civil war is inevitable.

The syllogism itself, of course, is never written out so clearly and concisely as it has been written out above: none the less, it is there. Readers who will take the trouble to read *Two Tactics of Social-Democracy*, together with *A Caricature of Marxism* and *The Military Programme of the Proletarian Revolution*, will not be able to doubt at the end of their reading that these works contain in a more diffuse, less logically concentrated form the proposition that has been stated in the preceding paragraph.

Sometimes, it is true, Lenin hedges a little. He occasionally says, not that civil war is inevitable, but that it is *almost always* inevitable; and in these passages he goes on to say that, in certain countries 'under certain conditions', the 'bourgeois' may see that resistance is totally useless, and may therefore capitulate in the early stages of the power struggle, before it has got so far as civil war.[84] It should be noted that he never suggested that there was another way by which civil war might be averted—namely by the 'revolutionary proletariat' refraining from adopting such extreme measures that the 'bourgeoisie' were driven to fight for simple self-preservation.

As late as 1919, for instance, Lenin urged the adoption of the following measures upon the Bavarian communists, who had just seized power in Munich: the formation of councils of workers and servants in the different districts of Munich; the arming of the workers and the disarming of the 'bourgeoisie'; the use of the stocks of clothing and other items for the benefit of the workers, farm labourers and small peasants; the confiscation of the farms and factories of the capitalists, and also their monetary wealth; the cancellation of mortgage and rent payments owed by small peasants; the trebling of the wages of farm-labourers and unskilled workers; the confiscation of all printing presses and all stocks of paper; the immediate introduction of the six-hour working day; the requisitioning of the bourgeois' 'surplus' accommodation, and the giving of it to the workers; the taking over of all the banks; the taking of hostages from the ranks of the 'bourgeoisie'; the giving of higher rations to the workers than those allotted to the bourgeois; and the mobilization of all workers for defence and for ideological propaganda in the neighbouring villages.[85]

That the Bavarian 'bourgeois' should therefore take up arms to prevent such measures being inflicted on them would be, under all the circumstances, an almost inevitable occurrence. It is an important point, and a detailed discussion of it will be found towards the end of this chapter.

When one turns to the question of the attitude of Marx, Engels and Lenin towards particular civil wars, it is fair to say that this was never uniform: it varied according to the type of civil war and also according to what they considered would be its probable effect.

Insofar as concerns civil wars of the first type (one between two factions of the ruling 'class'), they invariably disapproved of its *aim*; but they were prepared to applaud its *effect*, if that should be to the benefit of the revolutionary cause: hence the difference in their attitude towards the various wars which were waged by the feudal nobility. The three men were against the *aim* of all of them; because all these wars were concerned either with a lust for power ('reactionary' power), or else with plunder and territorial aggrandizement. On the other hand, they approved the *effect* of some, where those led to the emergence of a strong, centralized, national authority. Those civil wars, however, whose effect led to the marked diminution of the powers of the central authority (the king), and thence to their subsequent collapse (as happened in Poland), were strongly criticized by Marx and his followers, and continue to be so criticized by the USSR.

Where, however, the civil war is one of the second type (a fight between the 'oppressors' and the 'oppressed'), Marxist sympathies are invariably in favour of the insurgents; since the victory of the latter will lead, they hope, to revolutionary progress.

That this statement is true of the sympathies of Marx, Engels and Lenin is so obvious that it really does not require documentation. Sceptics, however, are referred to Marx's *Civil War in France* ('a war of slaves against their oppressors, the only just war known to history'), and to a whole string of Lenin's *dicta* in the same vein. In *Partisan War*, of October 1906, for instance, he explains his position in detail (roman original italics):

*No Marxist can consider civil war (or partisan war, as one of its forms) to be* in principle *abnormal or demoralising. A Marxist bases himself on the class struggle, and not on social peace. At certain periods of sharp political and economic crises, the class struggle develops into open civil war (i.e., into armed struggle between two sections of the people). At such times, a Marxist is* obliged *to support this civil war.*

Ten years later, in *The Military Programme of the Proletarian Revolution*, Lenin repeated essentially the same message in fewer words; while numerous passages in his other works are also couched in this vein. (See, in particular, the first section of his authoritative *Socialism and War*.)

Modern Soviet thinking agrees fully with this viewpoint; and those interested are referred to such sources as the section devoted to civil war in the second edition of the *Great Soviet Encyclopaedia*.[86]

## (1) *Revolutionary wars*

If revolutionary war is regarded by Marx and Engels, and also (and particularly) by Lenin, as one of the most important categories of war, it is also easily the most difficult to define. This is because Marx and Engels are vague in their use of this expression, while Lenin himself employs it in at least three different meanings. Moreover, he even uses it with two, and sometimes all three, different meanings in one and the same work.

Since, in the view of the Soviet Communist Party, the writings of Marx and Engels upon this subject are of little importance as compared with those of Lenin, it is to Lenin's writings that I shall confine myself almost exclusively; and his view of revolutionary war may be summarized as follows:

No war can be a 'revolutionary war' unless it is waged by a 'revolutionary party'. This is made clear in such works as *Several Theses* of October 1915, where Lenin says that, if the Russian 'proletariat' were to win power, and if it found itself unable to conclude a peace, the war that it would then be forced to fight would be turned into a 'revolutionary war'. Similar assertions can be found elsewhere in his writings.[87]

But a 'revolutionary party' is bound to follow a 'revolutionary policy', just as the British Labour Party will follow Labour policies, and the Conservative Party, Conservative policies. 'By their fruits ye shall know them!' The quotation comes from St Matthew; but the works of Lenin that I have just quoted demonstrate that, at least on this matter, Christian thinking agrees with Marxist thinking.

A 'revolutionary war' may therefore be defined as a 'war which is waged by a revolutionary party for a revolutionary purpose'. This definition automatically excludes from the category of 'revolutionary wars' those conflicts which have no revolutionary *purpose*, but which do have a revolutionary *effect*. The First World War, for instance, had an undeniably revolutionary effect, as Russian history demonstrates. Nevertheless, it is termed in Leninist parlance an 'imperialist' war, and not a 'revolutionary' one.

But a 'revolutionary party' may have all manner of 'revolutionary purposes', of which one, obviously, will be the making of the revolution in those countries where it has not yet been achieved. Other revolutionary purposes, according to Lenin, were the immediate ending of the First World War on a basis of no annexations and no indemnities, together with the instant liberation of all colonies and all protectorates;[88] the destruction of the power of the capitalists inside Russia;[89] and the introduction of universal labour conscription. He gave a great number of others, including the defence of Red Russia against the Whites and their Allied supporters.[90]

In one sense, therefore, Lenin's use of the phrase 'revolutionary war' amounts to no more than 'a war to be supported by Marxists'. Used in this sense, the expression 'revolutionary war' is synonymous with a 'just war' or a 'progressive war'; and in a letter to Zinoviev of August 1916, Lenin makes clear that this is so.[91]

In another sense, Lenin uses 'revolutionary war' to mean 'a war in defence of the revolution' or 'a war in defence of the "proletariat"'. In certain passages, he asserts that he is so using it; and interested readers are referred to his speech to the Conference of the RSDLP Groups Abroad, which he delivered in March 1915 (the section entitled 'Pacifism and the peace slogan'), and to his *Theses on the Agrarian Question Adopted by the Communist Party of France*, published in 1922.

Among examples of actual wars which would be 'revolutionary wars' in this particular meaning of Lenin's, we may cite the efforts made by the French Revolutionary armies to defend the new-born Republic against the onslaughts of the allied kings. This was called by Marx and Engels a 'revolutionary war'; and has continued to be so called by their successors. Another example is the civil war in Russia of 1918–20, when the Bolshevik armies were said by Lenin to have been fighting a 'revolutionary war'; because one of their aims was to defend the revolution against the Russian and the Allied 'bourgeois'.

These two wars are still regarded by Soviet political writers as prime examples of 'revolutionary war' in this particular sense.[92] However, the argument has been taken a good deal further than this; because, since the Soviet Communist Party believes that the USSR is the sole true guardian of the revolution and the sole true home of the 'proletariat', any war in which the USSR may happen to become engaged will be for the defence of the revolution; and the war itself may therefore rightly be termed a 'revolutionary war' by the canons of Leninist logic.

The third meaning sometimes given by Lenin to 'revolutionary war' is what the 'bourgeois' tend to think that he *always* means by it—viz 'a war to spread the revolution by force of arms'. Of course, there is no doubt whatever that sometimes he does use 'revolutionary war' in this sense; and one cannot doubt it because he explicitly says so.

Thus, in a footnote to *The Collapse of the Second International* (1915) Lenin writes (roman original italics):

*We Marxists have always stood, and still stand, for a* revolutionary *war against* counter-revolutionary *nations. For instance, if socialism is* victorious *in America or in Europe in 1920, and Japan and China, let us say, then move their Bismarcks against us—if only diplomatically at first—we certainly would be in* favour *of an offensive revolutionary war against them.*

In *Theses on the Question of the Immediate Conclusion of a Separate and Annexationist Peace* (January 1918) Lenin declared that, at that juncture, a 'truly revolutionary war . . . would be a war waged by a socialist republic against the bourgeois countries, with the aim—an aim clearly defined and fully approved by the socialist army—of overthrowing the bourgeoisie in other countries'.

Similar passages can be found elsewhere in Lenin's writings.

In whichever of Lenin's three meanings the phrase 'revolutionary war' is used by Soviet communists, the fact that they use it means (as it meant with Lenin) that the war in question has the Party's wholehearted approval. This statement is just as true of the third meaning (the 'revolutionary war' fought to thrust communism upon other nations by force of arms) as it is of the first and second. Moreover, communist approval of this third kind of 'revolutionary war' is just as automatic, irrespective of whether the war in question is a later extension of a war begun by others (as in the case of the French Revolutionary wars, and of the Russo-Polish War of 1920) or whether it is a war actually *initiated* by the communists—where the communists, that is to say, would be termed by Westerners the 'aggressors'. Of this third type of 'revolutionary war' the best examples (as we have seen above) are the operations in Georgia in 1921, and the seizure and subsequent 'sovietization' of Latvia, Estonia and Lithuania in 1940.[93]

However, for propaganda purpose, it is essential for the Soviet Union nowadays to pretend that Lenin never used 'revolutionary war' in this third sense; because if once the world at large were to believe that a communist government was prepared to spread revolution by force, the likely result would be an increased hostility to the Soviet Union and to communism. For a long time now, therefore, the USSR has stoutly maintained that, when Lenin spoke of 'revolutionary war', he was using that phrase in our second meaning ('war in defence of the revolution'); and it has cited the appropriate quotations to support its point (those that have already been quoted on p. 53).

Moreover, the Soviet Communist Party has never felt able to acknowledge to the world at large that Lenin ever used 'revolutionary war' even in our *first* meaning (i.e. as synonymous with a 'just' war); because that would involve admitting that Lenin *approved* of war under certain circumstances. This approval, shared by Lenin's successors, including the present rulers of the USSR, is highly inconvenient to the

Soviet Union in its efforts to present itself to world opinion as peace-loving. In particular, it could lose it a lot of support among those sections of the non-communist West which are pacifist or semi-pacifist by nature.

As a result, the phrase 'revolutionary war' is to be found used ever less frequently in authoritative Soviet publications. Thus, although the first edition of the *Great Soviet Encyclopaedia*, published in 1928,[94] has a full discussion on the subject, the second edition, which dates from 1951,[95] contains only passing references to the matter. The third edition, which dates from 1971, is even less forthcoming, though it still mentions it.[96] Similarly, the subject-index to the third Russian edition of Lenin's works, which appeared in 1935, contains no less than fifty-seven references to the various facets of 'revolutionary war'; but the similar index attached to the fourth edition, dating from 1955, has only half that number. In 1958, a fifth edition was published, with about three times as many items in it as the previous editions had had. Despite this, the subject-index, which came out in 1969, has no proper reference at all to 'revolutionary war'. If you look under 'Voina' ('war') there is no mention of it; and if you look under 'Revolyutsionniye Voiny', it refers you to civil wars, to wars of national liberation, and back to the entry on 'War' (sub-heading: 'Lenin's teaching on the subject of war'). But since there are 468 separate references shown under this particular sub-heading, and no specific mention of 'revolutionary war', a man has to be perversely enthusiastic about the subject, who will plough through all these references for Lenin's *dicta*. On the other hand, Marshal Sokolovsky's *Military Strategy* of 1963 avers that a third world war would be a 'revolutionary war', so far as the Soviet Union was concerned.[97]

It is important to note that this sharp reduction in the number of references to 'revolutionary war' to be found in the subject-indexes to Lenin's works has not been accompanied by excisions in his actual text. For instance, the article 'On The Slogan For A United States of Europe' still carries the assertion that, if the 'proletariat' should be victorious in one country, it would then rise up against the capitalists in the rest of the world—if necessary by armed force. Similarly, the footnote to *The Collapse of the Second International* still proclaims that Lenin would be in favour of an offensive 'revolutionary war' under certain circumstances.

In other words, it is the *label* which is thought undesirable in today's conditions: the underlying philosophy is regarded as still valid.

And indeed it obviously must be. For, as we saw at the beginning of this chapter, it is a basic doctrine of Marxism that wars are fought for the benefit of the ruling classes and in furtherance of their own class interests. And this is as true of the 'proletariat', when it becomes the ruling class of a country as the result of a revolution, as of any other ruling class.[98]

To those who may object that this is not so—that the 'proletariat', unlike all other ruling classes, would never contemplate resorting to war as a means of furthering its interests—one can only retort that authoritative Bolshevik opinion does not agree with them; and in support of this assertion one may cite not only the innumerable passages from Lenin, which have already been quoted and which will also be quoted later in this chapter (see, for instance, pp. 70-4 on the communist attitude to aggression and self-defence), but also the *Great Soviet Encyclopaedia*. The latter, indeed, has a long section on the way in which all ruling classes, *including the proletariat*, must necessarily seek to advance their own class interests whenever they engage in war; and it goes on to state that this was exactly what was done by the Soviet proletariat in the course of the Russo-Polish War of 1920 and again in the case of the operations in Georgia in 1921. Both these campaigns it labels 'revolutionary wars'; and it might well have gone on to give us further examples, if it had been published at a later date than in fact it was.[99]

(m) *'Wars of fraternal aid'*

The expression is my own: no communist would countenance it for a moment. The phrase is intended to describe those applications of armed force by the Government of the Soviet Union, whose object has been to effect a social revolution in the countries which were the target of it, irrespective of whether formal battles did or did not take place. It is therefore identical with 'revolutionary war' in the third of that phrase's meanings.

But, as we have seen, 'revolutionary war' is an expression which the Soviet leaders have been reluctant to use in public (that is to say, in circumstances where it would reach the 'bourgeois' world); and as time has gone by, this reluctance of theirs has grown. Whereas the first edition of the *Great Soviet Encyclopaedia* was prepared to describe the operations in Georgia in 1921 as a 'revolutionary war', more modern writers have not. And whereas Lenin himself employed the term on quite a large number of occasions, Khrushchev and his successors have refrained from doing so. Lenin's category of wars includes 'revolutionary wars'; Khrushchev's altogether omits it.[100]

Nevertheless, the fact is indisputable that the Soviet Government, on more than one occasion, has sought by the use of its armed forces to bring about fundamental changes in the social structure of other countries, or, to put it more bluntly, has tried to use force to 'sovietize' them. Moreover, on several of these occasions it has been successful. The changes in question in these countries' social structures may already actually have been attempted by the local communist party, as they were in Finland in 1918, or they may never even have been contemplated, as was the case in the Baltic States in 1940. In every case, however, it was asserted by the Soviet Government that 'the workers and peasants' of the country in question were trying to make a 'proletarian' revolution, were meeting with opposition from their capitalists and landlords, and wanted Soviet assistance.

And that is why Soviet communists do not find it necessary to use the word 'war' to describe affairs like these. For, if in 1918, Bolshevik Russia and Finland had been *at war* with one another, then the Bolshevik *State* would have been fighting the Finnish *State*. But from the communist viewpoint this was not what was happening. In Lenin's eyes, the Bolshevik State was merely supporting brother 'proletarians' who were engaged in a struggle against their capitalists and landlords, and who happened to be Finnish:[101] it was engaged in sending 'fraternal aid' to the Finnish revolutionary workers. Indeed it was almost these very same words that Stalin used to describe the process in question.[102]

Even in the case of the Russo-Polish War of 1920, an event which is always described as a 'war' by Soviet commentators (probably because it was an operation begun by the Polish *Government* and directed against the Soviet *Government*, the second stage of this conflict sees the appearance of 'fraternal aid' as a term used by Lenin to describe the purpose of the Red Army's continued advance. The Soviet Government may not have begun the war; but, once it had won some victories, it determined to make use of the opportunity to bring a communist revolution to Poland. That the attempt failed is not to our purpose here; we are here concerned simply to note that Lenin himself, describing the advance on Warsaw and the concomitant 'bolshevization' of Polish territory occupied by the Red Army,[103] told an audience in Moscow that the intention in marching on the Polish capital was to hand over power to the Warsaw workers, convene a Soviet of Workers' and Peasants' Deputies, and say to the Polish 'proletarians' and peasants, 'We have come to your aid'.[104] And he persisted in using this phrase about 'coming to their aid', despite the fact that the Polish workers and peasants showed precious little signs of wanting it.

The swallowing up in 1940 of Latvia, Lithuania and Estonia under pressure from the Red Army, together with the subsequent forcible imposition upon them of a communist regime, is described by the *Great Soviet Encyclopaedia* as sending 'fraternal aid' to those countries' workers and peasants;[105] while, in 1968, it was the bringing of 'fraternal aid' that was the purpose of the swoop into Czechoslovakia by the Soviet armed forces. Indeed, that is why we in the West were said to have fallen into 'bourgeois' error when we described this latter event as an 'invasion'. The reasons why the Russians indulged in this

C

operation are not to our present purpose: our concern here is only to note that a large-scale military operation by the Soviet armed forces was not described by the Russians as 'war' or 'invasion', but simply as 'fraternal aid' to fellow-communists; and the fact that for so long they were unable to identify the communists who allegedly asked for this 'help' from their Russian brothers has no bearing at all on the fact that, wanted or not, 'fraternal aid' was supplied.

The relevance of the above to future events can be put quite simply in a nutshell. The Soviet Union will not use the dread word 'war' to describe operations conducted by her armed forces, whatever their nature may be, *so long as the operations in question have been initiated by the Soviet Government*. This is because the Soviet Union is invariably and undeviatingly 'peace-loving'. By contrast, if the operations were the result of an attack launched upon her by another country, she would say unhesitatingly that she was engaged in fighting a *war*. And if this sounds merely like abstract academic theorizing, irrelevant to practical people, there could well be occasions when it might not be so.

For instance, I have no reason whatever to suppose that the Soviet Government has made any plans for the invasion and conquest of Afghanistan, or for the invasion and conquest of West Germany (though I also have no reason to suppose that the Soviet Government has not). But, for the sake of argument, let us assume the existence of such plans; and let us further assume that the United States is unable or unwilling to take any action to prevent their materialization. No one can doubt that, under such circumstances, the conquest of both these countries could be swiftly accomplished; but the relevant point is that, if this happened, it would not be described by the USSR as 'invasion', 'conquest' or 'war'. Once again, the Soviet Government would have been sending 'fraternal aid' to fellow 'proletarians' and peasants—in this case, to the 'proletarians' and peasants of Afghanistan and West Germany. Moreover, in order to lend verisimilitude to what Poo-Bah once described as a 'bald and unconvincing narrative', it might be considered prudent to wait until a strike or a riot provided incontrovertible evidence of the existence of dissident citizens, who can then be labelled 'proletarians' or 'peasants' just as easily as 'strikers' or 'rioters'. And, once you have found them, you can send them 'fraternal-aid'. *Verb.*, as the saying goes, *sap*.

## The communist attitude to aggression and self-defence, and to 'offensive' and 'defensive' wars

It will be thought odd that nowhere in the previous section has mention been made of 'offensive' and 'defensive' wars. Yet, as we all know, Marx and Engels frequently employed these terms, and Lenin did so not seldom. Why, then, have they been omitted from the previous section, which claimed to expound the categories of war most usually recognized by communists?

The answer is that the way that these terms were used by Marx, Engels and Lenin was such as to render them wholly incomprehensible to the ordinary 'bourgeois' Westerner, who has had no previous instruction in their specifically Marxist meanings. 'Attack' and 'defence', for instance, might seem to the average Westerner to be the complete opposite of each other; yet we have it on Lenin's authority that there is no essential difference between them.[106]

Faced with this situation, it seemed advisable not to proceed with a discussion of the Marxist concept of 'offensive' and 'defensive' wars until we had first examined what precisely communists mean when they speak of 'attack' and 'defence'; and such an examination therefore forms the subject of the first part of this section. But since the actual expressions 'attack' and 'defence' are most usually used by communist writers in connection with military *minutiae*, our actual examination is devoted, not to these two terms, but to their cognate terms in the field of international relations—aggression and self-defence.

One cannot acknowledge the right to self-defence without implying that, should it be exercised, one will support the persons who exercise it. Such support, of course, need not be physical; it can confine itself to purely moral encouragement; but unless one is prepared to accord at least so much support, one is surely wrong in saying that the person assailed has any actual *right* to resist his assailant; and one should say instead that it is a matter of common experience that men will generally defend themselves who are first attacked.

It is clear from what I have written in the previous section that there are many kinds of war where Marx and Engels could not possibly have acknowledged with any logic the *right* to self-defence. For instance, when Marx in 1848 proposed that war be declared on Tsarist Russia, he could hardly have maintained, simultaneously with that proposition, that Tsarism had the right to defend itself. He would certainly have agreed that Tsarism would undoubtedly do so, just as he always agreed that the 'bourgeois' would undoubtedly defend themselves against a 'proletarian' attempt at a revolution; but he could not then have logically agreed, in view of his original postulates, that Tsarism had the *right* to defend itself, in the sense of having the right to call upon all Russian subjects (including 'proletarians' and peasants) to come to the defence of the Romanov privileges against a liberalizing, reformatory invader.

Similarly, if Marx really regarded a war of 'slaves against their oppressors' as being 'the only just war in history', as he said he did,[107] it is hard to see how he could meaningfully have believed that the oppressors had any *right* to oppose the slaves.

On the other hand, there is no doubt whatever that Marx and Engels were generally of the opinion that a nation which was attacked had the right to defend itself, *whenever the aim of the aggressor was plunder or territorial aggrandizement or the fulfilment of dynastic ambition.*

However, the sharp lines of this thesis become slightly blurred when we look at the reactions of Marx and Engels to the Austro-Prussian War of 1866. Here Prussia was the aggressor; but although her aims in starting the war can be described not altogether unfairly as a mixture of territorial aggrandizement and dynastic ambition (or, at any rate, Bismarck's ambition), the fact that she was the aggressor did not enter into the calculations of Marx and Engels, when deciding which side to support. On the contrary, these calculations were based, as was usual with them, on a consideration of which side's victory would do most for the revolutionary cause.

From which it follows that, before one can decide whether in a given war the aggressed has the right to self-defence, one must first determine the aims of the aggressor. Where that aim is 'progressive' (the furtherance of the revolution, national liberation etc.), the attacked nation, according to Marx and Engels, does *not* seem to have any right to defend itself, though it may nevertheless proceed to exercise it. Where, however, the aim of the aggressor is 'reactionary' (plunder, territorial aggrandizement, dynastic ambition), the right of the attacked to self-defence is in principle admitted; and its attempts to exercise that right will usually be supported by communists.

In illustration of the first of these two statements, we may take the Risorgimento. From the Marxist point of view, this was a 'war of national liberation' on the part of the Italians, whose cause was therefore 'progressive'. However, so far as the question of aggression was concerned, it was the Italians, not the Austrians, who started the fighting. Despite this fact, neither Marx nor Engels, nor subsequently Lenin, bestowed upon the cause of the Austrian Empire one single jot of sympathy, as they surely must have done, if they had ever genuinely recognized as an overriding principle the right to self-defence.

In illustration of the second statement, we may take the wars of Napoleon Bonaparte. Whereas Marx, Engels and Lenin always held that the wars of the French Revolution were 'progressive', they condemned as 'reactionary' those of Napoleon I. This was because the aims of the latter were territorial aggrandizement, plunder and dynastic ambition. Consequently, Marxian support was given to all those peoples of Europe who resisted Napoleon's efforts to incorporate them into his empire, and Marxian recognition accorded to their right to defend themselves against him.

It will be seen, therefore, that, on the subject of self-defence, Marx and Engels produced no consistent, clear-cut body of doctrine. Was it really true that, when a 'reactionary' government was attacked by a more 'progressive', the former did *not* possess the right to self-defence? That proposition seems implicit in Marx's and Engels' writings; but I know of nowhere where they actually say so explicitly.

Similarly, although both men appear to be agreed that, where one nation attacks another for plunder or territorial aggrandizement, the latter is fully justified in defending itself, is this true of those instances where the nation which has been the subject of the attack is more 'reactionary' than its assailant? By Marxist reckoning, the old Roman Empire was more 'reactionary' than its barbarian invaders; on the other hand, the purpose of the latter was undeniably territorial aggrandizement, plunder and dynastic ambition. Engels tells us specifically that he approved of the *result* of these invasions; but whether he thought that Rome had a right to defend herself, he does not say.

Even in a cause which automatically acquired the fullest possible measure of support from both Marx and Engels (e.g. a war begun by a colony against the colonial power), I know of no instance where the two men definitely state that the latter had no right to defend itself; though it is clear that they hoped that, if it had, it would exercise it feebly and ineffectually.[108]

In the contrary case (where a would-be colonizer attempts to acquire a colony) the right of self-defence on the part of the attacked is generally recognized by Marxism; though, in any case, a war such as this can be brought under the general heading of the right to defend oneself against an attempt at territorial conquest.

However, when it came to wars between the major powers of Europe, where neither combatant, if it were victorious, was likely to want to colonize the other (in the sense of seizing and occupying the whole of its territory on a permanent basis), the question of which was the attacker, and which the attacked, was one that Marx and Engels raised very seldom. Instead, in such cases as these, the question that they usually put to themselves, in order to determine which side to support, was 'Whose victory is likely to do most for the cause of the revolution?'

Thus, despite the fact that the British and French were the aggressors, Marx and Engels supported their cause at the time of the Crimean War because they thought that a Russian victory would have led to a still greater strengthening of Tsarist reaction, and that this would have been 'an indescribable misfortune for the cause of the Revolution'. A Russian defeat, on the other hand, seemed likely to lead to a social revolution both in Russia and elsewhere in Europe. Hence, although neither Marx nor Engels wanted to benefit the French and the British 'bourgeois', they thought that a victory for Britain and France would be preferable to a victory for Russia; and the fact that the former had started the war was of no importance to them.[109] Indeed, I think it is fair to say that, taken as a whole, self-defence was a matter of nugatory importance to Marx, Engels and Lenin.

The above statement is likely to sound outrageous in the ears of those many people, both communists and others, who are accustomed to regard Engels and Marx as persons unwilling to countenance any war *except in self-defence*. Even those who have a somewhat more extensive acquaintance with the writings of those two men, and who are therefore aware that they undoubtedly approved of wars where the question of self-defence did not arise, even such people have a tendency to think that in most cases (though admittedly not in all) self-defence was the touchstone for Marx and Engels. The more I read what Marx and Engels themselves have had to say on this particular subject, the less I believe it to be true. Furthermore, there is one circumstance which supports me in my belief; and this is that, in saying what I have said above, I appear to have the backing of Soviet scholarship.

Before examining what Soviet scholarship actually has to say on the matter, I would remind my readers that the Soviet Politburo has for years been assiduously assuring us that the USSR is 'peace-loving', and that she will never engage in war unless attacked. Further, they have sought to prove the truth of these assertions by declaring that Soviet policy is founded on Leninism, which in turn is founded on Marxism; and that it was precisely because neither Marx nor Engels nor Lenin would, they say (in those speeches of theirs which are intended for world consumption), ever agree to take part in a war *except* in self-defence, that the same principle is observed by the USSR.

But if this is so, Marx, Engels and Lenin must have written a very great deal in defence of this thesis, in order to have had any chance at all of convincing the world of their day that war was no longer to be resorted to, unless one was first attacked; for in their lifetime war was regarded as a natural and inevitable, and even as a desirable, phenomenon. Furthermore, if they had actually written those reams and reams of polemics, it would clearly be in the Soviet Government's best interests to publicize them as much as possible; so that all might see how peace-loving is that philosophy which serves as the basis for the policies of the USSR. But when the Foreign Languages Publishing House in Moscow brought out an English version of the *Selected Works* of Marx and Engels in two volumes, the works that it selected lend little credence to the thesis advanced above.

It is not that these works avoid the subject of war. According to a most useful subject-index to be found at the end of each volume, they contain between them a total of thirty-seven references to the matter; and I myself, after a careful perusal of the text, have found two or three references more. Yet of all these thirty-seven or more references, there is only one which is concerned with 'self-defence' (it is listed, incidentally, under the heading of 'defensive war').

The *Selected Works* are supplemented by a *Selected Correspondence*, produced by the same publishing house. In this, there is a total of forty-two references to war given in the subject-index; but only two of these are concerned with 'defensive war'; and there are no additional entries to be found under the heading of 'self-defence' or anything similar. Nor does a careful examination of the actual text reveal any. Spread over the three volumes, this gives a total of seventy-eight references to war, of which those referring to 'defensive war' account for only three.

Two of these three references are concerned with the Franco-Prussian War; and it is noteworthy that, of the six wars which are specifically mentioned by name in these three volumes, the Franco-Prussian is the only one where Marx and Engels bother to introduce a mention of that question of self-defence, which for them was supposedly such an important principle. In the case of the other five, the works contained in these volumes do not devote a single sentence to it.

Moreover, even in the case of the Franco-Prussian War, the Prussians' right to self-defence is qualified by Marx. After saying that they may 'justly claim' some sympathy 'in a war of defence against Bonapartist aggression', he adds that 'they would forfeit it at once by allowing the Prussian Government to call for, or accept, the help of the Cossacks'.[110] The reason for this, says Marx, is that 'after their war of independence against the first Napoleon, Germany lay for generations prostrate at the feet of the Czar'.[111] This point of view may, or may not, be sound political reasoning; it is hardly an expression of unqualified support for the right to self-defence.

Nor does that right get further championship from the third reference to 'defensive wars' to be found in the volumes I was mentioning. This consists of that famous passage from Engels, where he says that 'the victorious proletariat can force no blessings of any kind upon any foreign nation without immediately undermining its own victory by so doing. This of course by no means excludes defensive wars of various kinds'. The first sentence is important in another context; and it will be examined in detail in a chapter entitled 'The Messianic Element in Marxism-Leninism', which will appear in another volume. Engels' second sentence tells us nothing, unless we assume that a 'defensive war' must always mean 'a war where one is first attacked'. But such an assumption, in the context of our discussion, would be a ridiculous tautology.

At the end of it all, the views of Marx and Engels concerning the right to self-defence may be summarized roughly as follows:

(i)  When two nations are 'reactionary' (or 'progressive') to a precisely equal degree, neither of them has the right to attack the other. If either does, its victim will be entitled to defend itself; and its efforts to do so will be termed a 'defensive' war, and will usually be supported by Marxists.

(ii)  If a 'reactionary' nation attacks another which is less 'reactionary' (or more 'progressive'), the latter has the right to defend itself; and its efforts to do so will be termed a 'defensive' war (or, in certain circumstances, a 'revolutionary war'), and will usually be supported by Marxists.

(iii)  If a 'progressive' nation attacks a 'reactionary' nation, it is extremely doubtful whether Marx and Engels allowed the 'reactionary' nation any right at all to defend itself.

(iv)  If a nation attacks another with the purpose of turning it into a colony, Marx and Engels generally allowed the latter the right to defend itself.

(v)  Nowhere in Marx's and Engels' writings is there any really clear exposition of their views on self-defence—still less is there any attempt to demonstrate the thesis that a Marxist is permitted to resort to war only if attacked first.

But, having thus considered the Marxists' attitude towards the right to self-defence, what about the other side of the coin? What about their attitude to aggression? Surely they, who condemn war as an evil, could never be willing to start one?

The answer, however, is that, whenever it has suited them to do so, they have had no hesitation whatever about committing aggression. Indeed, aggression was in the true revolutionary tradition. The French Revolutionaries, for instance, were very much in favour of wars to free peoples from the rule of oppressive monarchs; and they had no objection to starting a war in order to attain their objective.[112] Marx and Engels continued this tradition, and developed it; while, as we shall see, Lenin developed it further.

Of course, as is well known, neither Marx nor Engels was ever at the head of a government or commander-in-chief of an army. Neither man, therefore, had the power to begin a war, even if he so wished; nor to prevent the outbreak of a war which he opposed. All the wars that took place, or were prevented from taking place, during the lifetimes of these two men were the result of the schemes of kings and of cabinet ministers, who went on their ways regardless of any views which two eccentric and extremely obscure revolutionaries might wish to express on the matter. In view of the tremendous attention which nowadays is paid to all aspects of Marx's and Engels' thinking (and of which this present book is just one unimportant example), it is right to recall that, while they were still alive, Marxism was merely one tiny, schismatic section of an international socialist movement which, during the period in question, could itself exert almost no influence at all upon the counsels of princes and governments.

Consequently, with regard to those wars that actually happened between 1818 (the year of Marx's birth) and 1895 (the year of Engels' death), the attitude of the two founders of Marxism was necessarily extremely similar to that of the Athenians in the great harbour of Syracuse, when they watched the efforts of their comrades upon the sea, whose defeat or victory would destroy or advance their cause, but whose longed-for success they had no means whatever of promoting.[113]

As a result of this impotence of Marx and Engels with regard to the practical political decisions of their day, it is essential to remember, when considering their views on aggression, that, had they actually possessed the power to begin or prevent a war, they might not necessarily have exercised that power in the way that their writings suggest. Nevertheless, it should also be remembered that, after the October Revolution, Lenin did possess this power; and that the way in which he exercised it, and did not exercise it, follows remarkably closely the published views of Marx and Engels on the subject, as will be demonstrated later in this chapter (see pp. 70–4).

We may begin our task of assessing the views of Marx and Engels on the subject of aggression by summoning the evidence assembled in the course of the preceding sub-section, which went to show that they very seldom concerned themselves with who actually began a war. From this, we may reasonably infer that in their opinion it mattered little if one did so. Both men were well aware of the enormities of war; they were equally well aware of its extreme importance as a means of hastening social revolutions; but they were, it seems, practically never interested in the question of who was the aggressor.

It might be argued that, because they themselves were powerless to commit (or to prevent) aggression, it is a subject to which they would naturally not devote more than a tiny fraction of their attention. If this is true, it is quite uncharacteristic of them. They did not possess (and admittedly did not possess) the power to prevent the 'exploiting class' from behaving in the way it did; yet that did not prevent them from devoting pages and pages and pages to a minute examination of the details of that class's behaviour. And the reason that they examined it minutely was because they felt it was of importance; and if they had felt that the question of aggression was of remotely comparable importance, they undoubtedly would have subjected it to an examination of commensurate nicety.

But, before continuing further with the discussion, it should be made clear that 'aggression' is being used here in the sense in which it is used by the Soviet Union today; because this book is concerned with Soviet attitudes. The latest official Soviet definition of aggression that is available at the time of writing is to be found under the heading of 'Agressiya' in the new (the third) edition of the *Bol'shaya Sovietskaya Entsiklopediya* (Moscow, 1971). This definition may be summed up by saying that he who attacks first is the aggressor; and that no reasons of politics or economics can justify such an action.[114]

If this is so, Marx and Engels must surely stand *un*justified in the eyes of the Soviet encyclopaedia. To start with, they strongly urged Germany to declare war upon Russia in 1842, and again in 1848. It is true that the Germans did not take their advice; but this has nothing to do with the fact that, like it or not, Marx and Engels wanted aggression committed. Moreover, when Prussia did actually commit aggression by invading Schleswig-Holstein in 1848, the two men gave her action their hearty support.[115]

If we turn now to the other kinds of war recognized by Marxist thinkers, we have seen above that they thoroughly approved of civil wars between the 'oppressors' and the 'oppressed', 'wars of national liberation', and 'revolutionary wars'. But to approve of civil wars from the point of view of the 'oppressed', or of 'wars of national liberation' from the point of view of the colony, means that one must approve, and indeed definitely desire, the starting of such wars by the 'oppressed' and by the colonized peoples.

For otherwise there will be no war. Once the colonizers have completed their conquest and wholly subjugated their colony, their only wish is for law and order to prevail; so that they may administer their newly-acquired dominion with the minimum of trouble and expense, and provide conditions for their merchants and industrialists to flourish. The colonizers therefore, so far from starting a war, will do all they can to prevent such a thing from happening. The whole history of the British rule in India shows that the Raj was prepared to resort to war in order to *extend* that rule, but always tried to maintain peace in the areas it had already conquered. The histories of the French, the German, the Spanish, and the Italian colonial empires, as well as those of any other that one can think of, all point the same moral.

Similarly with civil war. The 'oppressors' (the rulers of the nation) have no wish to begin a war against the 'oppressed', so long as the latter are prepared to accept their station in life, and do what their rulers tell them. Civil war between the 'oppressors' and the 'oppressed' breaks out when the latter have had enough of their 'oppression', and rise up in arms to put an end to it.

The circumstances that cause them to rise up in arms, instead of remedying their grievances by legal methods, are not to our purpose here. Here we are concerned solely with the fact that, on those occasions when civil wars between 'oppressors' and 'oppressed' do actually break out, it is the 'oppressed' who are the cause of it doing so.

This is true even in those instances where the first shots are fired by the 'oppressors'. Thus, the 1905 uprising in Tsarist Russia was sparked off by shots fired by Tsarist forces. The reason they opened hostilities was that the general situation was so threatening that they hoped by this means to suppress the incipient disorders before they had had time to erupt (a hope which, in the particular instance in question, was certainly not justified by the event). Similar reasons operate in similar incidents elsewhere.

Therefore, to say that Marx and Engels approved of civil wars between the 'oppressors' and the 'oppressed', and also of 'wars of national liberation', is also to say that they approved of such wars being started. Those who wish for specific textual authority are referred to their writings on the subject of the Indian Mutiny for their views on 'wars of national liberation'; while *The Civil War in France* will provide the same service in a *negative* connotation, so far as civil wars are concerned. In other words, the Commune is there reproached with having *failed* to start a civil war; and its subsequent downfall is largely ascribed by Marx to its omission to do so. (The reader should be reminded yet again that, from the Marxian viewpoint, the American Civil War of 1861–5 was *not* a war between 'oppressors' and 'oppressed', but between two different sections of the American 'oppressing' class; and the fact that one of them happened to be considered to be more 'progressive' than the other, and hence to be very much favoured by Marx and Engels, must not lead us to apply in blanket fashion the views that they formulated about this war to other civil wars, such as those of Spartacus, which really were between the 'oppressors' and the 'oppressed'.)

When it comes to 'revolutionary war', there were no revolutionary governments actually in existence in the lifetimes of Marx and Engels. Indeed, in their view there had only ever been one truly revolutionary government, and that was the Government of Republican France before the usurpation of Napoleon I. Therefore, in order to judge their attitude towards aggression in a 'revolutionary war', we must perforce rely upon what they wrote concerning the wars of the French Revolution.

And the important thing to note is that they approved of them. Not merely did they naturally approve of the Revolutionary Government defending itself after it had been attacked; but they also approved when, after the Battles of Valmy and Jemappes, that same government went over to the offensive.

Now, Valmy and Jemappes stand in relation to the wars of the French Revolution as does Sedan (in Marxist opinion) to the Franco-

Prussian War of 1870. Consequently if, after 1870, the Prussian Government is to be convicted of having started a new war, a war of conquest, when it proceeded with the invasion of France (and Marxists do so convict it), then the French Government of 1792 must equally be convicted of starting a new war, when, after Valmy and Jemappes, it proceeded upon the invasion of Europe. Only the French Government of 1792 was not embarking upon a war of conquest; it was embarking upon a war designed, in Marx's and Engels' opinion, to spread its revolutionary principles by force of arms.

But this, by Marx's standards, was a new war; and it was therefore the French who started it. And since 'to start a new war' is 'to commit aggression', and since Marx and Engels were wholly in favour of the starting of it, we are forced to conclude that both men were wholly in favour of aggression, when committed by revolutionaries for revolutionary purposes.

To the above positive evidence we can add a great deal of negative evidence. For there were five main wars that were fought on the continent of Europe during the lifetime of Marx and Engels—the Crimean War, the Franco-Austro-Italian War of 1859, the Austro-Prussian War of 1866, the Franco-Prussian War of 1870, and the Russo-Turkish War of 1877. In the case of four of them, Marx and Engels were supremely uninterested in who was the aggressor. Russia was a participant in both the Crimean War and the Russo-Turkish War; and, as has been explained above, whenever Russia was engaged in war after the fall of Metternich, the two men invariably longed to see a Russian defeat. We would therefore expect them *not* to be interested in who was the aggressor in these two wars; and as a matter of simple historical fact, they were not.

The Franco-Austro-Italian War of 1859 was begun by the Italians; but as their aim in starting it was to win their independence, it was seen by Marx and Engels as a 'war of national liberation' on the part of Italy. Once again, they did not enquire into who was the aggressor.[116]

As for the Austro-Prussian War of 1866, Marx and Engels, seeking which side to support, carefully considered the probable effects of a Prussian victory, and also of an Austrian victory. The one criterion they did not use was who was the aggressor.

From which it follows that, in these four wars at least, aggression was not the one unpardonable transgression in the eyes of Marx and Engels. Indeed, so far from that being true, there is ample evidence in their comments on these wars to show that they had no objection to the commission of aggression, provided that either its aim or its probable effect was likely to serve their purposes.

By contrast, the Franco-Prussian War of 1870 provides the one example among the five wars that I have quoted, where the question of who was the aggressor carried weight with Marx and Engels. In this conflict, one of the reasons that they gave for supporting Prussia at the commencement of hostilities was that the latter was fighting a 'defensive war'.

But although this was indeed one of their reasons, it was not the only one: as we have seen (pp. 32–4), there were others that were also operative. Among the most important of these was surely the fact that, at the moment when hostilities began, the regime in France was thoroughly reactionary, while Bismarck's aims, as Marx and Engels saw things, were 'progressive'.

So long, therefore, as Bismarck preserved the purity of the 'progressiveness' of his war aims, and did not allow them to be sullied by the seizure of Alsace-Lorraine (which would have been 'territorial aggrandizement' in the eyes of Marxists), the support of Marx and his followers was given to the cause of the Prussians. It was only when the latter had defiled themselves by demanding Alsace-Lorraine, and when Napoleon III had been toppled from his throne and a Republic set up in Paris, that the support of Marx and Engels was switched from the cause of the Prussians, and given to that of the French.

But, until this happened, it was of the greatest consequence to the two men and their disciples that the support of the international labour movement should be given to the Prussians. At that time, however, the international labour movement was by no means composed exclusively of Marxists; and even the International Working Men's Association, for whose General Council Marx prepared his three famous *Addresses*, contained a great many members who were not Marxists. Some of the non-Marxists in this Association were outright pacifists, while another important section subscribed to the view that all war was basically wrong, and that the only legitimate reason for engaging in it was self-defence. On such people as these, many of the Marxian arguments in favour of the German cause would have made little impression; but they would respond immediately to the suggestion that the Germans were to be supported, because they were engaged in defending themselves against a French attack.

The Franco-Prussian War was the only major war of Marx's lifetime in which the international socialist movement had any part to play, however trivial. The International Working Men's Association did not exist before 1864; and Marx died in 1883. During those nineteen years, the only wars of any importance (apart from the Franco-Prussian War) were the Austro-Prussian War of 1866 and the Russo-Turkish War of 1877; and in neither of these wars was aggression a significant factor from the Marxist point of view, for reasons that we have examined already. It therefore seems to be no coincidence that the question of aggression and of self-defence should be raised by Marx so comparatively persistently in the case of the Franco-Prussian War; but that he should not have bothered to raise it in the case of the others.

And this leads to the conclusion (one which has already been stated) that Marx and Engels were perfectly willing to countenance aggression, and even to commit it, so long as it was done for purposes that met with their approval.

Lenin's developments of the Marxian thinking on self-defence and aggression resulted in these two terms becoming virtually indistinguishable, when used by him from about 1915 onwards, and hence virtually meaningless to the Western man-in-the-street. However, to this day the West has insisted on trying to ferret out of them the ordinary 'bourgeois' meaning; and, as a result, the usual Western notion of Lenin's understanding of the concepts 'attack' and 'defence', and 'offensive' and 'defensive' war, are horribly wide of the mark.

At least as early as 1908, Lenin was already saying that the question of who actually fired the first shot was of no importance, when it came to assessing responsibility for causing the war and for deciding which side to support.[117] The question was which side had offensive, and which side defensive, *aims*; and he quoted with approval an example given by Kautsky to the effect that it was difficult to say whether Japan was attacking or defending herself at the beginning of the Russo-Japanese War.[118] Since there can be no doubt but that in this war Japan was the aggressor, it is plain that Lenin's understanding of the meaning of 'offensive' and 'defensive' wars was somewhat different from that of the ordinary Westerner.

By October 1914, he was expressing his view as follows: 'It is absurd once and for all to renounce participation in war in principle. On the other hand, it is also absurd to divide wars into defensive and aggressive.' And he went on to say that when, in 1848, Marx urged Germany to declare war upon Russia, he had good revolutionary reasons for acting in the way he did; and that, if that war had materialized, it might have been termed by the vulgar an 'offensive' war; but that it would have been considered by communists to have been objectively 'progressive', and that communists would have supported it.[119]

A month later, he was attacking the argument of Axelrod that, when trying to assess the First World War, it was impossible to ignore the question of who actually started it. In Lenin's view, this was unmitigated rubbish. The British, the French, and the Russians had been busily arming for years before the war had actually begun. Was there therefore 'anything surprising that two robbers began the attack before the other *three* got the new knives that they had ordered'? (Italics original.)[120] The 'bourgeoisie' of all the combatant countries were equally guilty in Lenin's eyes; and the question of who fired the first shot was a matter of the utmost indifference to him.[121]

Indeed, he said so even more bluntly, and in even more picturesque language, in his *In the Footsteps of 'Russkaya Volya'* (13 April 1917), where the relevant passage is as follows (italics original): 'And when war is waged between two groups of predators and oppressors merely for division of the spoils of plunder, merely to see *who* will strangle *more* peoples, *who* will grab *more*, the question as to who began this war, who was the first to declare it and so forth, is of no economic or political significance.'

By the summer of 1915, Lenin had developed his argument to the stage where he could express it thus:[122]

*For example, if tomorrow Morocco were to declare war on France, or India on Britain, or Persia or China on Russia, and so on, these would be 'just' and 'defensive' wars, irrespective of who would be the first to attack, any socialist would wish the oppressed, dependent and unequal states victory over the oppressor, slave-holding and predatory 'Great' Powers.* (Roman original.)

By this argument, therefore, any country whose victory is desired by socialists is invariably fighting a 'defensive' war, irrespective of whether the country has been assailed or is the assailant.

That Lenin should hold this view with regard to the Indians, the Moroccans, the Chinese or the Persians should come as no surprise; for, at the time that Lenin was writing, Britain, France and Russia were colonial powers, and India, Morocco, Persia and China were their colonies or dependants. Under these circumstances, a war begun by the latter against the former would be a 'war of national liberation' in Marxist eyes; and all communists could be expected to welcome it warmly.

But why did Lenin call it a 'defensive' war? Is he using the word 'defensive' here simply as a term of approval, in the same way that, as we have seen earlier, he sometimes uses the epithet 'revolutionary'? Attractive though such a solution to the problem would be, it is not the correct answer. A clue to the proper solution is to be found in a passage in the first section of his *A Caricature of Marxism* (Autumn 1916): 'How then can we disclose and define the "substance" of a war? War is the continuation of policy. Consequently, we must examine the policy pursued prior to the war, the policy that led to and brought about the war.' This means that, as he tells us elsewhere, 'The character of the war (whether it is reactionary or revolutionary) does not depend on who the attacker was, or in whose country the "enemy" is stationed; it depends on *what class* is waging the war, and on what politics this war is a continuation of.' (Italics original.)[123]

If this strand of thinking is the warp of our present argument, there is another which is undoubtedly the woof. That other strand is the Marxist concept of the 'class struggle'. This, for our present purposes, may be reduced to the proposition that in any 'class' society the 'exploiters' and the 'exploited' are bound to be at loggerheads, as a result of the very nature of the system. This is because the 'exploiters' will want to pay their workers as little as they can, while getting the maximum amount of work out of them: by contrast, the workers will try to do as little as they can for the highest possible pay. The existence within a society of these two conflicting and totally irreconcilable objectives is bound to create an unending struggle between the two main 'classes'; and this struggle is known to Marxists as the 'class struggle'.[124]

In this struggle, as communists see things, the 'exploited' class is always on the defensive—that is to say, it is always trying to preserve itself, its wage and its few possessions from the rapacious onslaught of the 'exploiters'. Viewed in this light, the policy of the 'exploited' is *always a 'defensive' policy*.

Now, at certain times and under certain circumstances, the 'class struggle' may become exacerbated: it is then said to have become 'heightened' or 'sharpened', in communist terminology. Moreover, at certain conjunctions of time and circumstance, it may become so 'heightened' that it will take the shape of an armed struggle, and become a civil war.

If now we weave together the warp and the woof of our argument, and relate it to civil war, we shall find that one of the combatants (the 'exploited') has pursued policies which have consistently been 'defensive'. And since Lenin said that the character of *any* war (including a civil war) is to be judged according to what class is waging it, and what policies it is a continuation of, it follows that in the civil war which we have taken as our example, it is the 'proletariat' who will be deemed to be fighting a 'defensive' war, irrespective of whether they started it or not.

But this communist notion of the 'class struggle' is not confined to the struggle *within* a society; it also finds expression on the international scene in the shape of a struggle between countries. Such an 'international class struggle' can be waged between a colonial power (the 'exploiting' country) and a colony (the 'exploited'); it can also be waged between all the capitalist countries on the one hand (representing the 'international bourgeoisie') and all the socialist countries on the other (representing the 'international proletariat'). Or between one capitalist country and one socialist country.

But in such international conflicts the same premises are postulated by communists as are assumed in the case of the 'class struggle' within a given country: in other words, the 'proletarian' combatant is invariably assumed to have pursued a 'defensive' policy prior to the outbreak of hostilities. Hence, when the fighting begins, the war will inevitably be a 'defensive' war on the part of the 'proletarian' countries, by the same rules of Leninist logic which operated before.

If we now look back at the list of the categories of war which we considered in the previous section, we shall find that it consists of the following items: Wars of territorial aggrandizement, plunder and dynastic ambition; wars between independent sovereign states; 'imperialist' wars; 'world wars'; colonial wars; 'wars of national liberation'; 'national wars'; local wars; limited wars; civil wars; and 'revolutionary wars'.

The last seven categories are bound to consist of wars between the 'oppressors' and the 'oppressed'. Hence, in the Leninist canon these will be termed 'defensive' wars on the part of the 'oppressed', irrespective of whether they started them or not. In the case of the first two categories, these by Leninist definition are nowadays bound to be 'imperialist' wars; because Lenin believed that in 1914 the world was divided into 'oppressed, dependent and unequal States' and imperialist states—and the only change that has taken place since then is that a new category, 'socialist states', has made its appearance. But we have already seen that, when two imperialist countries are engaged in fighting each other, the question of which of them was the aggressor was of no importance to Lenin.

Since 'local wars', limited wars and 'world wars' are only varieties of 'imperialist' wars, that leaves to be considered only those wars which are fought between 'imperialist' countries and socialist countries. But such wars are 'revolutionary wars' or 'just wars', so far as the communists are concerned. In either case, it will be the socialist country which, by definition, will be fighting a 'defensive' war; while the 'imperialist' country will be said to be fighting an 'offensive' war.

But these were the only categories of war which were conceivable in Lenin's lifetime; for he would have deemed it impossible that any two socialist countries could go to war with each other. That being his attitude, it was no hyperbole, but mere iron-cold logic, which made him declare in 1914 that the distinction between offensive and defensive wars had become outmoded.[125] And it was the same iron-cold logic which, in 1919, led him to give a list of categories of wars which contained no mention of the terms 'offensive' and 'defensive'.[126] Why should he, when, as he stated bluntly in that same year, 'in view of the class character of such wars, the distinction between defensive and offensive wars has finally lost all meaning'?[127]

The above, however, should not blind us to one point. However the issue be fogged by this blurring of the distinction of meaning between 'offensive' and 'defensive' wars, Lenin throughout his life followed the Marxian dictum (and, for the matter of that, the French Revolutionaries' dictum) that a 'progressive' class or a 'progressive' country is fully entitled to start a war, if it wants to. He said so in 1908 in *Bellicose Militarism and the Anti-Militarist Tactics of Social-Democracy*; he said it again in 1915 in *Socialism and War*; and he repeated the statement emphatically that same year in *The Collapse of the Second International*. Nor were these the only occasions on which he made this statement.

If, therefore, aggression consists of firing the first shot, Lenin was perfectly willing to commit it; but this was on condition that he thought it would be successful, and that it was in a 'progressive' cause.

Modern Soviet thinking declares firmly that, when Marx and Engels classified wars as 'offensive' and 'defensive', they were not referring to who began them or who were the aggressors' victims. On the contrary, we are plainly told that, when classifying wars in this way, Marx and Engels were solely concerned with the policies underlying the war— that is to say, whether its aims were 'rapacious' (*zakhvatnicheskiye*) or 'liberating' (*osvoboditel'niye*); and that they condemned the one, but heartily approved the other.[128] In view of this, it is not at all surprising that, when they get to the Leninist period, Soviet writers follow Lenin's dictum, and regard the distinction between 'offensive' and 'defensive' wars as having finally lost all meaning. In other words, they scarcely mention these categories.

The subject-index to the latest edition of Lenin's works, for instance, contains no reference to either of them; and Soviet writing on war and the theory of war either omits them completely, or else treats them purely as synonyms for 'unjust' wars and 'just' wars respectively. This means that, from the official Soviet viewpoint (as also from Lenin's viewpoint), it makes no difference who is the first to attack; and it also means that there is no moral or ethical constraint operating to prevent the USSR from launching an attack on others.

From which it follows that, whenever it refrains from launching an attack on others, it must be withheld by reasons which have nothing to do with either ethics or morality. But since the Soviet Union has not attacked anyone since August 1968 (as a Western 'bourgeois' would see it), or since 1921 (as a Soviet communist would see it), it follows that restraining influences of a wholly amoral kind must have been operating on the Soviet Union between those dates and now. I myself believe that this statement is wholly and profoundly true. I believe that the USSR would willingly start a war even today, whenever she thought it would be to her advantage to do so; and I therefore believe that, since she has refrained from starting one since 1968 (or 1921, depending on your point of view), this can only be because she has *not* thought it would be to her advantage.

The reasons why she has not thought it to her advantage to start a war are varied and extremely complex: they are also extremely important. I shall therefore be examining them in detail at a later stage in this chapter. Here I am concerned only to repeat my own view that the reasons preventing the USSR from waging war on others are purely concerned with material and 'class' advantage—Lenin having, as we have seen above, effectively removed any moral inhibitions against doing so that she otherwise might have had.

But in that case, you may reasonably object, what about her views on aggression? Has not the Soviet Union over and over again condemned aggression by whomsoever committed? And since the word 'aggression' is nowadays to be found in hundreds and thousands of instances in Soviet writing, always with a pejorative meaning, does this not indicate that the USSR today has reversed Lenin's dictum, and now regards the distinction between 'offensive' and 'defensive' wars as having a very real validity? No, by no means.

The modern Russian for 'aggression', in the sense in which we are using it here, is *agressiya*; but this is very much a newcomer to the Russian language. Soviet sources date its first official acceptance as a Russian word at not earlier than 1911; and many Russian dictionaries published after that date contain no entry for it. Lenin, so far as I am aware, never made use of it; and certainly it is Stalin, not Lenin, to whom its first usage is attributed in that many-volumed dictionary of the Russian language published quite recently by the Soviet Academy of Sciences, despite the fact that, generally speaking, the dictionary is eager to attribute to Lenin as many words of political significance as possible.[129]

In fact, it was really only in 1933 that the word *agressiya* was commonly to be met with in Soviet speaking and writing. The reason for this is obvious. In 1933, the reconstruction and modernization of the Soviet armed forces had scarcely begun; and there were three powers in the world which were militarily formidable and also expansionist in outlook. These three were Germany, Italy and Japan. Germany and Japan in particular might reasonably be expected to indulge their expansionist tendencies at the expense of the USSR, and throughout the 1930s Soviet diplomacy sought for ways to prevent this. The policy of 'collective security', vigorously propounded by the Kremlin throughout this period, is an important example of this strand of Soviet foreign policy; while the attempted persuasion of world opinion to define, condemn and then physically prevent 'aggression' is yet another.

This attempt to define and condemn 'aggression' first took place in February 1933, at the disarmament conference at Geneva; and the

Soviet draft definition received considerable support. It defined 'aggression' (and *agressiya*) as:[130]

*The State which first commits any of the following acts: Declares war on another State; invades the territory of another State, even without declaring war; bombards another State's territory, whether by land, sea or air, or deliberately attacks its ships or aircraft; introduces any of its armed forces (whether land, sea or air) into another State's territory without the permission of the Government of the latter, or violates any of the conditions attached to such permission (with particular reference to the time and place of the stationing of such forces); or who sets up a blockade of the coasts and ports of another State.*

At Soviet insistence, the rider was added that no political, strategic or economic considerations can justify the commission of any of the above acts[131] (shades of Czechoslovakia!).

With the advent of the Second World War, people were far too busy in dealing with the results of aggression to have time to hold political debates about it; but when that war was over, the USSR discovered that, in relation to the Western powers, she was militarily in much the same sort of situation as she had been in 1933. As early as 1948, therefore, the World Peace Movement under Soviet direction was defining 'aggression' and condemning it. Once again, the definition was rigorous and far-reaching.

The outbreak of the Korean War in September 1950 reinforced the Russians' interest in defining and condemning 'aggression'. For the North Koreans had a reasonable chance of winning, if the Western powers (and in particular America) could be made to stop supporting the South Koreans. One way of doing this was to persuade public opinion in the Western countries that their governments had done wrong by sending troops to Korea; and one way of persuading that opinion was to assert that their governments had committed 'aggression' (an extremely emotive word among Western peoples) against the North Koreans.

This was not difficult. The American Government could hardly deny that its troops were engaged in 'bombarding the territory of another State, whether by land, sea or air', or committing a number of the other acts which the Geneva definition of 1933 had expressly declared to be 'aggression'. Nor could it plead that what it was doing was in the pursuit of some higher good, such as the defence of the liberty of the South Koreans; because the rider inserted in the 1933 definition at the Soviet Government's insistence made it plain that 'no political, strategic or economic considerations' could justify what had been defined as 'aggression'.

The 1933 definition with its accompanying rider therefore exactly suited the Soviet Union's requirements in 1950. Consequently, the USSR presented this definition and rider for the approbation of the United Nations in 1950, 1951, 1952 and subsequently. Not that the General Assembly accepted the Soviet proposals; but they commanded wide support among important sections of Western public opinion, especially that of the Left. As a result, the Americans were branded as 'aggressors' in a considerable number of influential Western publications, with noticeable effects upon the attitudes of Western governments.

But, if all the above is true, has not the Soviet Union herself been guilty of 'aggression', according to her own definition of it? Officially, of course, the Soviet Government would indignantly deny such a thing. For one thing, it has caused it to be asserted that 'aggression' is peculiar to 'class' societies, from which it follows that, by definition, the Soviet Union *cannot* be guilty of it.[132] For another, 'aggression' is the work of *states*, being committed by one *state* assaulting another *state*:[133] it cannot therefore apply to 'wars of fraternal aid', where the Soviet *Communist Party* sends 'brotherly help' to other *communist parties* or *proletariats*.

Third, authoritative Soviet sources now explicitly assert that the rules concerning 'aggression' are not applicable to civil wars,[134] nor to 'wars of national liberation'.[135] This means that the 'oppressed' classes (whether the 'proletariat' of a capitalist country or the native population of a colony or protectorate) are fully entitled to start a war without committing 'aggression', a proposition which we deduced earlier from the postulates of classical Marxism. But the Soviet dictum, as expounded today, carries a wider implication; for the North Koreans would not have committed 'aggression', if it had been they who had started the Korean War by invading South Korea. This is because the Korean War is described in authoritative Soviet writing as also being a 'war of national liberation'.[136] (Not that the North Koreans stand in need of this excuse, at least so far as the USSR is concerned; because it is the considered view of the latter that it was the *South* Koreans who started the war by invading *North* Korea.)[137]

Despite all this, however, there remain at least four occasions where the Soviet Union would appear to have committed 'aggression', even according to her own definition of that concept. These four occasions are the conquest of Georgia in 1921, the Russo-Finnish War of 1939-40, the Hungarian uprising of 1956 and the invasion of Czechoslovakia in 1968.

With regard to the Georgian episode, this was considered in the early days as a straightforward exercise in 'revolutionary war'; and the first edition of the *Great Soviet Encyclopaedia* describes it in just those terms.[138] But, as has been explained earlier, the phrase 'revolutionary war' has rather gone out of fashion nowadays among Soviet writers and speakers; because it is likely to startle and upset the 'bourgeois', and make them suspicious of the Russians' peaceful intentions (see pp. 54–5 for further details). Moreover, the very concept of 'revolutionary war', in the sense in which we are using it here, is not too easy to distinguish from 'aggression', in the Soviet Union's own definition of that word.

The latest edition of the *Great Soviet Encyclopaedia* therefore puts things differently. According to this new version, the Georgians themselves *asked* Lenin to send Red Army units into their country, so as to remove their existing government and put a communist one in its place.[139]

Unfortunately, however, it was not the Georgian *Government* which asked him, but the Georgian communists; and, according to the Russians' own definition of aggression, it is the *government* of a country that has to do the asking, if a charge of aggression is to be avoided. On the other hand, a sophist should be able without too much difficulty to exculpate the USSR from any charge of aggression against Georgia, by pointing out that the rules about aggression do not operate in the context of a civil war; that a few days previously there had been a communist uprising which the Mensheviks were successfully suppressing; and that therefore what was occurring in Georgia was obviously a civil war. Consequently, no aggression was committed by the USSR.

If we now turn to the Russo-Finnish War of 1939–40, any Soviet liability to the charge of 'aggression' here is neatly avoided by insisting that it was the Finns who started it. Since it was they who started it, it was clearly they who committed aggression upon the Soviet Union, and not the other way round.[140] *Q.E.D.*, as Euclid used to say, and in exactly the sense he meant it.

In the case of the Hungarian uprising of 1956, the Russians say that here, too, there can be no question of their having committed aggression; because their troops were sent into Budapest 'at the request of the Hungarian People's Government'.[141] The reason for doing so was to get them 'to help the Hungarian People's Army and the Hungarian organs of power' (i.e. the security forces) to restore order in the city.[142]

If, therefore, the Soviet account is correct, and if the Russian forces were indeed asked by the Hungarian Government to help suppress the uprising, there was obviously no aggression; and the sole point to be considered is whether this was so. Western historians do not believe that it is, because Imre Nagy and his colleagues were still the Government of Hungary when the request is alleged to have been made; and it is beyond question that these men did not make it.

If, however, one ignores this particular objection (and the Russians naturally ignore it altogether), then it is indeed true that the USSR committed no aggression when she used her troops in 1956 to suppress the Hungarian uprising; because she did what she did at the request of the Hungarian People's *Government* (my italics).[143]

The invasion of Czechoslovakia in 1968 also escapes the charge of being 'aggression', and for the same reason. This is because here, too, according to the Russians, members of the Czechoslovak Communist Party and of the Czechoslovak Government *asked* the USSR to send in troops (my italics).[144] It is true that neither then, nor subsequently, was the Soviet Union able to name the Czechs who had issued the invitation; and it is also true that those Czechs who were then members of the Communist Party or the Government showed no signs of wanting the Russian presence, still less of having actually asked for it. Nevertheless, if it is indeed correct that the USSR was asked to send 'immediate help to the fraternal Czech people'[145] (that ominous phrase), such an act cannot be classed as aggression, for the same reason that was applicable in the case of Hungary.

Despite all the above, however, the USSR shows signs of feeling slightly uncomfortable about the above four incidents. The charges of aggression levelled at her may be easy to refute legalistically, but not so easy, she now appears to believe, to refute in a convincing manner. In particular, that rigorous definition of 'aggression', for whose world-wide acceptance she fought so hard in the 1930s, the late 1940s and the 1950s, now shows an unhappy propensity to clash with the 'Brezhnev doctrine'. What is more, people in the West have noticed it. Indeed, quite soon after the invasion of Czechoslovakia, letters were appearing in Western newspapers, confounding the Soviet apologists by referring the reader to the USSR's own definition of aggression of 1933 and subsequently; and in particular referring to the rider that 'no political, strategic or economic considerations' could justify the commission of aggression. They then went on to point out that the action of the Soviet Army was incontrovertible aggression by that definition.

Letters of this kind cause great pain to the sensitive souls in the Kremlin. As a result a firm directive was issued; and the latest edition of the *Diplomatic Dictionary* has had a significant change made in its article on 'aggression'. Whereas previous editions had carried that splendid rider that 'no political, strategic or economic considerations' could justify 'aggression', the new edition retains the actual definition, but has quietly dropped the rider.[146] The new edition of *Kratkii Politicheskii Slovar'* goes further, and declares that aggression can only be committed by 'imperialist' states, thus disposing of the whole problem at one fell swoop.[147]

In view of the above, it is beyond question that the USSR has more than once committed acts of aggression; and that it can escape the charge of doing so only by resorting to sophistry. Furthermore, the aggression it has committed must be classed as aggression by *its own* definition of the concept, as well as by that of the West.

Nor should we be surprised that this is so. As this whole, rather lengthy section has pointed out, Marx and Engels were willing to countenance aggression if its commission was likely to further causes they favoured. Lenin wholeheartedly agreed with them. Furthermore, he not merely countenanced it; he practised it. It was at Lenin's command, for instance, that the Red Army invaded and conquered Georgia in February 1921.[148] Brezhnev claims to be a Leninist, and probably is. There is at least no doubt that the Soviet invasion of Czechoslovakia in 1968 is plumb in the Leninist tradition.

## War is the continuation of policy by other means[149]

Any reading of Lenin on the subject of war, however superficial, is bound to reveal how frequently he quoted the famous dictum of Clausewitz. What is more, modern Soviet writing, especially that published by the Soviet Ministry of Defence, reiterates Clausewitz's words. Therefore, both for Lenin and for the USSR of today, the notion that war is the continuation of policy by other means has clearly got great significance; and it is therefore necessary to try and establish just what that significance is.

One complication, however, bedevils our quest from the outset. For it appears certain that Lenin at least saw two quite different meanings in Clausewitz's epigram; and consequently, before we can really measure the influence that Clausewitz has on the Soviet attitude to war, we must first disentangle the two separate concepts of Lenin.

The first asserts that war is a means by which policy may be continued. As Clausewitz also expressed it, and as Lenin noted with approval, 'War . . . is policy which has exchanged the pen for the sword.'[150] The second concept relates to the way in which communists should react to a war. To take the second one first, it is all very well to know that wars are divided into 'just' and 'unjust', and into 'wars of national liberation', 'imperialist' wars, and so on; but when a part of the world erupts into armed hostilities, how can one tell for certain which is which?

In many cases, there can be little doubt. If a 'proletarian' government is involved in war, then that is a 'just' war, so far as that government is concerned; if an 'imperialist' government is involved, the war is 'unjust'. But what if none of the combatants is either 'proletarian' or 'imperialist'; how shall we judge them then?

Even in the modern world, where so much of our globe is dominated by 'imperialism' or 'proletarianism', such a situation is by no means to be considered impossible. The war between India and Pakistan, for instance, which broke out in 1965, or the interminable wars between Bolivia and Paraguay which raged in the Gran Chaco in the 1920s and 1930s; were these wars 'just' or 'unjust'? And which (if any) of the combatants was 'progressive', and which 'reactionary'?

Lenin himself, of course, was concerned with an earlier period; and for him the crucial war was that of 1914–18. This was because, although he himself had labelled it an 'imperialist' war right from the very start, large numbers of other revolutionary socialists refused to agree with him. It therefore became necessary to convince them.

The means that he chose for this purpose was the preaching of the message of Clausewitz: 'War is the continuation of policy.' Therefore, said Lenin, in order to judge the war, one must look at the policies that preceded it; for by these was the war begotten.[151] Consequently, over and over again in Lenin's writings one finds the exhortation to his fellow-communists to assess the war by looking at the policies of the combatants in the years that preceded its outbreak.

As he put it in *War and Revolution*, which he wrote in May 1917, 'From the point of view of Marxism . . . the main issue in any discussion by socialists on how to assess the war and what attitude to adopt towards it is this: what is the war being waged for, and what classes staged and directed it.' He went on to say: 'War is a continuation of policy by other means. All wars are inseparable from the political systems that engender them. The policy which a given state, a given class within that state, pursued for a long time before the war is inevitably continued by that same class during the war, the form of action alone being changed' (pp. 398–400). And he came to the conclusion that the First World War was being waged by the capitalists of the various combatant countries in pursuance of those same policies of self-enrichment which they had pursued before the fighting began: Germany wanted colonies; Russia wanted Constantinople; Britain and France wanted to maintain their financial pre-eminence. It was therefore a war waged by groups of 'bourgeois' in pursuance of 'imperialist' policies; and consequently it was an 'imperialist' war, an 'unjust' war, in which no decent citizen of any of the combatant countries should allow himself to take part.[152]

It is plain that Lenin's criterion for assessing war is very different from that of the ordinary non-communist. The age-old cry of 'My country, right or wrong' is probably not heard so frequently now as it used to be; but there is still at work a powerful instinct to rally to the defence of one's native land, if it finds itself in danger, particularly if the danger has arisen as the result of foreign attack.

In Lenin's lifetime, the instinct was incomparably stronger; and that is why he devoted a great deal of his energies to combating it. In his opinion, the only time when it is right to defend one's country is when it is engaged in a 'just' war: indeed, he said, to proclaim that one is defending one's country is to proclaim simultaneously that the war in question is 'just', and that it is being fought in the interests of the 'proletariat'.[153]

But when one's country is engaged in a war that is 'unjust', then, said Lenin, one has a positive duty—not merely to refuse to take part in it, but also to do one's utmost to work for one's country's defeat. In *Socialism and War*, there is a section entitled 'On the Defeat of One's Own Government in an "Imperialist" War', where Lenin declares bluntly that: 'A revolutionary class cannot but wish for the defeat of its own Government in a reactionary war, and cannot fail to see that the latter's military reverses must facilitate its overthrow.' Ten years earlier, in an article written to commemorate the fall of Port Arthur, that grievous and bloody setback to Russian arms, he had written, 'The proletariat has cause to rejoice. The disaster that has overtaken our mortal enemy [the Tsar] not only signifies the approach of freedom in Russia, it also presages a new revolutionary upsurge of the European proletariat.'

Such exultation at the defeat of one's fellow countrymen must inevitably appear as something akin to treachery to an ordinary Westerner. A Marxist's loyalties, however, are to the international 'proletariat', not to the land of his birth. As Marx and Engels put it in *The Communist Manifesto*: 'The working man has no country.' Therefore, although a communist can be held to betray the 'proletariat', he cannot possibly be held to betray his country, according to the communist way of thinking, *unless the country in question is a 'proletarian' one.*

Thus, a British communist today would not be regarded by his fellow-communists as having betrayed Britain if he passed British defence secrets to a member of the communist bloc: on the contrary, they would regard him as having done no more than his duty. Moreover, as Philby's memoirs clearly indicate, this is the view that he had of his actions himself.

On the other hand, a Soviet communist who handed Russian defence secrets over to the West would be regarded by *all* communists as a traitor; though their attitude would not be nearly so unanimous if he handed them, not to the West, but to another communist country (for instance, China); because in that case both the countries involved would be 'proletarian'. Nor is such a thing impossible. The Chinese Communist authorities not long ago detained two Soviet sailors on charges of spying. They may, or may not, have been guilty; but the point is that it was not *a priori* inconceivable to the Chinese communists that Soviet communists should spy on them.[154]

But although war is a continuation of policy, it cannot be maintained seriously that every policy that is continued with will land us in a war. The question therefore poses itself: When does a continuation of policy erupt into armed conflict?

It takes two to make a quarrel. Therefore, if one party to a potential dispute gives way to the demands of the other, there will be no quarrel, or, in other words, there will be no war. There was no war in 1940 between the Soviet Union and the Baltic States, because the latter accepted all of the Russians' demands; there was also no war between the Soviet Union and the countries of Eastern Europe in the years after 1945 for precisely the same reasons.

Of course, there have been instances in history where communities have waged war purely for the love of the fighting; but this is not true of the Soviet Communist Party, and it is important that the fact should be recognized. Soviet communism uses war as a means of gaining its objectives; but if it can gain its objectives without fighting, it would far prefer to do so. Lenin noted, with exclamations of approval, a passage in Clausewitz to the effect that an aggressor is always peace-loving, and that he would far prefer to walk in and occupy peacefully the territory of another nation, rather than have to fight for it, if only he could.[155]

Therefore although, if the question be put 'Do Communists renounce war?', the answer can only be 'No' (and those who doubt it are referred to the innumerable passages where Lenin asks this self-same question and replies that they do not), nevertheless, if the alternative question be put, 'Do communists *want* war?', the only correct answer is: 'No—not if they can get their own way without it.'

This means to say that, war being the continuation of policy, and the cause of war being the pre-war policy of the one side coming into collision with the pre-war policy of the other, it logically follows that fighting will only actually break out if the two sets of policies are on a collision course *and neither side will give way.*

Thus, Britain and Germany could easily have gone to war in 1938 instead of in 1939. The policies that each was pursuing were the same in both years: in the final analysis, the two sets of policies were set on a collision course (although the appeasers pretended otherwise). The reason that these policies did not result in a collision in 1938, but did in 1939, was that in the former year Britain gave way at Munich, whereas in the latter year she stood firm.

Lenin implicitly says the same sort of thing (and thereby agrees to the correctness of my thesis) whenever he writes about the making of the revolution and of what would happen subsequently. For, among his writings dating as far back as 1905, there are to be found passages where he asserts that a civil war is inevitable (or almost inevitable) in connec-

tion with the making of the revolution in any country.[156] He continued
to make such assertions throughout his life.[157]

Confronted with these statements, one is bound to ask 'How did he
know? Why was Lenin so sure that this would happen?'

Certainly, if one is making a revolution, one would be wise to expect
opposition; and it would be only prudent to anticipate that, in certain
circumstances, the opposition would become so stubborn and so
determined that civil war would break out. But surely one would do
one's utmost to prevent this? Surely it could be no help to the new
regime to have a civil war on its hands? And, in any case, if one's
strategy has been effective, and one has seized power without any undue
difficulty (as Lenin did in the October Revolution), surely one would
then proceed to govern in a way that would rally the support of the
whole population, thereby removing civil war from the order of the
day?

Lenin, however, reasoned completely differently. He had been much
interested in the fate of the Paris Commune of 1871, which he, together
with Marx and Engels, regarded as the world's first 'proletarian'
revolutionary government; and he spoke and wrote on the subject on a
number of occasions that stretched from 1904 to 1919.[158]

As a result of his reading of the history of the subject, including what
had been written by Marx and Engels, Lenin came to the conclusion
that the Paris Commune had failed because it had been too 'soft'.[159]
Since, in his eyes, the Paris Commune was an attempt at a 'proletarian'
revolution, he inferred from this that, for a 'proletarian' revolution to
be successful, it was essential to be merciless and hard.

Moreover, in Lenin's opinion, a revolution has not been successfully
accomplished merely when power has been seized: there still remains
the possibility of a 'bourgeois' counter-attack. In order to prevent this,
in order to make sure that power remained in the hands of the 'proletariat', it was essential to *smash* the 'bourgeois', and in particular, to
smash the departments of State through which they ruled the country.
Thus, early Bolshevik policies included the disbandment of the old
army; the disbandment of the old police; the replacement of 'bourgeois'
judges with 'proletarians' (despite the fact that the latter had had no
legal training at all); the nationalization of the banks and of a number
of industries; and the substitution of worker commissars for 'bourgeois'
ministers of state.

In addition to the above measures, it was necessary, according to
Lenin, to inspire the reactionaries with fear; to support the authority
of the armed 'proletariat' against the 'bourgeois'; and to allow the
'proletariat' to suppress its opponents *by force*.[160]

In his opinion, these measures should be implemented with all the
weight and authority of the newly-created 'proletarian' state, whose sole

purpose (said Lenin) is not to provide freedom for its citizens, but to suppress its enemies.[161]

Elsewhere Lenin tells us that the bourgeoisie must be exterminated as a 'class'.

Of course, such expressions as 'smashing the bourgeois' and 'exterminating the bourgeois as a class' do not imply that every single 'bourgeois' in the country is to be rounded up and shot; though it should not be forgotten that, during the Russian Revolution and before the outbreak of the civil war, a great many 'bourgeois' were indeed shot on no better grounds than that they were 'bourgeois'. Nevertheless, we should be guilty of a gross exaggeration if we were to imply that Lenin's policies involved, or were meant to involve, the killing of every 'bourgeois' to be found in Russia. What, then, was actually involved in them?

The most important elements involved were roughly as follows: The sacking of upper- and middle-class persons from most jobs in industry, commerce or the Civil Service which carried any sort of responsibility; the dismissal of judges and police chiefs, as well as officers of the old armed forces; and the confiscation of factories, businesses and shops, usually without compensation, as well as of holdings of land of more than a few acres. In addition, people's houses and flats were either taken away from them completely, or else the owners were pushed into one of their rooms and forced to surrender the rest. Finally, ration cards were denied to all those considered 'bourgeois'; and without a ration card in the cities of Russia in the years immediately following the Revolution one was condemned to near-starvation.

Now, it is clear enough that people exposed to such treatment are bound to resist; it is also clear that Lenin *knew* that they would resist and that he had foreseen their resistance as early as 1905.[162] But the fact was, that he positively *wanted* them to resist, for that was the easiest way for him to smash them. Indeed, that is why he said, and said repeatedly, that a revolution could not be successfully accomplished without a civil war.[163]

But a civil war would only break out, *in fact*, if he continued with his particular policies. Since, however, he did continue with them, and since the 'bourgeois' could only have avoided war by surrendering their lives and property, we get two sets of policies continuing on a collision course which eventually produced a war. If Lenin had been more concerned to avoid war than to carry out his policies, he could have conducted a tactical withdrawal, as he did with NEP; but he was convinced from his reading on the Paris Commune that, immediately after a 'proletarian' revolution, it was more important to smash the 'bourgeois' than to avoid civil war. So he continued with his policies; and civil war resulted.

## War is the tool of policy

But war is not only the continuation of policy; it is also the tool of policy. So said Clausewitz, and Lenin agreed with him.[164]

The extent of their agreement, and the emphasis that both men put upon the fact that war is merely a tool of policy, is indicated by the heading that Clausewitz gave to the sixth chapter of the third book of *On War*. This heading runs 'Der Krieg ist ein Instrument der Politik' ('War is a tool of policy'); and Lenin copied out this headline into his notebook, along with a great deal else from the body of the chapter, and he added the comment that this sixth chapter is the most important in the whole book.

But a tool is, by definition, subordinated to its wielder: it is a means by which the latter achieves his purposes. That being so, we should expect to find that both Clausewitz and Lenin looked on war as being subordinated to the purposes of policy; and this is what we do find. Thus, in section 24, chapter 1, book I, Clausewitz asserts roundly that 'the political intention is the objective; war is the means'. The Soviet translation goes further by adding the Russian words *zhe tol'ko*; so that, in the Soviet version, the sentence runs: 'The political intention is the objective, but war is *only* the means.' (Italics mine.)[165]

When we get to the sixth chapter of the third book (the one which Lenin thought to be the most important) Clausewitz is more emphatic still. 'It would be silly,' he says, 'to subordinate the political viewpoint to the military viewpoint, because it was policy that begat the war. Policy is the master mind; war is only the tool—and not the other way round. Consequently we have no option but to subordinate the military viewpoint to the political.'[166]

This being so, it is no wonder that Clausewitz should conceive of war as being not merely a tool of policy, but also its *flexible* tool, and as responding immediately to the changes demanded of it by changes in policy. As Clausewitz himself declares in a striking passage:[167]

*So policy turns all-devouring war into a mere tool; and out of the terrible battle-sword, which needs two hands and the whole of one's strength to lift it, and which is fit only for delivering one single blow and no more, it makes a light, manageable sword, and at times even a rapier, with which it can thrust or feint or parry as it thinks fit.*

Lenin, as we know, ignored a great deal of the contents of Clausewitz's volumes; but these two passages he obviously thought important, because he copied them out in full into his notebook.[168] We may take it, therefore, that on this particular point Lenin was in agreement with Clausewitz.

But if war is a tool of policy, and subordinate to the latter's aims, it should only be resorted to when it is the best means available in the given circumstances for attaining the policy's objectives: when it is not, peace should be employed instead.

The idea of employing peace as an instrument of policy is likely to sound strange to Westerners; yet peace is regarded by communists as just as much a tool for gaining their ends, as war ever was by a Machiavellian Renaissance prince. In Lenin's view, it was ridiculous to think of peace as being a thing somehow apart; and plain silly not to be able to realize that, if war is the continuation of the policies of peace, so peace is the continuation of the policies of war.[169] Peace to him was a means of attaining his objectives, as Brest-Litovsk was to show; and it has been regarded similarly by subsequent generations of communists, a point we shall deal with later in this book in the chapter concerned with peace.

But, to return to the main stream of the argument, it is surely true that, if you regard all wars as 'organized violence', as Engels did, then the particular form of violence that you employ is simply a minor variation on a given theme; and that this is true whether you are organizing a strike, or trying to whip up a demo, or whether you are waging conventional or nuclear war. It is only a question of what tools you use in order to attain your objective, which is the bringing down of the existing house (capitalist society) and the building of a new one (communism).

The best analogy that I have been able to think of is indeed concerned with houses. I live in an old-fashioned, tumble-down sort of house with oak beams and inglenooks and all that; and a little while ago one of the beams had gone, and I had to replace it. I did the replacement on a 'do-it-yourself' basis; and I had to go through the *destructive* business of knocking out the old beam, and the *constructive* business of putting in a new one. When a friend came round in the evening and asked 'What have you been doing?', I answered, 'I have been replacing an old beam', because that was my objective. I did not go into details of exactly what tools I had used—that at one moment I had used a hammer; at another, a saw; and that at a third I had used a screwdriver. I assumed that my friend had understood this, and had expected me to select the tool that best suited my purpose at the moment. I therefore did not particularize.

In the same way, communists expect that their leaders will survey the tools that are lying to hand in their workshop (war, peace, neutrality, disarmament, sabotage, strikes, subversion and all the rest of it), and will select the one that is most apt for their particular purpose. As Marshal Sokolovsky's authoritative *Military Strategy* puts it: 'Policy, by evaluating military and political factors, selects the most propitious moment to start a war, taking into account the strategic consider-ations.'[170]

But, given that it has been decided that, for the attainment of the policy's objectives, war is the tool most suitable in the given circumstances, it follows that its employment must be directed to attaining those aims as quickly and as economically as possible. And once the goal has been reached, the war must be stopped.

The goal, of course, may be vague, almost open-ended; or it may be narrow and precise. Thus, one aim of communist policy is the setting up of a communist society in every quarter of the globe. This may be described as a vague and open-ended policy; for none knows quite what a communist society is, nor how much effort and money must be expended before the 'bourgeois' countries go communist, if ever they do. On the other hand, the goal may be exceedingly precise, such as the acquisition of a piece of territory which is considered essential for the proper defence of Leningrad.

Various tools, including peace and war, have been tried by the Soviet Union in the various attempts it has made to achieve these goals. In the case of the establishment of a world-wide communist society, no tool has as yet been perfectly successful; in the case of the acquisition of Finnish territory, diplomacy was tried first in 1939, and war was embarked upon only when diplomacy failed.

And the war was successful. On 12 March 1940, the Finns accepted defeat, and surrendered to the Russians the territory that the latter wanted. And once they had got that territory, they stopped the war.

An even more remarkable example of tailoring the war to suit the particular objective was China's attack on India in 1962. The Chinese aim was to settle the dispute about the frontier in the way that they thought was right. They tried to do this first by means of diplomacy; and when diplomacy failed, they resorted to war. Two points about this campaign should be noted. The first is that the Chinese were determined to achieve their aim; and they were not going to baulk at war, if war was necessary to achieve it. The second is that, once the aim was accomplished, the war was stopped. The Indian army was defeated; the way into India lay open; and it was widely assumed at the time by foreign commentators that the Chinese would march down into it and possibly 'communize' it. Instead, having achieved their objective, they halted their armies; and they signed an armistice that recognized their gains. As Lenin said: 'Peace is the continuation of *the same policies* [i.e. of the policies that led to the war], with *the record written into it* of those changes in the relationships between the rival forces that have been brought about by the military operations.'[171]

These two wars have a common element, in that diplomacy was tried first and war was the second choice. This follows the predilection of Marx, who declared that the communists would gain their ends by peaceful means if they could; but that, if they could not, they would achieve them by force of arms. That he might relinquish his objectives rather than resort to war was not, however, an idea that ever occurred to him. Nor has it occurred to subsequent communist leaders.

But this is the crux of the matter. The Soviet leaders will pick war as their tool, whenever they think that it is the one that is best adapted for getting them what they want. But this means, of course, that they have got to be victorious: losers in war do *not* get what they want.

In view of this, at some stage in our enquiry we must investigate the factors which, in Marxist opinion, go to make for victory in war; and we must also consider the general principles which Marxists believe to underlie the successful use of violence.

## Strategy is the tool of policy

But it is not only war that is the tool of policy; strategy is governed by it too. This is a dictum which Soviet military writing is never weary of repeating. Thus, the five editions of *Marksizm-Leninizm o Voine i Armii*, dating from 1936 to 1968, all contain a passage asserting this principle; so do the three editions of Sokolovsky's *Military Strategy*; so does the *Great Soviet Encyclopaedia*.

The notion, like many others in Soviet military thought, derives from Clausewitz. It is one of the several passages upon which Lenin seized with avidity,[172] so it presumably became absorbed into Soviet military thinking partly as a result of respect for Lenin's authority, and partly as a result of that careful study of Clausewitz which prior to the Second World War was almost obligatory for every Soviet officer.[173] Not that Clausewitz has even yet been totally discarded; references to his work are still to be met with frequently in Soviet writing; and the entry concerning him in the latest edition of the *Great Soviet Encyclopaedia*, though stopping this side of idolatry (his 'bourgeois' reactionary tendencies are noted with some asperity), still, on the whole, creates the impression on the reader that Clausewitz's work was not merely valuable in some long past historical era, but that it is still valuable today.[174]

The question of how this Clausewitzian corpuscle became absorbed in the Soviet bloodstream is not, however, more than one of purely academic interest. What to us is pertinent is not the means by which Soviet military thinking became possessed of this particular notion, but the extent to which it has digested it, and the uses to which it has been put.

The main sweep of the doctrine can be stated roughly thus: Since the attainment of a given political objective underlies the waging of every war, it is clearly essential to devise a strategy that will not only help to win the war but also attain the objective. At the very least, it must do its

D

utmost not to win the war in such a fashion that the political objective is rendered impossible of achievement.

Thus if, to take a somewhat crude example, the political objective of a war conducted by a slave-owning society, such as Ancient Rome, was the capture of slaves, it would be remarkably foolish, if not downright self-contradictory, to adopt a strategy of mass slaughter of the enemy as a means of achieving victory. Whether or no it be true (and the modern age would obviously conspire to deny it) that the only good Indian is a dead one, it is plain commonsense that the only good slave is one who is very much alive.

Or if, to take a more up-to-date example, the Soviet forces were to march into Western Europe, and if the purpose of them doing so was to strengthen the Soviet economy by capturing intact the French and German factories and research laboratories, it would signally fail to achieve its object if it blasted the territory of Western Europe with a stonk of nuclear weapons. This is not to say that the USSR would never use nuclear weapons in an advance into Western Europe; it is merely to say that, if ever it were to do so, the political objective underlying its military operations would be something other than the capture intact of the Western European economy and its incorporation into that of the Russians.

The above examples are given from a deliberately classless (i.e. non-Marxist) viewpoint: those adduced by Soviet military writers are invariably based on 'class'. One of their favourites relates to the period at the beginning of the Second World War, which in the Britain of the time was generally nicknamed the 'phoney war'. The phoniness consisted of the fact that from 3 September 1939 until Hitler's invasion of Norway in April 1940, the British and French on the one hand, and the Germans on the other, indulged in few manifestations of open combativeness, although we were supposed to be at war. This is explained by the USSR as being the result of the strategy adopted by the British and French Governments, which itself (they say) was dependent upon the policy that guided those governments' actions. In the Soviet view, this policy consisted in trying to secure the destruction of their 'class enemy' (and therefore bitterest foe), the USSR by themselves avoiding battle with the Germans, luring Nazi Germany into a major war with Russia, and by then sitting back and husbanding their resources until Hitler's Reich and Stalin's Russia had both bled themselves white. Thereupon the French and British, their resources intact, would step forward to administer the *coup de grâce* to Communist Russia and, as a kind of afterthought, would destroy Nazism; though the Soviet writers are always quick to allege that the ruling classes of France and the United Kingdom were always inherently sympathetic to Hitlerism, which they regarded as a reliable bulwark against communism, the principal danger (as they perceived things) to their class predominance and to their privileges. Some variations of this theory therefore allege that, having once got Hitler to declare war upon Russia, the 'bourgeois' British and French Governments would at once have proceeded to ally themselves with Hitler in an anti-communist crusade.[175] But whichever the version the reader may prefer, the strategy adopted by the French and British during the 'phoney war' flows (so the Russians aver) from the policy adopted; and the policy adopted was to sit back and do nothing, and let Nazi Germany and Soviet Russia fight it out to the finish.

Even this last is a relatively straightforward example of policy influencing strategy which Westerners, though they may reject its premisses, should be able to understand without any difficulty. It is not, however, the commonest example which is adduced by Soviet commentators when they wish to show that strategy is the tool of policy. Their favourite example derives from another facet of this concept altogether, which in turn derives from another facet of Clausewitz. This is where he argues that the amount of effort that a nation will put into the conduct of a given war will depend directly on the importance to that nation of the political aims for which that war is fought. If, for instance, the aim of the war is merely the annexation of some small area of territory of no great value even to the would-be annexer, then the amount of effort to be put into the attempt to seize it will be limited; if, on the other hand, the value of that piece of territory is of absolutely vital importance to the nation that is attempting to seize it, as was that piece of Finnish territory to the Russians in 1939, then the nation concerned will put into the struggle every ounce of effort of which it is militarily capable. By contrast, the defending side, the original owners of the territory, will fight like hell to retain it in their possession if its retention is judged to be vital to the well-being of the State, but will try much less hard to do so if it is not.

In Clausewitz's view there is only one circumstance which could cause the war's political objective to be so crucial, so fundamental, that the war itself would be literally a war to the death; and consequently in his opinion there is only this one circumstance where the combatants will exert themselves to the utmost (or, as he himself describes it, where 'war assumes its Absolute form'). This is where the motive underlying the war is not some piece of material advantage (a piece of territory, a customs concession, a privileged access to a market) but a war of hatred—a war, that is to say, where the political objective is the extermination of the one side by the other. Clausewitz assumed that this sort of war, which was not uncommon in earlier times, had become extinct by the early nineteenth century when he sat down to write *Vom Kriege*. The Russians do not.

This is because the Soviet view of war is based upon their view of the nature and effects of 'class'. So long as there are 'exploiting' and 'exploited' classes still in existence, so long will the 'class' antagonisms between them burst into open war from time to time. Up to 1917, such a war between the 'exploited' and 'exploiting' classes could only take place *within* a given society, because until that date there was no country where the 'exploited' formed the government, and hence no country that could mount a military campaign on behalf of the 'exploited's' interests with all the resources of a nation-State behind it. Before 1917, therefore, any war between the 'exploiters' and 'exploited' was bound to be some form of civil war.

Now a civil war has always been regarded by Marxism-Leninism as the most cruel, most far-reaching form of war. Lenin gave that description of it in a speech he made to the First All-Russia Congress on Adult Education; and he went on to explain that the reason for this is that civil war is the means whereby the oppressed class directs its strength to destroying the oppressor class *utterly*, and to destroying the economic conditions necessary for the continued existence of that class.[176] Naturally enough the oppressors will resist, and will make use of any successes they may obtain to carry out savage reprisals against the insurgents. Just as the latter's aim is the destruction of the exploiters, so these in their turn seek the extermination of those members of their working-class that dare to try and remove them.[177] It is this determination of each side to make a complete end of the other that gives civil war that characteristic of thorough and relentless cruelty which made such an impression on Lenin.

Since the October Revolution, however, the 'exploited class', which in modern conditions is described by Marxism-Leninism as the 'proletariat', has held power first in one country and then in a number. Consequently, ever since the October Revolution, the 'proletariat' has been in the possession of an army and navy and of all the resources of a nation-State with which to oppose the 'exploiters' (which in modern conditions Marxism-Leninism terms the 'bourgeoisie'). The first use that the Russian proletariat made of these facilities was to destroy the Russian 'bourgeois', as Lenin had recommended, and to complete its work by destroying the economic conditions necessary for its continued existence. But though the *Russian* 'bourgeois' had been destroyed, the French, British, German, American, Japanese and innumerable other 'bourgeois' had not; and sooner or later, so Lenin taught, war between them and Bolshevism was inevitable.[178]

But such a war, being a war between the 'exploiters' and the 'exploited', would be every bit as cruel, every bit as momentous, as a civil war; for the simple reason that, as Marxism-Leninism views things, war between a capitalist country and a communist country would not be just a war between two States (e.g. between the United States of America and the USSR), but a war between two mutually antagonistic *classes* which happened to be fought on a world-wide scale rather than within the confines of a given country. Wars of this kind were described by an authoritative Soviet work of the late 1950s as 'revolutionary class wars' and as being 'the highest form of the class struggle'; because the aims pursued in them were 'the most decisive of all political aims' (or in other words, the destruction of Soviet communism, if capitalism were the victor, or the destruction of Western capitalism, if it was the Russians who won).

If this is so, wars of this kind are obviously going to be wars of life and death for both sets of combatants: they will be what Clausewitz described as 'wars of hatred'; and, being such, they cause the countries engaged in them to exert every ounce of their strength, to deploy the utmost efforts of which they are capable, in order to attain victory and avert defeat. The result will be that the strategy employed by *both sides* will be the most decisive, the most fundamental, the most all embracing, of which the combatants are capable. Put into the language of the second half of the twentieth century, this means that such a war would be bound to be all-out nuclear.

But this will be true only if one side or the other (or both) believes that it is fighting for its very existence. If one side or the other believes that the victory of its opponent will mean the end of its own way of life, it will stop at nothing in order to avert defeat; which means that, if it possesses strategic nuclear rockets, it will certainly employ them. For many years, it was the profound conviction of the leaders of the Soviet Communist Party that *any* war between East and West was bound to be of this kind: no authoritative announcement on the nature of war that was published in the Soviet Union failed to contain this message.

It was based upon the assumption, which the Russians for years regarded as axiomatic, that a war between East and West would be started by the Americans, and that their purpose in starting it was to launch an anti-communist crusade. This, if successful, would (the Russians believed) involve the suppression of the existing Soviet system in the USSR, the abolition of the communist dictatorship, and the imposition upon a defeated Russia of a bourgeois-liberal, capitalist regime modelled upon that of America. Repeated calls for war of this kind, or else for some kind of preventative war, were regularly made by prominent American politicians during the late 1940s and the 1950s; and these were seen by the Russians as confirmatory evidence of the correctness of the above-mentioned assumption.

It should be added here that, as the Soviet Union sees things, if the United States today were suddenly to decide to wage a war of this nature, the only way it could do it would be by strategic nuclear bombardment. The United States armed forces, as they stand today, do not possess anything like the numbers of men, equipment and munitions to allow an assault to be launched on the USSR *with conventional means only*. Consequently, if the USA wanted to wage an anti-communist, ideological war, the only way it could do it would be by an all-out, highly intensive, surprise nuclear bombardment; and it is precisely against this possibility that Soviet military writing today takes the greatest pains to warn its Soviet readers.

The logical possibility that a war of a similarly ideological character might be started by the Russians does not seem to have occurred to the Soviet mind, if we may judge by their published writings. As we have already seen, however, there is nothing in Marxism-Leninism to discourage the starting of another world war for the purpose of forcibly spreading communism except that clause which insists on war not being started except when victory is certain. At no time since 1945, however, has the Soviet Union been able to count upon victory as being certain in any such conflict. Indeed, until the early 1960s its chief ideological opponent, the United States of America, was virtually unassailable by Soviet arms. Consequently, the Soviet failure to discuss in the open literature the question of whether (and, if so, when) a third world war might be started by the Soviet Union coincided with a Soviet inability to fight such a war convincingly—though that is probably not the only reason why the open literature did not discuss the subject.

However that may be, the fact remains that, had the Politburo convinced itself that the time had come to embark upon a 'revolutionary war' of this nature, the only possible means of waging it victoriously, and without incurring unacceptable damage to Russia, would have been by means of an all-embracing, all-powerful, totally destructive nuclear first strike; for only so could the Western powers have been prevented from retaliating. Furthermore, since the aim of the war would have been the destruction of the enemy's political, economic and social system, the appalling havoc wreaked by the nuclear missiles would have actually served to further the war's objective. Once again, therefore, we have a situation where a 'fundamental' objective requires the use of 'fundamental' means of warfare.

Recently, however, there has been a change. Since about 1969 the Kremlin leaders seem to have been willing to recognize that not every clash between East and West is bound to be based on a political objective that seeks the total destruction of the loser's form of society. In other words, the realization has dawned upon the Politburo that limited war between capitalism and communism must nowadays be considered possible. Naturally, such a war must seek to attain no more than limited objectives; but provided that the objectives are indeed limited, then the means employed for waging the war may be expected to be limited too. Of course, the danger still exists—as the Politburo is very fond of stressing—that in the course of the war either (or both) of the combatants may decide to seek a much more far-reaching objective than that which they sought at its outset: in other words, the political objective may 'escalate'. In which case the means of warfare too would escalate, perhaps to a point below the nuclear threshold, or perhaps to the point of an all-out nuclear exchange.

The notion that limited war between capitalism and communism is possible appears to have first been made by the Soviet Navy. The Soviet admirals operate in the sort of conditions where a brush between them and the NATO navies is not wholly inconceivable, but where the issues at stake are likely to be minor. An incident off the island of Mauritius, for example, or a clash with the Guinea patrol might revolve round matters of a certain degree of importance, but round none that were fundamental. If one side or the other were forced to back down in such a conflict, it might lose face, or suffer a check to its foreign policy, but the continued existence in its own country of its particular form of social system would not be at stake. Consequently, in any such conflict the most 'fundamental' of all forms of warfare, a strategic nuclear bombardment, would *not* be employed.

Similarly, in the 1973 Arab-Israeli War the possibility existed of American troops and Soviet troops becoming engaged in fighting each other. Here, the issues for both sides were of considerably greater importance than any involving Guinea or Mauritius, but they would still have fallen a long way short of being *fundamental*. Consequently, although the subsequent fighting was likely to have been a great deal more intensive than any involving bits and pieces of Africa, there would have been a strong probability that an all-out nuclear war could have been avoided. Similar considerations would have applied if the United States' armed forces had been used to attempt to seize the Arab oilfields at the start of the energy crisis. Failure to seize them would not have been absolutely vital to the American way of life, which has in fact continued to exist, despite the fact that an attempt to seize the oilfields has not even been made. On the other hand, a successful seizure would not have meant the end of the reign of the Soviet Communist Party in the USSR; so, once again, a resort to strategic nuclear bombardment could probably have been avoided.

Ever since 1969 or 1970, therefore, the Kremlin has been prepared to concede that a conventional war between East and West is possible. This, however, is subject to the proviso that the war in question must be 'local'. Once the war has spread to being global, once it has become a 'world war', in the sense that the bulk of our planet has become involved in it, the issues for which it will be fought (the Russians believe) are bound to escalate sharply to the extent of becoming 'fundamental'. And, as we have seen, fundamental issues demand fundamental means of warfare, or, in other words, nuclear rockets.

But the question of whether to use them is a question of strategy. Yet, as we have seen, the answer to it has already been predetermined by the basic question of policy that lies at the root of the war. In other words, the strategy to be employed in the waging of the war has been settled from the very outset by the nature of the war's political objective which, in other words again, can only signify that strategy is the tool of policy.

It remains only to be pointed out that, if the war is going badly, the need to avoid defeat will exert a reciprocal influence on the nature of the underlying policy. Where the goal for which the war is being fought is of relatively minor importance for the likely loser, the effect on the latter's policy may not be great. If, for example, the USSR and the Americans were engaged in a conventional, 'local war' over some small island in the Pacific, either side might prefer to concede defeat, and renounce an objective which would be, after all, of no *fundamental* importance to it, rather than alter its strategy and turn to nuclear bombardment as the only means available for avoiding defeat.

If, on the other hand, the consequences of defeat for the loser would be so serious that the whole of life as he knew it would come to an end, he would alter his strategy regardless of his original intentions, and use all means available to him to prevent his enemy winning.

### The factors that make for victory in war

According to Marx, it is the economic base, the productive process, that is the ultimate determinant of the course of human history; but although he considered it the ultimate determinant, he did not consider it the only one. On the contrary, politics plays its part; and so do all other forms of human activity.

What really happens, in the opinion of Marx and Engels, is that the economic base of a particular community affects the political structure of that community, together with its ideology, its art, and (among other things) its armies. Let us take the case of art. The productive process in Europe in the eighteenth century was largely confined to agriculture. The wealthiest people were therefore the great landowners; and these tended to live in splendid palaces set in small towns or else in the depths of the country. Those of them who happened to like music kept their own musicians; and these were expected not only to play other people's compositions for their employers, but also themselves to compose. The type of work they composed necessarily depended upon the musical establishment which their employers happened to keep; and this in turn naturally depended to a great extent upon their employers' income.

The very wealthiest, such as the Esterhazy, could afford to maintain whole orchestras; but the general level was a small ensemble of ten or a dozen players. As a result, we find that the eighteenth century excelled in the composition of pieces for small orchestras; whereas today, under different economic conditions, fewer such pieces are written. Moreover, the eighteenth century had neither wireless nor television and, deprived of this source of entertainment for the long winter evenings, the land-owners had to have others. Those who not merely liked listening to music, but themselves could play an instrument, commissioned their tame composers to write music for them to play. Trios, quartets and quintets were the obvious answer; for this allowed the formation of an intimate and agreeable ensemble, in which the other partners would be members of the landowners' family, together (as often happened) with the composer himself to provide useful professional stiffening.

It is therefore no accident, if you accept this Marxist interpretation of the effect of economics on music, that the eighteenth-century com-posers wrote such enormous quantities of chamber music. Haydn, for instance, wrote nearly two hundred works of this genre; Mozart, over a hundred. And if economics can have such an effect upon art, seemingly the most ethereal of human activities, what effect will it not have upon warfare, where the gross corporeality of massed armies has to be sustained by such obviously economic phenomena as arms, ammunition, rations, petrol, signals equipment, and the transport needed to convey the whole lot of them from the place of their manufacture to the individual soldier in the field.

But if economics affects the superstructure (whether politics, art or armies), these in turn reflect on the economic process, and are the cause of changes in it.[179]

For instance, improvements in weapons, which have been continually introduced throughout the ages, themselves affect the structure of a society, and therefore, at one remove, affect the productive process. A good example of this is to be found in *Anti-Dühring*, where Engels points out that firearms could not be introduced on to the field of battle until industry had first adapted itself to provide for their manufacture. Hence these weapons, once produced, tended to be the weapon of the manufacturers (the townsmen), while the landowning nobility clung to its traditional weapons. But, as it so happened, the newly invented firearms tended to be more effective than the traditional weapons; and thus their adoption by the townsmen contributed to the victory of the latter in their struggle against the feudal nobility. One important result of their victory was that they acquired greater freedom of action; and this in turn gave a further stimulus to industrial production, which in turn led to the appearance of still better weapons.[180]

This view of war as something which is constantly changing in

D*

response to changes in industry and technology, and in turn affecting the whole industrial process, is extremely characteristic of Marxism. As Marx himself put it, 'Is our theory that the *organization of labour* is determined *by the means of production* confirmed anywhere more splendidly than in the man-slaughtering industry?' (Italics original.)[181] In other words, an efficient man-slaughtering industry can only exist if it has a strong industrial base. So, once again, economics is the ultimate determinant.

Applied to war as a whole, this means that the side with the stronger economy will gain the victory, *provided that the war continues for a considerable time*; but when we are speaking of short-term military activities, such as particular battles, the result may be decided by short-term factors (including such intangibles as human bravery), because in those cases the long-term workings of the economic determinant will not have been accorded the time required to make their influence decisive.

Thus, in the Arab-Israeli Six Day War of 1967, the economic potential of the two sets of combatants was roughly equal: indeed, if anything, the combined economic *long-term* potential of the Arabs was likely to be somewhat stronger than the Israeli. Yet this advantage to the Arabs, which Marx would see as being ultimately decisive, had no effect upon the actual course of the war because the Israelis, by a brilliant, lightning campaign, secured the victory before this factor could be operative.

I would like to work out to the end this particular strand of the argument, even though it is out of place at this particular juncture of my thesis, by observing that a war resembles a piece of string, in the sense that its actual duration is what you say it is. One can argue, for instance, that the Second World War was merely a continuation of the First World War, with the years between 1918 and 1939 representing a temporary armistice; one can further argue that the First World War was itself a continuation of the Franco-Prussian War of 1870. In which case, the whole period from 1870 to 1945 can be seen as one of prolonged conflict between Germany and France, punctuated by two cease-fires.

If this point of view be applied to the Six Day War, then the whole period from 1948 (the first armed clash between the Arabs and the Israelis) to the present day and beyond is seen as one long war between the two combatants, of which the Israeli victory of 1967 was merely a single episode. Regarded in this light, the war is not yet over; and as it continues year after year after year, the long-term economic advantage which Marx would see as accruing to the cause of the Arabs may yet have time to make its effects felt. Some might say that the Israelis have understood this; and that their acceptance, however tentative, of the

American peace plan after the fighting of 1973 was a cautious acknow-ledgment that Marx might perhaps be right.

But to return to the main thread of my argument, I was saying that, in Marx's opinion, despite the fact that economics was the ultimate determinant, human factors could *in the short term* prevail against economics; and that examples of this could be found in a number of battles. Thus, the Abyssinians defeated the Italians at Adowa in 1896, despite the fact that the latter had good contemporary equipment, while that of the Abyssinians was primitive. At Isandhlwana in 1879, a Zulu 'impi', possessed of no firearms at all, defeated and almost completely annihilated a British force which, in addition to rifles, was equipped with field guns and rocket-carriers. In 1587 (to go back a bit in time) Sir Francis Drake inflicted crippling losses on the Spanish fleet at Cadiz, although his little fleet of twenty-three was far outnumbered and outgunned by the Spanish defences.

Nevertheless, even in the case of individual battles, economics has a great part to play. This is because it is the industrial base of the combatant country which provides that country with its weapons; and where that base is small and poorly developed, the weapons will be poor, too. Marx and Engels were perfectly well aware of the part played by military technology on the battlefield; and had there been any likelihood of their forgetting it, the Prussian victory over the Austrians at Sadowa (which occurred when they were both in their middle age) would have been ample reminder of it.

Moreover, this reminder was buttressed by the innumerable colonial wars which stud the nineteenth century; for these were frequent and obvious examples of the power of technology in war. Considered as soldiers, the Zulus and the Matabele were every bit as courageous as the British redcoats, and were very much more numerous on the field of battle. Nevertheless, despite their occasional successes in particular engagements, they lost their wars against the forces of the British, and were driven to ultimate surrender. This failure on their part was due, above all, to the fact that their opponents were armed with efficient firearms, against which they had to contend with spears and shields.

However, although both Marx and Engels regarded the economic base as of tremendous importance in war, nevertheless they conceded that, as has been said above, other factors could influence the course of the fighting, particularly in the short term. Of these other factors, the most important, in Engels' opinion, was 'the quantity and quality of the populations' of the respective combatants.[182]

The importance of having a large population in wartime is easy to understand. For one thing, its existence permits the raising of a big army; and, *all other things being equal*, the combatant with the bigger army is likely to be the victor. For another, the more populous country will probably have the stronger industrial base: its economic resources are likely to be greater than its enemy's, its commerce more highly developed, its productive capacity bigger, and its technology more advanced. It is not to belittle the personal qualities of the Americans to say that one of the reasons why their economy is so productive, and so very highly developed, is that they have a population roughly four times that of Britain, four times that of West Germany, and nearly five times that of France.

Having dealt with the importance of the *size* of the population of a combatant (its 'quantity', as Engels described it), we must now turn to what he labelled its 'quality'. When that quality is high—which, in the context of war, means that the people are brave, hardy, intelligent, resourceful, well disciplined and good at organization—then the fortunate possessors of that quality will have an advantage in combat. In the case of the Arab-Israeli Six Day War, the advantage was great enough to give Israel a brilliant victory; though in that particular conflict the advantage that Israel received from the high quality of her own troops was further increased by the *low* quality of the troops of her opponents. For, whatever the reasons for the poor showing of the Egyptian Army, no one attempts to dispute that it fought badly; and this in turn contributed greatly to the notable Israeli success. By contrast, the fact that in 1973 the Egyptian Army fought incomparably better, undoubtedly contributed greatly to the Israeli Army's difficulties in that campaign.

A further example of the contribution which the low quality of a combatant can make to the victory of his enemy is to be found in the campaign of Alexander the Great against the Persians. An important reason for the former's magnificent victory was the superior quality of the Macedonian equipment, especially the arms and armour of the phalanx, together with the tactics that the phalanx evoked. It is not to be doubted that the Persia of Darius was capable of the manufacture of equally effective equipment, but the fact remains that it did not actually make them. The Persian failure to manufacture good equipment, together with a failure to evolve tactics that could cope with the Greek invaders, was due to a failure of 'quality' in the Persians themselves. As Marx said: 'War puts nations to the test . . . and pronounces its sentence of death on those social institutions that have become ossified.' In Alexander's campaigns the Persian Empire was tested; and its social institutions were condemned, and sentenced to death.[183]

To return to the advantage conferred by *high* quality, this was a cause of the British airmen, in September 1940, defeating Hitler's numerically superior air force in the Battle of Britain. Had the British lacked that high quality, had they been possessed of that timorousness of soul which marked the Egyptian officers in 1967, had they not had the skill to fly their machines so as to evoke the best of which these machines were capable, the Luftwaffe would have won the Battle of Britain, and the Germans would have won the war.

Nevertheless, human valour, however consummate, is not in itself sufficient to confer victory when faced with superior weaponry. The followers of the Mahdi in the Sudan were brave in the highest degree; and Kipling himself pays tribute to their soldierly qualities.[184] But despite the presence of this high quality in their troops, the Dervish forces were beaten at Omdurman, because they possessed no field artillery and no machine-guns, while the British had an abundance of them both.

But the chief reason why the Sudanese were short of artillery and machine-guns is that they did not have the industrial base necessary for their manufacture. Moreover, since a non-industrialized country is, generally speaking, a poor country, they did not have the money with which to buy them. Seen in this light, therefore, it was the lack of an advanced industrial economy which was responsible for the Mahdi's defeat.

Thus, the argument has turned full circle; and we are back with the proposition that, despite the fact that human virtues and failings can undoubtedly exert some influence on the course of a battle (and even on the course of a war, if it is finished quickly), in the long term the war will be decided by the relative strengths of the combatants' economies; and he who has the stronger industrial base will emerge the victor.

If the above is true (and Marx and Engels were fully convinced that it was), then the only gambit open to a country which is faced with an enemy with a stronger economy than his own is to resort to some form of blitzkrieg so that, by making the war a 'lightning war', it may hope to achieve victory before the long-term advantages of the enemy's superior economic potential can make their influence felt upon the battlefield. From the Marxist viewpoint, therefore, Hitler was undoubtedly right to launch a blitzkrieg in 1940; because in that year the combined economic potential of Britain and France was greater than that of Germany and Austria. Consequently, his only hope of success lay in defeating the British and French before they had time to realize that potential. The reason why he failed (so a Marxist would say) was because he had omitted to think the thing through properly, and, in particular, had not perceived the necessity of acquiring the means of 'blitzing' his 'krieg' across the Channel. Had he done that, Britain must undoubtedly have fallen; and he could have turned against Russia a year or two later with every chance of success.[185]

The above is an exposition of the factors making for victory and defeat in war, as Marx and Engels saw things. If I have erred at all, then I have done so in the direction of allowing more weight to the human factor than Marx and Engels themselves were wont to give it. This is especially true of such purely spiritual qualities as courage and steadfastness, which Marx and Engels almost completely ignore.

For even where Engels, in that famous quotation from *Anti-Dühring*, asserts that 'the quantity and quality of the population' is an important factor in making for victory or defeat, he goes on to make quite clear that, in his opinion, both the quantity and the quality are ultimately due to economic causes, which is why he describes them as 'human *material*' (my italics) and lumps them alongside 'armaments material'. Nor are such qualities as courage and steadfastness of any great interest to him. The 'quality' of the population which concerned Engels in *Anti-Dühring* turns out to mean a nation's social structure and its means of livelihood. The Americans, he said, won their War of Independence because of their skirmishing tactics; they adopted skirmishing tactics because most of them were hunters; and the cause of their being hunters was economic. Whether they were braver than the British 'redcoats', or more resolute, are questions with which Engels did not concern himself.

On the other hand, there are good reasons for believing that Marx and Engels, in their public writings and speeches, tended somewhat to over-emphasize the importance of economics, as compared with the weight which they gave it in the quiet of their own hearts. In which case it is possible (and I certainly hope it is true) that the summary of their views on victory and defeat, as expounded in the preceding paragraphs, comes even closer to what they *really* thought on the matter than a collage of their published writings would seem to suggest.

The reason why in their published work they tended to over-emphasize the importance of economics as a determinant, not only in war, but in every sort and kind of human activity, is best explained by Engels in his famous letter to J. Block of 21–2 September 1890, where he says:

*Marx and I are ourselves partly to blame for the fact that the younger people sometimes lay more stress on the economic side than is due to it. We had to emphasize the main principle vis-à-vis our adversaries, who denied it; and we had not always the time, the place or the opportunity to give their due to the other elements involved in the interaction.*

The result has been that most of Marx's and Engels' own writings on the subject of war do concentrate very largely on the economic element —except, of course, where their concern is with the political results that would flow from defeat or victory in a given conflict (i.e. whether they were likely to help or hinder the revolutionaries' cause).

But the result of this concentration upon economics has been that their disciples have fastened upon it to the virtual exclusion of almost everything else. As Engels himself said later in that same letter:

*Unfortunately, however, it happens only too often that people think they have fully understood a new theory and can apply it without more ado from the moment they have assimilated its main principles, and even those not always correctly. And I cannot exempt many of the more recent 'Marxists' from this reproach, for the most amazing rubbish has been produced in this quarter too. . . .*

There is one circumstance which sharply distinguishes Lenin's world from that of Marx and Engels, so far as war is concerned. This is that, during the lifetimes of the latter, war was still generally restricted to a comparatively small proportion of the populations of the combatant nations. In the Crimean War, the Austro-Prussian War, and even the Franco-Prussian War, the vast majority of the inhabitants of the countries that were engaged in them lived out their lives untroubled by any fighting. This state of things was ending by the time that Lenin was born, and was finally ended by the outbreak of the First World War.

Even prior to 1914, however, it had virtually come to an end for certain people; for, seen through the eyes of a dedicated Russian revolutionary (that is to say, seen through the eyes of someone like Lenin himself), the Russo-Japanese War of 1904–5 blended with the 1905 uprising to produce two years of fighting which involved a great slice of Russia. Moreover, during all this fighting, Lenin's attention was focused on the grey masses of the workers, for it was upon them and upon the peasants that he pinned his hopes of victory in any uprising— the workers to seize power, and to hold it in the cities, and the peasants not to allow themselves to be duped into helping to suppress them. Therefore, he wrote a number of works at this period which were concerned with armed insurrection, and whose purpose was to teach the masses of the workers how to combat the Tsarist troops and the Tsarist police.[186]

As a result of these experiences, Lenin acquired the view that wars were now once more an affair of the whole population; and that this was so, whether they were 'ordinary' wars between ordinary nation-States, or whether they were armed uprisings or civil wars in which, according to Marxist doctrine, the mass of numbers of the 'proletariat' was an essential requirement for victory.

This view was given a sharp fillip when he came to study Clausewitz. In book VIII, chapter III, of *On War*, he lit on the passage which describes how war at the time of the Tartar invasions had been an affair of the whole people; how in the Middle Ages the people were very much less concerned; how in the eighteenth century their influence was virtually nil; but how the wars of the French Revolution and of

Napoleon Bonaparte restored to the people that total commitment in war which Lenin appeared to think was justly theirs. At any rate he gave great emphasis to this passage, which was one of those that he copied out into his notebook.[187]

He read Clausewitz at some time in 1915. Three years later, the civil war in Russia allowed him to study Clausewitz's theory at first hand. He found him justified. In Lenin's view, the chief reason why the Bolsheviks won that war was because those who supported them believed in the cause they were fighting for, while the bulk of the troops opposing them did not.

To what extent this view is historically accurate is not to our purpose here. Our present purpose is to appreciate the emphasis that Lenin gave to this 'factor making for victory', and to the still greater emphasis that is given to it in the USSR today. It asserts essentially that if soldiers believe wholeheartedly in the personal significance for each one of them of the cause for which they are fighting, they will fight like the very devil; while if they do not, they will not; and it further asserts that, in this latter case, their lack of will to fight may result in wholly nullifying whatever inherent superiority may have been conferred on them by better equipment.

Put at its baldest, this statement is obviously true. If a soldier of even the most modern army is unwilling to pull the trigger, he can easily be killed by a Stone Age savage armed with a Stone Age club. Indeed the sentiment, admittedly expressed in a somewhat more sophisticated manner, has already had its validity demonstrated in the preceding paragraphs. What was the British defeat at Isandhlwana but a failure to pull the trigger, however caused?

But such a failure, though it led to the loss of a battle, was not sufficient to cause the loss of the war. As we have seen, the British Army pulled itself together after the defeat at Isandhlwana, and went on to win the war; and Marx and Engels always assumed that, in this sort of circumstance, this sort of consequence would follow. Lenin's thesis asserts, however, that this 'failure to pull the trigger' can be so widespread and last so long among the troops of one of the combatants that it can lose, not merely a battle, but the war itself; and the events of the civil war in Russia of 1918–20 were cited in support of his thesis.

According to Lenin's version of what happened, the Bolshevik Government was faced by two armed enemies, of whom one was a section of the Russian population that is usually termed 'the Whites', while the other consisted of British, French, Czech, German, Japanese and American soldiers who had been sent by their respective governments to suppress communism by force.

So far as the Whites were concerned, time and again they recruited armies which, once brought into proximity with the Reds, simply melted away. They might be, and often were, equipped with weapons greatly superior to those at the disposal of the Bolsheviks; because the highly developed economies of the imperialists had lavished these arms upon them. But since the rank-and-file of the Whites were often unwilling to use them, then on those occasions their superior technical efficiency counted for nothing. And, in Lenin's view, such occasions occurred sufficiently frequently to give the Reds the victory. This is not to deny that there were thousands of White supporters who were committed wholeheartedly to the cause of the defeat of the Reds, and who were ready to fight and die for it; but it is to say that these were not nearly sufficiently numerous, and not nearly sufficiently resolute over prolonged periods of fighting, to allow the Whites to win. The White forces had the latest equipment in plenty, but they could not get the bulk of their troops to use it with any spirit of self-sacrifice or even adequate determination.

The case of the other section of the Reds' enemies was analogous, but not identical. These, it will be remembered, consisted of the governments of a number of imperialist countries who had sent their troops into various parts of Russia in an attempt to exterminate communism. (This, at least, was Lenin's view of the matter; and it is Lenin's views that concern us.)

But these troops, too, were unable to gain the victory, despite their superficially enormous superiority in training and equipment over the Red forces opposed to them. In certain cases this was because they had little stomach for the fight: the mutiny of the French in the Black Sea is an obvious example here. But the fundamental reason for their failure is that the Allied invasions were very small-scale affairs; and, according to Lenin, the real reason that they were no bigger was that the proletariats of the various imperialist countries would not allow their governments to wage a sustained military campaign on a scale large enough to achieve the downfall of Bolshevism.

By contrast, said Lenin, the 'proletarian' Red Army knew that what it was fighting for was of the greatest personal concern to every man in it; because if it failed, their Workers' and Peasants' Government would be swept away, and in its place would be brought back the 'class' tyranny of the bourgeois.

From the above circumstances Lenin drew the conclusion that not merely in the context of the Russian Civil War, but in that of all wars in general, now that war was once more the affair of the whole of a combatant's population, the attitude towards it of the combatant countries' workers and peasants was going to be decisive, for the simple reason that they were by far the most numerous section of the population; and Lenin declared that their attitude was going to vary according to the 'class' composition of the various combatant governments.

For, as we have seen earlier, it is a basic premiss of Marxism that wars are waged to further the interests of the combatants' ruling classes; and in slave-owning, feudal or bourgeois countries the rulers' interests (so Marxists say) have nothing in common with those of the peasants and workers. Consequently, the workers and peasants living in a 'feudal' or 'bourgeois' country have nothing personally to gain by fighting wars (except sometimes in the event of an attempt to invade and occupy their country by another 'feudal' or 'bourgeois' country with the aim of territorial conquest). Once the workers and peasants have had it explained to them that this is indeed the case, they will be most reluctant to risk their lives on behalf of their 'bourgeois' masters; and this reluctance will be particularly marked if the war in question should chance to be directed against a 'proletarian' country, or in other words a country ruled by fellow-workers and peasants. By contrast the 'proletarian' inhabitants of a 'proletarian' state can be relied upon to lay down their lives with enthusiasm if the interests of their country should demand it, because in such a state their country's interests are always the same as their own.

Lenin's addition to the theory concerning the 'factors making for victory' may therefore be summed up by saying that in modern times, where war is once more an affair of the whole people, the morale of the populations of the combatant countries is an important factor in deciding the outcome of the war; and that this is particularly true where a 'proletarian' country is engaged in fighting the 'bourgeois'. In such a case, the theory avers, the troops of the 'proletarian' country will fight with wholehearted, revolutionary enthusiasm while those of the 'bourgeois' countries will be particularly reluctant to serve.

In 1942, Stalin formulated his 'permanently operating factors which decide the outcome of a war'. These were 'the stability of the rear', 'the morale of the army', 'the quality and quantity of the divisions', 'the armament of the army', and 'the organizational abilities of the command personnel'.[188]

It was not denied that there were other factors, such as surprise, which could affect the course of a war; but these were described as 'temporary attendant factors' (Garthoff translates them as 'transitory factors') which could indeed produce momentary tactical successes (and even important ones), but which could not determine the outcome of the war as a whole.[189] The Second World War is cited as a case in point: the Germans, by means of surprise, achieved important successes in 1941; but the 'permanently operating factors' ultimately worked in Russia's favour, and so the Russians won.[190]

It is probably true that the reason that Stalin downgraded the importance of surprise was because the Red Army had in fact been

tactically surprised in the summer of 1941, and had suffered severely
as a result. And this state of affairs was due to Stalin's own personal
decisions. But Stalin in his heyday was invariably officially portrayed
as being infallible. If, then, surprise is an important factor in ensuring
victory in war, Stalin, by allowing the Germans to achieve it, had shown
himself to be fallible. Therefore it had to be proclaimed to the Russian
people that surprise is *not* a factor of major importance; and that victory
is won, instead, by due attention being paid to the 'permanently
operating' factors.

It should be added that, even if the reason for the downgrading of the
importance of surprise was really that which has been put forward in
the preceding paragraph, the *effect* of this was extremely serious on the
development of Soviet strategy and military doctrine. For, so long as
Stalin lived, it was never possible for a Soviet officer to do other than
denigrate surprise, nor discuss rationally the effects it might really have.
For, so far as higher authority was concerned, there was nothing to
discuss. The highest authority of all had roundly asserted that surprise
was no more than a 'temporary attendant factor'; and thus it remained
until that highest authority was dead.

But to return to the 'permanently operating factors', Stalin was a
sound 'vulgar Marxist'; and the 'permanently operating factors' are
sound 'vulgar Marxism'. The first factor, 'the stability of the rear',
denotes not merely the ability of the civilian population to withstand the
privations of war and such things as aerial bombardment, but also its
capacity to manufacture and distribute those items of munitions and
equipment which an army requires for fighting.[191] As Engels remarked
in *Anti-Dühring*: 'Nothing depends on economic conditions so much
as an army and a fleet. The armament, the personnel, the organization,
the tactics and the strategy depend above all on the level of production
and on the means of communication at a given moment.' This remark
is usually quoted by Stalinist commentators in connection with the
first 'permanently operating factor'.[192]

The next three of the 'permanently operating factors' are self-
explanatory. The last of them needs comment only to the extent
necessary to explain that *nachal'stvuyushchii sostav armii* (which I,
following Raymond Garthoff and others, have translated as 'the command personnel') in fact applies to almost every officer, certainly to all
who are in command of even the smallest detachment. The com-
mentaries make quite clear that this is so.[193]

The above demonstrates that Stalin's errors with regard to Marxian
doctrine concerning the factors that make for victory in war are errors
more of omission than of commission. He has introduced nothing new;
he has left two factors out. Or, to be accurate, he has totally omitted one
factor, and downgraded another to the rank of a 'temporary, subsidiary

factor'; and it is these two factors which we must proceed to examine now.

To take the second one first, the downgrading of the factor of surprise cannot possibly be justified if we are speaking of war in general, not even if we are speaking of it before nuclear weapons were invented. It has always been perfectly possible for a war to be over and done with in the course of a few weeks by virtue of the factor of surprise: this is especially true when we are speaking of small countries which have not got the expanse of territory needed to absorb the shock of the surprise attack, and still allow a regrouping of the shattered forces and a preparation for a *riposte*. The Six Day War between Israel and Egypt is a good illustration of my meaning.

However, if we are speaking of surprise purely with relation to Russia in a defensive role, *and purely with relation to a non-nuclear war*, then it is just possible that Stalin may have been right when he said that surprise was only a temporary and subsidiary factor among those making for victory.

Of course, the subsequent development of nuclear weapons and the means of their delivery have contradicted Stalin even in this respect, because they have made the factor of surprise important in any war. We should therefore regard it as natural that Stalin's successors should have denounced his concept of the 'permanently operating factors', and should have assigned to the role of surprise a very much greater importance than he was prepared to do.

The factor that Stalin totally omitted is one that is really basic to the views of Marx, of Engels and of Lenin on the subject of what is necessary for victory. This is the strength of the combatant country's economy, *taken as a whole*. For, such highly desirable aids to victory as 'the quality and quantity of the divisions' and 'the army's weapons and equipment' are all themselves dependent upon a strong industrial base. Engels, as we have seen, related everything, including strategy and tactics, to 'the level of production and the means of communication at a given moment'; and a modern formulation would probably include 'the level of research and development among the things to be so related'. But all these things are themselves ultimately dependent upon the strength of the economy in general.

Why, then, did Stalin omit this? Since he himself left us no explanation, all we can do is to guess. My own guess is as follows: Right from the very moment of the October Revolution, the Soviet Union has always been well aware that its own economy, taken as a whole, has not been as strong as that of the West as a whole. Certainly, at the time when Stalin formulated his five 'permanently operating factors', there was no doubt whatever that the economy of the USSR, shattered and ravaged by war, was nowhere near as strong as that of America. Nor could it be doubted that, if the strength of the British and the French economies was added to that of the United States, the economy of the Soviet Union would have been at that time in a position of staggering inferiority. In which case, if Stalin had proclaimed to the world that one of the 'permanently operating factors which decide the outcome of a war' was the strength of the combatants' economies taken as a whole, he would have been proclaiming that, if the USSR were to become involved in a war with the capitalist countries, she would have been almost bound to lose.

The above, as I have admitted, is no more than my own guess; but I am confirmed in my belief in its probable correctness both from what the late Mr Isaac Deutscher said to me in this connection, and also because the deductions that one can make from it fit in well with what we know of Soviet strategic thinking, and serve to illuminate it. So it is to modern Soviet thinking that we must turn before very long; and Mr Deutscher's comments will be set down in the final section, when we draw together the various threads of this long and complex chapter.

The denunciations of Stalin's personality cult that followed the Twentieth Party Congress led to his 'permanently operating factors' being subjected to severe criticism. But since the bulk of them were, as we have seen, perfectly sound in principle, his critics were forced to retain their essence while pretending that they had not done so. Thus, one textbook of the period speaks of the importance of the 'quality and quantity of the *troops*', instead of 'the quality and quantity of the *divisions*'; another affirms that Stalin's were important factors, but said that they were not '*permanently* operating'. Those interested are referred, above all, to the second edition of *O Sovietskoi Voennoi Nauke*, where there is to be found the most detailed criticism of Stalin's views on warfare with which I am personally acquainted.[194]

His enemies, however, had legitimate ground for complaint when they objected to surprise being considered as no more than a temporary and subsidiary factor in assuring success in war. As they rightly pointed out, it cannot possibly be so described in the nuclear age; and therefore the factor of surprise has been very considerably upgraded in modern Soviet thinking on the subject of war.[195]

There has also been an important return to the values of Lenin's time in the present emphasis on the enormous importance of morale in war today. This is really a change of *style*, rather than a change of content; because Stalin's 'permanently operating factors' included at least two— 'the stability of the rear' and 'the morale of the army'—which bore on this very point. Furthermore, he gave them weighty emphasis. Why, then, the change in the manner of presentation?

The reason seems to be that the international situation confronting the USSR, insofar as the threat of a large-scale war is concerned, is generally portrayed to the average Soviet citizen as much resembling that confronting Russia at the time of the civil war and Allied intervention of 1918–20. War, he is told, is unlikely; because the Soviet armed forces are so strong, and indeed so obviously strong, that they are likely to deter aggression. If, however, the American imperialists should choose to ignore the USSR's imposing military capability, and should decide to launch an attack on her as a means of extinguishing communism, then the war that would result would be an all-out war between the Soviet Union and America, in which the allies of both would be involved. Seen like this, it would be a war of the Western coalition against the coalition of the socialist countries.

Geography, too, is said to work in favour of the USSR. She is big enough, if need be, to endure the nuclear rockets' incinerating blast, and still survive the ordeal. Countries only slightly less big are likely, it is implied, to prove incapable of such survival; while the small countries will be totally extinguished. Since the United States has a surface area of only 3,548,974 square miles, while that of the USSR amounts to about 8,650,000 square miles, the difference in size should be big enough (by Soviet calculations) to serve as a powerful factor making for the latter's victory in any global conflict of the future.

But, of course, the Soviet Union today has by no means abandoned, as a factor making for victory, such a traditional Marxist concept as the quantity and quality of the arms, ammunition and equipment. The armed forces of the USSR are supplied with weapons of first-class quality and admirable design. Nor is there any shortage of them. Moreover, they often give evidence of bold and imaginative thinking on the part of their research and development teams.

In the same vein, great attention is paid by the Politburo to the development of the Soviet economy. In particular, it is especially concerned with those sections of it which are geared to the needs of defence. It is as aware as were Marx and Engels that wars are won and lost in the research laboratory and in the factories; and it is sparing no effort to see that it wins the next one, of whatever kind that may be.

Generally speaking, therefore, modern Soviet notions of the factors that make for victory in war have undergone no change of intrinsic importance since the days of Marx and Engels—with one exception. But, apart from this one exception, the other factors are much as they were when the Founding Fathers of communism expounded them to their disciples: there have been some differences of emphasis, but that is all.

The one exception, however, is extremely important. It is now asserted that, because of modern technology, a war can be won in a very short space of time, and before the long-term factors have had time to operate. That is to say, the strength of the combatants' economies, taken as a whole, is no longer of decisive importance. That this was true of battles was never denied by any of the classical Marxists, who also admitted that in certain exceptional circumstances (and notably when one of the protagonists was a small country) it might also be true of wars.

But modern Soviet writers are asserting that it is likely to be true nowadays even of wars in which the protagonists are very big countries; and that it will *certainly* be true in the case of a war that is nuclear. This is because, in their opinion, the basic assumptions on which Marx and Engels tacitly based their conclusions no longer hold good today.

For why did the founders of communism believe that in a war, as distinct from in a battle, the long-term factors would almost certainly be decisive? For one thing, because they felt that a war could be ended swiftly only in those cases where the initially victorious combatant could press his advantage home on his wavering enemy, occupy all his territory, seize his workshops and his arsenals, and deprive him of the means of resistance. Such lightning success, however, could normally be achieved only when the victim was a small country: in other instances, the war would be more prolonged and the long-term factors would be given their chance to operate. Modern Soviet doctrine declares that a hail of nuclear rockets on an enemy's territory, aimed at his cities and industrial bases as well as at his military installations, would be completely and utterly effective in depriving him of the means of resistance, and also extremely speedy; and that this is so, whether the enemy in question is a big or a little country. Provided that one of the combatants has a sufficient store of missiles to 'overkill' his enemy, then (so the theory goes) the latter is very unlikely to be able to resist for long; though it is also true that, by his own retaliatory nuclear strike, he may put an end to the resistance of his opponent. It is the Soviet Union's boast that it does possess enough rockets to allow it to annihilate its enemies—and not merely their troops, their arsenals and their bases, but also the whole of that urban and industrial complex which serves to nourish their armies. All, all would be gone.[196]

In this connection, the reader must be made aware that Soviet strategical thinking does not (or, at any rate, claims it does not) regard the achievement of a lightning victory in a nuclear war as being necessarily the prerogative of him who first presses the button. In their published writings, at all events, the Soviet military make the claim that it is perfectly possible in such a war for the victory to go to the defender, provided he has prepared sufficiently in peacetime both to withstand the nuclear strike of the aggressor, and to return his blow with interest. Therefore, although surprise has certainly been upgraded since Stalin's time, it has not yet been promoted to the leading position, at any rate in the published writings. What these assert is that, in the conditions of nuclear war, total victory and total defeat can be achieved extremely quickly, and that aggression is by no means certain to confer victory.[197]

## The suppression of the vanquished

But there is no point in winning a famous victory, if the fruits of that victory are soon to be snatched away from you, and the victory itself undone. History knows not a few examples of such notable reversals of fortune, where the most splendid triumphs have been brought to dust and ashes in the course of a few months or years.

The empire of Gustavus Adolphus, wrested from his neighbours by a series of brilliant campaigns, outlasted his death by a beggarly three-quarters of a century. That of Napoleon I was gone within his lifetime. The conquests obtained by Germany as the result of the Franco-Prussian War remained in her possession for less than fifty years; and the process of Germanization of Alsace-Lorraine, so dear to the heart of Bismarck and von Bülow, had not had time to take root in the people's consciousness before the First World War reversed it.[198]

The view adumbrated in the preceding paragraphs was one that was shared by Marx. As has already been demonstrated, it was his view that every war contains within itself the seeds of another war; and that the spoils of victory 'can never be fixed finally and fairly, because they always must be imposed by the conqueror upon the conquered, and consequently carry within them the seeds of fresh wars' (see pp. 22–3).[199]

Consequently, the communist leaders have always been subjected to strong doctrinal pressures to prevent the wars, in which they have become embroiled, from giving rise to new ones.

Such pressure has been particularly strong in the case of wars that were wars between capitalism and communism, or which the Bolsheviks believed to be such. A capitalist victory in this kind of war entailed, the Russians asserted, the end of the Soviet regime in Russia and its replacement by some other. This 'other', in the communist view, must necessarily be some form of society which was either capitalist or quasi-capitalist in character, and which would put an end to the dictatorship of the Communist Party.

That such is the view of the Kremlin even today can be shown quite easily by reference to contemporary Soviet writing. Thus, one book published in Moscow in 1971 says that the chief aim of the imperialists is to destroy the socialist system; and that they intend to achieve this aim by means of war.[200] Another source quotes American authors to demonstrate to its readers that the destruction of the existing Soviet regime would be the principal aim of the United States in the event of another world war.[201]

Nor are such views mere self-justificatory outpourings. If the Whites had won the civil war, for instance, there can be no doubt that they would have suppressed the Bolsheviks, and destroyed the communist regime. Yet a White victory would have been impossible without the support of the West. *Objectively* speaking, therefore (to use a favourite communist adverb), it would have been the Western support which would have been responsible for the Bolsheviks' downfall; and this would have happened, the communists think, irrespective of whether the Western statesmen intended it or no.

Lenin, of course, was convinced that the Western governments intended it. The total destruction of communism, in his opinion, was the chief reason why the West supported the Whites: and his view has been echoed by subsequent Soviet leaders. Nor is this view entirely without foundation. A glance at the memoirs of contemporary Western statesmen shows quite clearly that, though they mostly thought it to be impracticable to send large quantities of their own troops to bring about the downfall of communism, yet if this could have been accomplished by other (presumably White) troops, a big section of Western public opinion would have been delighted.[202]

Twenty-one years later, a 'bourgeois' Western nation again invaded Russia. No one doubts that, if Hitler had been victorious, he would have put an end to communism; and here, therefore, is yet another example which helps to confirm the Politburo in its belief that its view is right.

And even after the Second World War had ended, a further example of the same anti-communist campaigning made its appearance in the West. This time, as it happened, it manifested itself in words only; but it manifested itself vociferously, and the Russians took note of it. The example to which I refer was that strong movement in certain political circles in the United States, which was most in evidence while that country retained an effective monopoly of atomic weapons, and which urged preventive war on the USSR. For while the American atomic monopoly continued, it always seemed just possible for the Americans to enforce a change of system on the Soviet Union and destroy the communist dictatorship. There was no lack of American citizens who believed that the thing should be attempted. Calls for war against Russia were commonplace in the immediate post-war years.

The above considerations therefore made it imperative for the Russians, right from the very beginning of Bolshevik rule, to find a solution to that problem which I expounded at the start of this section. That is to say, how was a war that ended with a Soviet victory to be stopped from engendering another war that might end with a Soviet defeat?

The solution that was adopted by the Politburo from the very first days of communist rule in Russia, and that has been applied to all the wars in which the USSR has participated, was the enforced 'sovietiz-ation' of conquered territory. The Soviet system, controlled by a communist party, is of all political systems the best adapted to prevent-ing subsequent revolt. Indeed, it was designed by Lenin precisely for that purpose; because it was his opinion that, in the early days of a communist seizure of power, 'counter-revolution' was a distinct possi-bility, and means therefore had to be discovered for preventing such a thing from succeeding. Rule by the Party along the general principles of what Lenin termed 'the dictatorship of the proletariat' was intended to be, and has proved to be in practice, the most effective means of preventing' counter-revolution'; and world history bears witness to its efficacy.[203] For never yet has a truly communist government, operating on the Soviet model, been driven from power by purely internal opposition: armed force, applied from without, has always been a pre-requisite in those few cases where a communist government has actually been evicted from office.

That being so, it could confidently be expected that, if a conquered territory were to be made to submit to a 'dictatorship of the proletariat', it would remain communist in character to the end of time. And since it is contrary to the tenets of Marxism-Leninism to suppose that war could ever break out between two communist countries, it follows that if, by whatever means, a Soviet regime could be imposed on a capitalist country, that country, by ceasing to be capitalist, would cease to want to wage war against the USSR. And even supposing that it did, and that it contrived to be victorious, nevertheless, being no longer capitalist, it would not seek to make use of its victory to restore capitalism to Russia.

Enforced 'sovietization' of occupied territory was naturally also congenial to the early Bolsheviks for a totally different reason. This was that, at the time of the October Revolution, they looked forward to all the world, and not just Russia, being speedily converted to communism. Therefore, whenever this or that piece of territory was captured by Bolshevik forces, any resistance to 'sovietization' that might be offered by the inhabitants of the aforesaid area was taken as evidence of counter-revolutionary contumacy, and not of the fact that, viewed objectively, communism was not wanted.

As a consequence, resistance was always suppressed; and the full rigours of the 'dictatorship of the proletariat' were imposed by military conquest. This happened in the various parts of Russia where the Red Army was victorious in the course of the civil war: it happened in Georgia after the suppression of the Mensheviks; it also happened in Poland in 1920, in those areas which the Russian forces had captured, and which were then turned over to the Revolutionary Committees for 'sovietization' to be applied to them.

The activities of the Revolutionary Committees in Poland are sufficiently fully documented to allow us to get a fair idea of what happened. Soviet sources alone are quite sufficient to make it plain beyond any doubt that the chief purpose of these committees was to impose the Soviet system of government upon the areas for which they were responsible, irrespective of whether the areas in question wanted the Soviets or no.[204]

In 1921, Georgia was forcibly 'sovietized', following upon the defeat of the forces of the Menshevik Government by units of the Red Army. While this undoubted historical fact has tended to become obscured by the passage of time, so that people today regard Georgia as being just as much a part of the USSR as Moscow itself, and never question whether this has always been so, the following points, taken from Soviet sources, might make them reconsider: First, Georgia had a Menshevik, not a Bolshevik, government, when the Red Army invaded;[205] second, prior to the invasion, that government had been strong enough to suppress a Bolshevik uprising;[206] third, it was because of this fact, because the local Bolsheviks could not muster sufficient support from among the native Georgians, that they had to summon outside help in the shape of the Red Army.[207] To these facts, one may add that Professor Carr, a man not normally noted for his sympathy with Menshevism, agrees that the 'sovietization' of Georgia was 'enforced'.[208]

Nor were the above examples of enforced 'sovietization' merely something done in the heat of the moment. Tukhachevsky, writing in 1926 (i.e. five years after the 'bolshevization' of Georgia), refers to the process of compulsory 'sovietization' of areas occupied by a victorious Red Army, and refers to it moreover completely casually. It is clear from the tone of his writing that the notion that conquered territory should be 'sovietized' was to his mind so self-evident a proposition that there was no need to digress from his main theme in order to propound it.[209] The same notion is to be found enshrined in his *Voprosy Sovremennoi Strategii*.[210]

In 1931, moreover, a book was written by V. K. Triandafillov, who at that time was Deputy Chief of the General Staff of the Red Army. His work is entitled *Kharakter Operatsii Sovremennykh Armii (The Nature of the Operations of Modern Armies)* and towards the end is to be found an important section dealing with political work in the field.

He states flatly that 'the sovietization of areas captured from the enemy is a very important task for our political organs';[211] and he goes on to remark that 'large-scale pursuit operations can, under favourable conditions, lead to the freeing of over 6,000 square kilometres of territory in a period of three or four weeks. This means that, in the space of two to three weeks, one must arrange for the sovietization of the whole of a smaller State, or the large part of a bigger one.'[212] He admits that the '*complete sovietization*' (my italics) of such an area is a long-term task; but he insists that the initial deployment of the Soviet political organs must take place quickly.[213]

*The number of such workers that will be needed for sovietization will be huge. From the frontier to the River Sana, Polish territory comprises 5 voevodstva and up to 90–100 uezdy; and in Western Byelorus it is much the same. So 500–1,000 men will be needed for forming the necessary political apparatus; and therefore sovietization will be impossible without making use of local workers and local revolutionary organizations. The consolidation of the Soviet system and the Soviet political apparatus wholly depends on the tempo at which revolutionary social (obshchest-vennye) organizations can be formed, such as trade unions, Committees of the Poor in villages, etc, etc. The final consolidation of the Soviet system in conquered territories will only take place as the result of the formation of their own powerful Communist Parties (p. 167).*[214]

If we now consider the events in Eastern Poland in 1939, Trianda-fillov's words acquire an especial significance. For, in that year, units of the Red Army invaded Poland from the east, at the same time as the troops of Nazi Germany were invading it from the west. The two armies met, and halted on a line which split pre-war Poland roughly in half. After this had been successfully accomplished, there began in the area held by the Russians that 'sovietization' of occupied territory which Triandafillov wrote about.

The details of this process in Eastern Poland between 1939 and 1941 have been sufficiently well documented in English sources to need no further elaboration here.[215] The only comment that I need to make is that complete sovietization, as Triandafillov testified, is a long-term process; and that the first stage consists of the liquidation of those persons in the occupied areas who might, by temperament, position or education, be minded to resist. The first stage, therefore, consists of wholesale arrests, aimed at the physical destruction of certain social categories.

Details of the exact categories of persons whom the Soviet Communist Party wanted to see eliminated are not so exactly documented in English in the case of Eastern Poland as they are in that of Lithuania, which a year later was itself invaded and sovietized. Here the categories are clearly listed in an order dated 28 November 1940, and bearing the number 0054, which was circulated by the Soviet Lithuanian People's Commissar for the Interior. The categories were:

1. Members of Russian pre-revolutionary parties—Mensheviks, followers of Trotsky and anarchists.

2. Members of contemporary Lithuanian political parties, including students belonging to student organizations.

3. Members of the state police, gendarmerie and prison staffs.

4. Officers of the former Tsarist Army and other anti-Bolshevik armies of 1918–21.

5. Officers and military judges of the contemporary Polish and Lithuanian Armies.

6. Volunteers of all armies other than Bolshevik.

7. Persons removed from the Communist Party.

8. Refugees, political emigrés and contraband runners.

9. Citizens of foreign states, representatives of foreign firms, etc.

10. Persons who have travelled abroad. Persons who are in contact with representatives of foreign states. Persons who are Esperantists or philatelists.

11. Officials of Lithuanian Ministries.

12. The staff of the Red Cross.

13. Persons active in parishes; clergymen, secretaries and active members of religious communities.

14. Aristocrats, landowners, wealthy merchants, bankers, industrialists, hotel and restaurant proprietors.

In Lithuania, the lists included about 700,000 persons out of a total population of 3,000,000. In Poland they were extended to include all of university standing, teachers, doctors, engineers, the forestry services, well-to-do peasants and very many very poor peasants, certain categories of workmen, the families of soldiers of all ranks who were thought to be with the Polish Army or interned abroad, refugees from the German-occupied parts of Poland, and 'speculators'—a term applied to small merchants and traders.

Both the registration and the deportations which followed it automatically included the families also of all persons enumerated above, again a perfectly normal proceeding under the Soviet code.[216]

Hitler's invasion of Russia put an end to further developments; and the 'final consolidation of Soviet power', which in Triandafillov's opinion could only take place with the aid of a powerful local communist party, had to wait until the end of the war, when a Polish Communist Party was assembled in Moscow, and from there despatched to Warsaw in the wake of the Russian armies. It was from these armies that it derived that 'power' that Triandafillov thought essential, if the Soviet system in a conquered territory were finally to be consolidated.

In 1940, Latvia, Lithuania and Estonia were accorded similar treatment. Specific details have already been given in respect of Lithuania; the tale in the other two countries was in all essentials the same.

Thus we see that, from the October Revolution down to Hitler's invasion of Russia, all territory that was occupied by the Red Army was subjected to sovietization.

Nor was Finland an exception, as might at first sight appear. We hear nothing about the 'sovietization' of those portions of Finnish territory which Russia acquired through the Winter War, for the simple reason that all except a tiny fraction of the Finnish people living in those areas abandoned their homes and fled to unoccupied Finland before the Russian administration moved in.[217] There was therefore nothing for the NKVD to 'sovietize', except their own barracks and their own troops; and that is why we do not hear about it.

The only exceptions to the rule about automatic 'sovietization' were in those areas which were subjected, not to a full-scale invasion, but to a brief and limited raid. Thus, in 1929 in China, Soviet forces crossed the frontier and occupied Chinese territory; but this operation was merely a large-scale raid designed to force the Chinese Government of the time to change its mind about the Chinese Eastern Railway. (See pp. 6–7 for details.) Soviet occupation of this area was therefore not so much temporary as momentary; and no programme of sovietization was introduced as a result.

When the Second World War was over, the countries of Eastern Europe were sovietized by the Russians, an occurrence which, according to Stalin, was only to be expected. As he said to Milovan Djilas: 'Whoever occupies a territory also imposes on it his own social system. Everyone imposes his own system as far as his army has power to do so. It cannot be otherwise.'[218]

Nevertheless, for all their apparent appositeness, Stalin's words present my argument with a very serious challenge. For in fact I have quoted Stalin out of context. The passage, as Djilas gives it to us, is prefaced by a comment of Djilas's own, and also by a preliminary sentence of Stalin's, which alter the picture considerably. The complete text runs:

*Stalin presented his views on the distinctive nature of the war that was being waged: 'This war is not as in the past; whoever occupies a territory also imposes on it his own social system. Everyone imposes his own system as far as his army has power to do so. It cannot be otherwise.'*

It will be seen that Stalin's remarks, in their full version, contradict flatly what I have been saying throughout the preceding paragraphs. For it has been my contention that, from the October Revolution onwards, sovietization of captured territory has been standard Russian practice; yet Djilas makes Stalin say that the Second World War was the first in which it had happened.

Of course it is true that, seen at first sight, Stalin's words are nonsense, and therefore present no challenge. For there have been many wars in the history of mankind where the victors have imposed their own social system on the enemy territory they occupied. Cyrus the Great imposed the Persian social system upon the empire of Croesus the Lydian; the

Ancient Romans thrust theirs upon the defeated Etruscans; and, somewhat nearer in time, the Arabs enforced their Islamic system on the countries of the North African littoral. To say, as Stalin said, that the Second World War was the first in which this had happened is plainly wrong.

It has to be remembered, however, that Stalin was a Marxist-Leninist; and, in the eyes of a Marxist-Leninist, there are no differences of importance between the social system of the Persian Empire of 547 B.C. and that of the Lydians: both were founded on slave labour; and both therefore shared the same 'mode of production', to use the Marxist phrase. Consequently, when Cyrus imposed 'his own social system' on the Lydians, the difference between it and the Lydian system was absolutely negligible, in the Marxist view. The same thing is true, *mutatis mutandis*, of the Ancient Romans and Etruscans, and of the Arabs and the inhabitants of North Africa. The same thing would also be true, with two important exceptions, of every war that has ever happened prior to the October Revolution.[219]

But the events of the October Revolution created an entirely new situation in world affairs. For the first time there was a communist state in existence, and one, moreover, endowed with all the normal apparatus of a State, including a standing army. For the first time in human history, therefore, it became possible for communism to fight a full-blown war against capitalism, and thus for war to produce a change of social system that was of real significance to a Marxist.

For, supposing that the communist state was at war with a 'bourgeois' state and happened to be victorious, it could then 'sovietize' the 'bourgeois' state; and such a change from capitalism to socialism would naturally be regarded as of great significance by every Marxist-Leninist. Contrariwise, if the 'bourgeois' were the victors, they would make use of their victory to destroy the soviet system, and force the defeated communists to accept a return of the 'bourgeois' order. This, too, would be a significant change, as the Marxists view significance.

If the above is correct, Stalin, as a Marxist-Leninist, was not talking nonsense: his words were approximately correct, apart from a few inaccuracies. For there were, of course, inaccuracies. Marxism-Leninism asserts roundly that Cromwell imposed on England 'his own social system'; and that the Cromwellian social system was revolutionary. It also asserts that the French Revolutionary armies destroyed feudalism, and imposed their own 'bourgeois' order in the territories they occupied as a result of war. These, then, were the two exceptions to which I referred when assessing Stalin's statement in my last paragraph but two; and if these are taken into account, it is *not* true to say what Stalin said.

Furthermore, there are other inaccuracies in his statement. We have already listed (p. 54) the occasions when the Red Army imposed on other countries its own social system, which meant for those countries a change from capitalism to communism. Yet Stalin's statement clearly takes no account of them. Why was this?

If we look back at the list of enforced sovietizations which have been discussed in the preceding paragraphs, only the affair with Poland in 1920 and the Winter War with Finland in 1939–40 are obvious, full-blooded *wars*. The conquest of Georgia in 1921 was over in less than ten days. From the point of view of the victor, so brief a military encounter may be described as a 'brush with the enemy'; it can hardly be termed a 'war'. In any case, Stalin, a Georgian himself, may even have succeeded in persuading himself, for obvious psychological reasons, that the Georgians actually *wanted* to be ruled by communists; and if he did, he would picture their resistance as counter-revolutionary contumacy by a handful of Menshevik heretics rather than as an actual war.

When the Red Army entered Eastern Poland in September 1939, unquestionably no war was waged between it and the Poles. The latter, poor fools, even believed that the Russian troops were on their way to fight against the Nazis, and welcomed them into their territory. They did not wage war against them, and Stalin knew it.

In 1940, the Baltic States were absorbed into the Soviet empire without any act of war. Individual acts of resistance, yes; but nothing which, in ordinary everyday language, would be classed as '*war*'. How could there be? The total population of the three countries was at that time only about 5,000,000. How was such a tiny handful to wage war against Soviet Russia?

If, therefore, we except the Russo-Polish War of 1920 and the Russo-Finnish War of 1939–40, Stalin's words are literally correct (except, of course, for the lapses about Cromwell and the French Revolutionary armies). But why should we except these two particular wars, which were, as it happened, the biggest wars that the Soviet Union had had to fight in the timespan that Stalin indicated? The answer, I think, is as follows: So far as concerns the war of 1920, it was one of those 'battles long ago' which Stalin had largely forgotten. He had good reason to forget it. It was a failure so far as the USSR was concerned: the war was a failure; the sovietization was a failure; and Stalin cannot be wholly exculpated from his share of the blame for both of them. He would hardly admit to 'imposing his own social system' with regard to this particular war, when the imposed system lasted no more than a month or two.

Reasons for excepting the Russo-Finnish War are even easier to come by; for sovietization of Finnish territory never actually took place. (I am using 'sovietization' here, as elsewhere in this section, as meaning 'the enforced conversion to communism of the conquered inhabitants'.)

Admittedly, the Soviet troops and civilians, entering Finland, brought with them their 'soviet' system of government and administration. But the areas they occupied had been almost totally abandoned by their native inhabitants. It was therefore upon deserted towns and villages that the 'soviet system' was 'forcibly' imposed by the Russians; and, in such circumstances, one might as well speak of the 'forcible introduction of the English system' by the troops of the British Eighth Army upon the lifeless stones and rocks of the Western Desert during the North African campaign.

We therefore reach the position where, *provided it be accepted that Stalin was speaking informally in the course of casual conversation*, his words can be taken as a correct statement of the thought that was in his mind.

And there is little doubt, I think, that Stalin *was* speaking informally. The remark was made, not at a conference in his office, but at a dinner party in Stalin's villa at ten o'clock at night. Toasts had been drunk; Stalin was in playful mood—he had been teasing Tito, and making fun of Djilas. Serious conversation had also been taking place; but it was clear that neither Stalin nor his audience was speaking with pedantic accuracy, weighing their every word.[220]

If this be granted, then Stalin's statement was correct enough; and we can pass on from analysing it to discussing its implications.

And its implications are central to our discussion. For if my analysis of Stalin's utterance be accepted as correct, it means that he viewed a war between a capitalist state and a communist state as one in which, automatically, the victor would destroy the vanquished's form of society, and replace it with one of his own. This notion, projected on to the screen of our present era, would mean that if a third world war were somehow to break out (and assuming, of course, that this war would be between the Soviet bloc and the Western bloc), the Russians, if victorious, would impose communism on the West; while if the latter won, it would impose capitalism on Russia.

In view of this, it is interesting to see that modern Soviet writing on the subject of a third world war forecasts exactly that.

Thus the latest edition of the *Great Soviet Encyclopaedia*, published in 1971, declares that 'wars between States with opposing social systems [e.g. wars between capitalism and communism] arise out of the aggressive efforts of the Imperialists to destroy the social achievements of the peoples of the socialist camp'.[221] While in 1968 Sokolovsky asserted bluntly that 'in a new world war, the imperialist bloc would strive for the utter defeat of the armed forces of the socialist States and the liquidation of their political system, establishing instead capitalist systems and the enslavement of these countries'.[222] Innumerable other quotations of this nature can easily be found.

E

But to say that the imperialists would destroy communism and impose capitalism if they were victorious in a third world war is not to say that, if the communists won, they would necessarily destroy capitalism and impose communism. Perhaps they would; but before we accept it as gospel, some sort of proof is needed.

Proof, as it happens, is not very hard to come by; though the chain of supporting evidence covers a good deal of ground. To begin with, it is a commonplace in Soviet writing on the subject of a war between capitalism and communism to say that this 'would be, in its *political* essence, the decisive clash between two opposing world-wide social systems' (italics mine).[223] Indeed, the whole of our present era (that is to say, peace time as well as wartime) is described as being one of '*conflict between two opposing social systems* . . . of the downfall of Capitalism . . . and of the *victory of Socialism and Communism on a world-wide scale*'. (Italics original.)[224] Clearly, the downfall of capitalism and the victory of socialism and communism on a world-wide scale are *political* events; and it can hardly be doubted, either, that they would be decisive, so far as the pattern of the future development of human society is concerned. The first of these quotations, both from Sokolovsky's opus, is therefore reinforced by the second.

Nor is this somewhat apocalyptic view confined to military publications of five or six years ago. The latest edition of the *Great Soviet Encyclopaedia* (1971) has the same message to preach. In the encyclopaedia's version 'a new world war . . . will be a struggle for *the very existence* of the two opposing world-wide systems, the socialist and the capitalist. *This war will decide the fate of all mankind*' (italics mine).[225] In 1973 Marshal Grechko repeated the statement that a new world war would decide the fate of humanity;[226] while in 1974 Rear-Admiral Shelyag spelled out the message in detail, and, quoting from the officially adopted *Programme of the Communist Party of the Soviet Union*, asserted bluntly that a third world war would mean the end of imperialism.[227] Since imperialism is, by the Soviet Union's own definition, the highest form of capitalism, it means that the result of another world war would be to abolish capitalism as we know it. Such a result, one is bound to admit, would be every bit as 'decisive' for Western society as Soviet commentators are fond of claiming for it.

Indeed, so often have the words 'decisive', 'decide' and 'decision' been used by the Russians in connection with a third world war that they have become with them almost stock expressions. Such a war, they assert, would be a war of *decision*: it would *decide* the basic conflict of the modern world, the conflict between socialism and capitalism.[228]

This view of a war between East and West as being decisive is not generally to be found in 'bourgeois' writing. The latter depicts it as being catastrophically *destructive*; but the question of its decisiveness is not as a rule considered (still less, the question of its decisiveness in respect of *what?*).

Indeed, Western writing on the subject of war is still very similar to what it was when it was ridiculed by Lenin. The 'bourgeois', he said, conceive of war as being a simple attack that disturbs the peace, followed by a peace which ends the war: 'They had a fight! Then they made friends again!'[229]

But if indeed, having had their fight, socialism and imperialism made friends again, how could that 'basic conflict' between the two rival ideologies have been *decided*? Obviously, under such circumstances the basic conflict would continue to rumble away unchecked beneath the peace-making, and nothing whatever of importance would have been decided at all. Yet Soviet writing continually insists that something of fundamental importance *will* be decided in a war between East and West; and the only thing of real importance that *could* be decided by such a conflict is whether the Western way of life or the Marxist-Leninist way of life is going to predominate on this planet. It must be borne in mind that the war in question is being definitely postulated as one in which strategic nuclear missiles are employed; for if it were not, it would not be being fought with 'decisive' means, and hence would not be aimed at attaining 'decisive' objectives (see pp. 89–96).

This being clearly understood, let us now look at the question in another way. It is a basic Soviet premise that all wars are bound to be waged for definite political objectives. Given that this is so, what political objectives can conceivably be pursued by means of world-wide nuclear war except the total destruction of one or the other social systems? Can it seriously be contended that, with Moscow, Washington, London, Paris, Bonn, Berlin, Leningrad, Kiev, New York, New Orleans, Kharkov, Birmingham and scores upon scores of other cities reduced to radioactive ruins, with all ports and aerodromes destroyed, all factories blasted, the victors at the end of such a holocaust would set their sights no higher than to demand of their beaten enemy some small cession of territory, such as Staten Island, Novaya Zemlya or the Cherbourg Peninsula? Making the big assumption that at the end of a third world war there would be any victors or vanquished left on this planet, and that the world's population would not have ceased to exist, how can it be supposed that such a terrifying mountain of a conflict should engender such a mouse-like solution?

The Russians, for one, make no such supposition. A third world war would mean, in their opinion, the total destruction of the capitalist system.[230] It would 'inevitably end with the victory of the progressive communist socio-economic system over the reactionary capitalist socio-economic system, which is historically doomed to destruction'.[231] It would 'lead to the death of capitalism as a social system'.[232] Nor is this an eccentric point of view. Wars do tend to have this kind of apocalyptic effect. The Second World War, it will be remembered, put an end to the then existing social system in Nazi Germany.

Should, therefore, a third world war break out, the horrifying physical destruction of cities, towns and villages and the laying waste of the whole economic complex of an advanced industrial nation is seen by the Russians as a principal means whereby the doom of capitalism can be accomplished:[233]

*The reserves of nuclear weapons . . . accumulated in peacetime may be used to full measure by the belligerent parties from the very first minutes of the war to destroy and devastate enemy objectives over the entire depth of his territory, in order rapidly to achieve the main political and strategic goals at the very outset of the war.* (Roman mine.)

Another Soviet author puts it thus: 'Nuclear weapons, especially strategic rockets, are the decisive means for attaining the main strategic aims of the armed struggle, and hence the *political* aims of the war.' (Italics mine.)[234]

Nuclear weapons are incapable of anything except destruction. From which it follows that, in the Soviet view, the mass destruction of a country's economy serves to achieve not only the strategic aim (i.e. winning the war) but also a *political* aim. But what political aim can be accomplished by destroying *in toto* another country's economy? Unless we are talking about trifling political objectives such as the acquisition of Staten Island or the Cherbourg Peninsula, the only political aim that the Russians could possibly have, would be the destruction of the Western socio-political system.

Elsewhere in Sokolovsky's *Military Strategy* we find the following passage: 'As a result of the rapid development of industry, science and technology, the means of conducting war have become so powerful that the chances of attaining *the most decisive political goals by war* have enormously increased.' (Italics mine.)[235]

Seemingly, therefore, in times gone by, 'the most decisive political goals' were unlikely to be obtained by war; and strikes, propaganda, subversion and revolutionary uprisings had to be used instead. Conventional war was a sufficient instrument for destroying capitalism in a single country (such as, for instance, Poland), but not for destroying it over the whole of our planet.

There is probably a great deal of truth in this statement; for, even if the Russians in times gone by had fought a conventional war against the Americans and their Western European allies, and somehow succeeded in beating them, the task of 'sovietizing' so huge an area, with a politically conscious population still more or less intact, would have been more than even the Soviet Union could reasonably have hoped to accomplish. If, however, America and her allies could be smitten into nuclear dust, the few defenceless, cowed survivors could easily be 'sovietized'.

But even supposing the 'sovietization' of the Western world would be a prime aim of Soviet policy in the event of a third world war, how actually would the Russians try to accomplish it? The destruction of Western cities, of Western communications and transport systems and of the bulk of Western industry may create the conditions in which 'sovietization' could be accomplished, but it would not of itself suffice to achieve it.

Fortunately, Russian sources provide us with the answer: the first stage of 'sovietization' will be accomplished by means of the ground forces, who will seize and occupy the conquered enemy territory. This, it will be remembered, was the initial means on which Triandafillov relied in his memorable essay (see pp. 115–16). Sokolovsky's work contains a number of passages in which it is stated that, for *final* victory, it is not sufficient to destroy the enemy's military potential, his cities and factories; it is also necessary to *occupy his territory*.[236] This task, says Sokolovsky, must be entrusted to the ground forces, who thereby play 'a very important part in achieving the fundamental objectives of the war'.[237] It is for this reason, he says, that 'the ground troops become the largest branch of the armed forces';[238] for, without a wholesale occupation of the territory of the beaten enemy, no final victory is possible. And in order to occupy the whole of North America and Western Europe, large numbers of men will be necessary.

I am well aware that I may appear to my readers to have relied too much in my documentation on Sokolovsky's *Military Strategy*. And indeed I very well may have done. Nevertheless, there was one good reason for quoting from *Military Strategy* whenever I could. This is that Sokolovsky's work is the only *Soviet* view of our subject that is readily available in English. It therefore seemed to me better to quote from Sokolovsky (perhaps somewhat monotonously) than branch out into other Soviet publications which are available only in Russian. I will add, however, that, had I done so, I would have found no difficulty in finding passages which would have exactly paralleled the Sokolovsky passages. To take a very recent example, Lt-Gen. Zavyalov, writing in *Red Star*, has no hesitation in asserting flatly that a war between the imperialists and the socialist states would 'inevitably become a world war and, in terms of its political content . . . a struggle with the most decisive objectives'. He then goes on to declare without any qualification that such a war would be thermonuclear.[239]

For, all Soviet authors, writing on the theme of war, state and re-state the basic proposition, derived from classical Marxism, that the ending of the enemy's will and ability to resist does not denote final victory. Each war, according to Marx, contains the seeds of another war; and no victory can be final until this other war has been fought. The Treaty of Versailles was believed by many Englishmen to mark the final victory over Germany: Hitler believed otherwise.

If, therefore, one side in a war were compelled to sue for an armistice, and hostilities came to an end, would not that side employ the subsequent peace to rebuild its armies, improve its arms and munitions, and then, when an opportunity presented itself, launch a war of revenge? It was Marx's and Engels' view that it probably would. It is the view of the Soviet leaders today that it will never be given the chance.

For, first of all, in modern nuclear warfare it is extremely likely that there would be nothing on which to rebuild. Homes, factories, arsenals, ports, railways, cities, concatenations of cities, and the millions of their inhabitants, will have vanished in nuclear dust. Indeed, it is the declared intention of Soviet military doctrine to see that this is so, so far as its enemies are concerned. A dozen mushroom clouds above the territory of its opponent, and a sterile desert beneath.

Second, if the Soviet Union were to win a nuclear war, it would take energetic steps to prevent the resurgence of its enemy by imposing on what was left of the population some form or other of communism (in the Western sense of communism, i.e. the kind of system under which the citizens of the USSR exist at present). In the words of *Military Strategy*, there would have to be established 'an appropriate order', by which it means the establishment of an appropriate political system.[240] That system, which we in the West inaccurately term 'communism', is admirably designed to prevent the populations subjected to it from indulging in activities uncongenial to those in power. Since those in power would be the nominees of the Soviet Communist Party, the preparation of a war of revenge against it would be quite impossible.

This, then, would be victory. The price that would have to be paid would make it pyrrhic, so long as the West retains a nuclear deterrent; but, once it had been achieved, it would last for ever: the KGB would see to that. In this sense, therefore, the KGB must be reckoned as one of the factors making for victory, as the Russians see things; for it is they who would make impossible that war of revenge which alone could turn victory sour. The beaten Americans would be mad to fix their hopes upon some future 'Day of Reckoning', as the French after 1871 fixed their hopes upon '*le jour*'. The 'appropriate order' would be established in the United States; and the war would be over for good.[241]

## The Soviet view of violence, and hence of the use for war

What I have written so far may have tended to give the impression that the Soviet Union will employ war whenever the factors making for victory are weighted heavily in her favour. This is very far from being true; and it is as important not to err in this direction as it is not to err in the opposite direction, and assume that the Soviet Union will never resort to war under any circumstances.

For if the USSR were indeed ready to wage war whenever she thought she could win, she would by now have attacked Afghanistan, Finland (for the second time) and other countries bordering her territories such as Iran, Iraq, and even China. In each case, there have been moments during the course of the past fifty years when an attempt at military conquest on the part of the Soviet Union would have been bound to have been successful, and when it was beyond the power of the capitalist countries to have done anything to prevent it. Nevertheless, no serious attempt in these directions has ever been made by the Soviet Government in all the years of its existence.

It is therefore clear that there are influences at work which serve to restrain the USSR from an uninhibited use of force. One of these is that, for the first twenty-three years of its history, it has been weaker than the capitalist nations; while from 1945 onwards, it has been subject to the nuclear deterrent. Another restraining influence is the Soviet concept of violence and of the uses to which violence can be put. But before going on to examine this concept, it must be pointed out that the Russian language has only the one word *nasiliye* to do duty for the two similar, though not identical, English words 'violence' and 'force'.[242] Since it is the *Soviet* concept of violence which we are now about to examine, and since Soviet concepts are indigenously expressed in Russian and not in English, it is obvious that what we are really about to examine is the Soviet concept of *nasiliye*. It is true that I have chosen to render this term into English by the word 'violence'; but if any reader prefers to substitute 'force', he is obviously entitled to do so.

From the Marxist point of view, the classic formulation of the effects of violence on the course of human development is to be found in the *Anti-Dühring* of Engels, which, it must be remembered, was written expressly for the purpose of refuting Herr Eugen Dühring's theories, including the theory that the main determinant of the course of history is force.

Surprising as it may seem in the light of what we have been saying throughout this chapter so far, such a theory ran completely counter to Marx's basic tenet; for he believed that the course of history was principally determined by economic development. Moreover, in 1878 (the year in which *Anti-Dühring* was written), Dühring's theory was acquiring a degree of popularity which was most unwelcome to Marx and Engels and their followers. Consequently, it had to be refuted.

The line of argument by which Engels hoped to have refuted him is well expressed in this summary of it, to be found in an official handbook published by the Soviet Ministry of Defence:[243]

*The course of history is determined in the last analysis by economic development and not by violence, and the main motive force of history is the broad masses of the people, and not armies. This, however, is not to belittle the enormous progressive significance of violence (including violence applied by military methods), if this violence facilitates the destruction of outdated economic institutions, and if it smashes dead, fossilised, political forms.*

The last part of that argument was summed up more pithily by Marx, when he wrote: 'Force is the midwife of every old society when it is pregnant with the new. Violence is itself an economic power.'[244]

But if the *real* determinant of the course of history is economic development, and if violence merely facilitates this development by helping to destroy outdated political and economic forms, it follows that violence can only usefully be applied, when its intended effects conform with the tide of history. As King Canute knew, but as his courtiers did not, no human being can turn back the tide; and if violence is employed in an attempt to do so, the result will be self-defeating.

A thorough appreciation of the above is so essential for a correct understanding of the Marxist view of violence (and hence of war) that, at the risk of wearying the reader, it is worth repeating in a slightly different form. For the example above was a reference to reactionaries, not to revolutionaries: Canute's courtiers urged him to *turn back* the tide, not to assist its flow. Yet the task of a Marxist revolutionary (as the revolutionary himself understands it) is to help the tide of history to flow *onward*.

On the other hand, he can only facilitate this flow by taking the proper action at the proper moment: the wrong action, if taken even at the right moment, will serve merely to obstruct it, as will also the right action taken at the wrong moment. This statement applies to *all* kinds of action, including the two particular kinds of action which we call 'violence' and 'war'. Therefore, to revert to Marx's metaphor of the midwife, a Caesarian operation (a particular form of violence) is possible only at a certain stage of the pregnancy: an attempt to remove the foetus from the womb within three or four months of that foetus' initial conception would merely fail to produce the desired result (the birth of a healthy infant).

This is why Marx and Engels insisted that, though they had no objection to violence, they advocated its employment only in those circumstances where they thought a judicious use of it would be successful, in the sense of successfully delivering a healthy revolutionary child. Under such circumstances, however, they not merely permitted violence, but they were eager for it to be used; and this is true, whether we are talking about violence committed upon one man, or 'organized violence' committed upon nations, which in normal parlance is 'war'.

The same attitude lies at the back of Lenin's writings on the subject. For instance, concerning the attempted assassination of the Austrian Prime Minister, Count Stürg, during the First World War, he explained to Franz Koritschoner in his letter of 25 October 1916, that 'We [communists] *do not at all oppose* political killing' (italics original); but he went on to say that it should only be used provided that this was part of a concerted plan for an uprising, or some other revolutionary undertaking, that would bring nearer the victory of communism. Since, however, the attempt in question was a single, isolated, uncoordinated act, Lenin condemned it. 'It is,' he wrote later in the same letter, 'only a mass movement that can be considered to be a real political struggle. Individual terroristic acts can be, and must be, helpful only when they are directly linked with the mass movement.'

Lenin himself certainly had no objection to putting into practice his theories concerning the murder of individuals; while, since his death, subsequent Soviet leaders have followed his example. In Stalin's time, we may instance the many thousands that were shot in the course of the purges and during the 'pacification' of the Ukraine. More recently, there were the murders of Stefan Bandera and of Dr Lev Rebet in Munich, who were killed by agents of the KGB sent specially from Russia for the purpose.[245] Whether these innumerable killings were 'directly linked with the mass movement' can only be a matter of opinion; but no doubt those who ordered them were sincerely convinced that they were.

Like Marx and Engels, Lenin applied to war the same notion of the uses of violence which he applied to the murder of individuals. Indeed, it is only logical that, if Engels was right when he said that war was merely 'organized violence', the same considerations that apply to violence must necessarily apply to war.

Lenin put this concept into the following words:

*Socialism is against violence being used on nations. That is indisputable. But socialism is in general against violence being used on people. However, no one except a Christian anarchist or a Tolstoyan has ever deduced from this that socialism is against revolutionary violence. This means that, to talk about 'violence' in general, without examining the conditions which distinguish reactionary from revolutionary violence is to be a philistine who has renounced the revolution, or else it means deceiving oneself and others by sophistry.*

*The same holds true of violence being used on nations. Every war is*

E*

*violence used on nations, but that does not prevent socialists from being* in favour *of a revolutionary war* (roman is original italics).[246]

We have already examined the Soviet concept of 'revolutionary war', and seen what a range of meanings is encompassed by it. Here we are concerned only to note that the Soviet leaders will seek deliberately to engage in any of its forms, only if they think that they are likely to be victorious, and only if it accords with the Marxist precepts on violence which I have sketched in outline above.

But who can tell what act will help the tide of history to roll forward, and what murder will be 'directly linked with the mass movement'? Clearly, this must be a matter of opinion. In Lenin's day, the opinion that decided the issue was the opinion of the Central Committee, with Lenin's as the leading voice; in Stalin's day, it was largely Stalin's opinion; but since his death, opinion has become more collective, so that probably most of the Politburo have a hand in its formation nowadays, with some *éminences grises* in the Kremlin closets giving *sotto voce* assistance.

It is clearly less easy to identify the nature of the opinion of a group of people than that of a single individual. However, with regard to the Politburo one thing at least is certain. The broadening of the base of decision-making in the USSR today has led to increased attention being paid to those whose ideology is strongly coloured with the tints of Russian nationalism. These people tend to regard the 'proletarian' revolution as being coterminous with the USSR, and to see the interests of the former as being identical with Soviet interests. 'What's good for the USSR is good for communism', is the way that many of them look at it; and it was the way, incidentally, that Stalin thought, and that so often prompted his actions.

Therefore, in the eyes of those who share this opinion, the tide of history rolls onward when it is furthering the aims and ambitions of the Soviet Union, whatever they may be. Consequently, they will be eager to employ violence, and ready to go to war, only *pro bono sovietico*, and will be reluctant to fight to convert the heathen in distant 'bourgeois' lands. On the other hand, they will fight with the greatest enthusiasm in defence of their own country.

This is the first time in all this long disquisition on war that this section of opinion has so far been mentioned. Previously, we have examined what Marx thought, or what Engels thought, or what Lenin thought; and we have taken their views as the basis for our discussion. But these three men, whatever they were, were not nationalists. Lenin, for instance, was concerned to defend Russia simply because, by defending her, he was 'defending the Revolution', in the literal meaning of that expression. In other words, if the enemies of Soviet Russia had succeeded in totally subduing her, Bolshevism would have been snuffed out.

But if men of the type to which I am now referring, men with a good deal of Russian nationalism in their make-up as well as communist fervour, if such men today are solidly represented in the higher echelons of the Party, is it not grossly negligent on my part to have made no mention of their existence in the earlier sections of this chapter?

It is my belief that the answer to this question is no. We have been concerned earlier in this chapter with examining the Soviet view of the origin of war: modern Soviet nationalism has nothing to say on this question that is out of line with accepted Marxist doctrine. We have also explored the Soviet attitude towards the inevitability of war, the revolutionary effect of war, the evils of war, the categories of war, the factors making for victory in war, and the question of aggression and self-defence. On these points, too, modern 'Soviet nationalism' agrees with Leninist doctrine.

Consequently, it is only when we get to the subject of this present section that the attitudes of 'Soviet nationalism' differ significantly from those of Marxism. And there is no doubt whatever that on the question of the use of force (or of resorting to war) it can differ significantly enough. It therefore logically follows, in my opinion, that it is only when a proposal to employ force is acceptable both to the tenets of 'Soviet nationalism' and to those of 'Marxist zealotry' that it is likely to be put into effect, especially nowadays.

Moreover, such a conclusion is conformable to daily experience. Serious undertakings are not usually embarked upon at the prompting of one motive alone. This is so, even in the case of an individual; and it is still more so in the case of whole communities. For a nation to be spurred to a deed of high resolve, such as the deliberate embarking upon a war, success must bring great moral satisfaction, coupled with material gain. As George Bernard Shaw made Napoleon say in *The Man of Destiny*: 'When [a man] wants a thing, he never tells himself that he wants it. He waits patiently until there comes into his mind, no one knows how, a burning conviction that it is his moral and religious duty to conquer those who possess the thing he wants. Then he becomes irresistible.' Shaw had in mind Victorian Englishmen engaged in building an Empire; but his words apply to Soviet citizens 'strengthening the camp of Socialism'. It is a fair bet that violence will *not* be seen by the members of the Politburo to help the tide of history to flow onward, unless it brings gain to the 'Soviet nationalists' as well as joy to the 'Marxist zealots'.

The facts of Soviet history seem abundantly to confirm this hypothesis, except perhaps during the years immediately following the October Revolution. But after about 1920, 'Soviet nationalism' had to be gratified as well as 'Marxist zealotry' before war could be begun.

Georgia is a case in point. When the Red Army was sent into Georgia to conquer it, and to make it part of the new Soviet Russia, this was gratifying to the 'Marxist zealots': a few more million people had now been converted to communism. But it was also gratifying to the 'Soviet nationalists'; because that which had been part of the old Russia, but had broken away (obviously under evil influence), had now been reunited with the mother country. Furthermore, as a result of the operation the Batumi oil refineries had been recovered and were now securely in the possession of Soviet Russia, and safe communications were now assured with Soviet Armenia. This too was gratifying to 'Soviet nationalism'.

The Russo-Finnish War of 1939-40 brought notable gains to the 'Soviet nationalists', and a few to the 'Marxist zealots'. The point of the war was to conquer territory which was considered vital for the proper defence of Leningrad; it was not a crusade to conquer souls for communism. The acquisition of this territory was probably not displeasing to the 'Marxist zealots' either; but the point is that, unless the 'Soviet nationalists' had seen a great deal of old-fashioned nationalistic benefit to be had by invading Finland, it is most unlikely that the invasion would ever have been ordered.

The events in Eastern Europe after the end of the Second World War are further confirmation of this thesis. The gains to 'Marxist zealotry' were very considerable: scores of millions of human souls and thousands of square miles of territory had been brought within the orbit of communism; and the world-wide victory of the latter had been considerably advanced. At the same time, the acquisition of these territories had also brought immensely important gains for the 'Soviet nationalists'. This was because the countries of Eastern Europe formed a buffer zone of great defensive significance for the USSR. They also represented economic gains, because the skills of their peoples and the output of those peoples' factories were set to work for the benefit of the USSR. There is plenty of Western literature describing in detail the way in which, immediately after the war, the Soviet Union exploited Eastern Europe with a degree of exploitation that would have been thought excessive even in Dickensian England.[247]

When the Cuban crisis burst upon the world in 1962, there was risk of war between Russia and America. The gains for 'Soviet nationalism' to be expected from such a war were very scanty, if indeed there were any at all. Cuba, as seen from a 'Soviet nationalist' viewpoint, was a 'small, far-away country of which we know nothing'; and its ruler, Castro, was dangerously independent-minded. Moreover, the Cuban economy produced nothing that was of vital importance to the Russian economy; and, being so far away from the USSR, the Cuban leadership could not be easily controlled. Why, then, go to war for such miserable prospects of advantage? And if to this argument is added the force of the military arguments (that the Soviet Union had no chance of winning a conventional war in that part of the world, and that a nuclear war with the United States would be as disastrous for Russia as for America), there is no wonder that the USSR backed down.

Of course, the USSR should not have got itself into a position where it was going to have to back down; but this was due to Khrushchev's lack of foresight (or, as the Russians say, his 'voluntarism'); and, as we all know, he was subsequently dismissed for it.

We may therefore conclude from the above examples, and from others which can be adduced, that the USSR will only resort to force when it can see gain for the 'Soviet nationalists' as well as joy for the 'Marxist zealots'. Of course, that does not answer the question of what the 'Russian nationalists' would regard as being gain. A significant improvement in the safety of the Soviet Union is clearly one form of gain that they would recognize; so, too, is an acquisition of territory that is economically profitable and easily controllable (and hence preferably adjacent to the USSR). Beyond that (though less powerful as a motive), one may say that anything that would bring honour and glory to socialism may well be regarded as gainful by the 'Soviet nationalists'; but this is subject to the important proviso that it is the Soviet form of socialism that is thus exalted, and not some heretical version such as that of Mao Tse-tung.

The same forces also work in the reverse direction. That is to say that 'Soviet nationalists', and to a large extent 'Marxist zealots', are as much concerned to preserve their existing gains as to seek to acquire new ones. This means that they will refrain from starting a war, however immediately profitable it may seem to them, if they fear that the result of doing so may be to endanger the USSR.

For instance, it can hardly be doubted that the Bolshevik leaders were always keen to see Latvia, Lithuania and Estonia incorporated into the Soviet Union; nor that such an acquisition would have been acceptable to 'Soviet nationalism' as well as to 'Marxist zealotry'. Between 1917 and 1919, attempts were made to set up communist governments in all three of the countries in question; but the attempts were suppressed by the local non-communist inhabitants, with help from the British Navy.[248]

Between then and 1940 (the year in which they were forcibly incorporated into the USSR and 'sovietized'), the Red Army was capable at almost any time of invading them and conquering them and occupying them, thus realizing Bolshevik ambitions; but it received no orders to do so. This was due mainly to the Russians' fear that such an operation would bring a renewed intervention by the capitalist countries, which might put Soviet communism at risk. It must never be forgotten that, from 1917 until 1939 or after, the USSR was militarily weak by comparison with the capitalist countries; and, what is more, she knew it. Lenin, for instance, confessed this weakness on quite a large number of occasions, while Stalin's avowal was made in dramatic terms which have since been frequently quoted.[249]

Furthermore, Latvia, Lithuania and Estonia lie along the Baltic coast, and thus could easily have received support from units of the British Navy, that bugbear of the old-time Bolsheviks. The Kremlin, therefore, would not risk an operation which might endanger Soviet security. But once the capitalists in Europe had become embroiled in the Second World War, there was little risk involved in annexing these three countries, and great profit to be had by doing so, on account of their strategic significance. This time, therefore, the Red Army received its orders; and Latvia, Lithuania and Estonia became Soviet territory.

In the modern world, the threat of nuclear retaliation plays the same part as did the fear of capitalist invasion in the years immediately following the Revolution. The destruction of the major cities of the Soviet Union would not be regarded with pleasure by the 'Soviet nationalists', nor indeed by the 'Marxist zealots', even if the USSR were to be the victor in the war that caused it. They would therefore try to avoid participation in any conflict that was nuclear or that threatened to escalate into nuclear; but, on the other hand, they would fight like fiends if ever the Western countries were to be so foolish as to invade them; and in that case they would accept the destruction of their cities as the necessary price to be paid for keeping the Soviet homeland inviolate.

There is, moreover, yet another reason, also deriving from the theories of Marxism-Leninism, which further serves to act as a restraining influence on the USSR. This is that, as the Soviet communists see things, history is on their side. Therefore, if only they leave well alone and give history sufficient time to effect its purposes, the world-wide triumph of communism is certain to come about. This, indeed, is the essence of the doctrine of 'peaceful coexistence'.

It is true that the triumph of communism will come about more slowly if left to its own devices than if speeded up by war, but it will come about nevertheless; and if war under certain circumstances may indeed do much to hasten it, under other circumstances (e.g. a nuclear exchange) it may actually retard it. A war between East and West might very well be nuclear; so war is not an appropriate instrument for hastening the triumph of communism in the West *under present circumstances*, as the Soviet leaders view things.

Better, therefore, be patient; and wait for that arch-enemy, capitalism, to sicken and die of its own endemic diseases. It would be nice to see, in one's own lifetime, the wicked punished and the virtuous rewarded; but virtue will be triumphant in the end. So, according to this argument, Time and the laws of history must be left to do the best they can, while one gives them such help as is possible without hazarding one's present gains.

The attitude that underlies this argument was nicely summed up by W. S. Gilbert in the opening chorus of *The Mountebanks*.

> We are members of a Secret Society,
> Working by the moon's uncertain disc;
> Our motto is: 'Revenge without Anxiety',
> That is, without unnecessary risk.

It is not a heroic attitude, but a nuclear world can do without heroics; and we must be grateful indeed that, on the whole, the Russians have decided to dispense with them.

Meanwhile, they think that the forces of capitalism are being weakened by the imperialists' own propensity to resort to war, which their Marxism-Leninism tells them is imperialism's besetting weakness. The revolutionizing effects of war can be observed at the present time, so the Russians believe, in the United States of America as a result of the latter's involvement in Vietnam. And who is to say that the Russian belief is wrong? Indeed, is it not even possible that these revolutionizing effects of war, coupled with high unemployment and negro dissidence, may produce an actual 'proletarian' revolution in the USA? It must look like that from the Kremlin.

In any case, if the Americans' will to fight was effectively undermined so far as the operations in Vietnam were concerned, is it not quite likely that it will also be undermined (and equally effectively) so far as concerns any possible operations in Europe? In other words, if American public opinion becomes disenchanted with the use of force as an instrument of policy, as it became with regard to Vietnam, will it not come to prefer the surrender of Western Europe to resisting by force any Soviet attempts to seize it? And, *in those changed circumstances*, may not the seizure of Western Europe come to seem to the leaders of the Soviet Communist Party a speedy, a certain, and hence a desirable, means of hastening the processes of history?

But, as has been shown above, until those circumstances have in fact changed, and have been seen to have changed beyond any possibility of doubt, history will have to proceed at its natural pace; for the Russians will not risk the hastening of them.

### The changes wrought in the theory by nuclear weapons

From the point of view from which we are here considering the Soviet attitude to war, the advent of nuclear weapons has made surprisingly little difference. Modern Soviet writers do indeed have plenty to say about the revolutionary changes caused by the invention of these weapons; but most of the changes they mention refer to strategy and tactics, with which we are not really concerned.

So far as concerns the subject of this chapter, the main effect of the advent of nuclear weapons has been to reinforce Soviet caution. Whether or not the USSR would win a nuclear war, there can be no doubt that she would suffer terribly as a result of having to fight one, *so long as the West retains a second-strike capacity*. Moreover, the degree of destruction which the USSR would experience is too great to be acceptable to any Russian, whether a 'Marxist zealot' or 'Soviet nationalist' or any other.

Consequently, one can be quite certain that it will be the policy of the Soviet leaders *not* to engage in nuclear war, if they can possibly avoid it; nor to engage in a war of conventional weapons that is likely to escalate further.

To this policy there will probably be two exceptions. The first is that, if the USSR or one of the 'satellites' were attacked, she would resist the attack to the utmost of her ability. This means that she would resort to nuclear weapons almost as a matter of course on present showing;[250] though it is just possible that, if only she could be persuaded to give further attention to the merits of the doctrine of 'flexible response', she might be prepared to oppose a conventional attack with purely conventional weapons, especially in view of her own overwhelming superiority in the size of her conventional armies. It would depend a good deal on who was the attacker (i.e. whether it was, for example, the Chinese or the forces of NATO), or for what purpose the Russians believed the attack was being launched. The graver the threat to Russia, the more likely that the rockets would fly. In any case, there can be no doubt that, if the enemy country resorted to nuclear rockets, the Soviet Union would unhesitatingly reply in kind.

The second exception is that, if the West's second-strike capacity could somehow or other be neutralized, the Soviet leaders might contemplate preventative war or pre-emptive strikes (to say nothing of nuclear blackmail), in order to further their long-term aims in connection with their 'imperialist' enemies. However, so long as the West's second-strike capacity continues to be effective, it is safe to say that only an attempt to invade the USSR or one of the 'satellite' countries would induce the Soviet leaders intentionally to discharge their missiles. Of course, that does not dispose of the possibility that Soviet nuclear rockets might be fired by some kind of accident; or that the Soviet leaders might press the nuclear button because they believed (wrongly) that the West was about to attack them.

The other effect of the nuclear age upon the Soviet attitude to war is that they now believe that nuclear weapons allow a war to be won extremely quickly, before the long-term factors that make for victory have been given a chance to operate.[251] From the point of view of the Kremlin, this is extremely important; because traditional Marxism-Leninism has always postulated that victory and defeat are ultimately decided by the strength of the combatants' economies. Since at no time has any responsible Russian argued that the economy of the Soviet bloc is anything other than weaker than that of the 'imperialists', it follows that, according to traditional Leninism, if a war breaks out between the USSR and the countries of the Western Alliance, it is the USSR that will lose. And since all the present leaders of the Soviet Union, both political and military, have been most carefully tutored in the tenets of traditional Leninism, this is a most uncomfortable deduction, so far as they are concerned.

It is therefore only natural that they should have fallen with whoops of joy upon this new doctrine, which teaches that the long-term factors can be bypassed. As a result, Soviet military thinking has concentrated upon developing the blitzkrieg, though it naturally makes no use of that distasteful term. But, whatever the term it uses, the fact is indisputable that present-day training in the Soviet armed forces is directed almost exclusively towards the inculcation of speed and of surprise, and of what may be termed 'the infliction of instantaneous destruction' upon the enemy and upon all that is his.[252] Rivers must be crossed without stopping; tanks must advance unceasingly; surprise landings by helicopter in the rear of the enemy must be practised; tactical nuclear weapons must be used to smash down enemy resistance as soon as possible; while the whole range and strength of the strategic nuclear arm must be directed to ensuring that the enemy's factories, his supply dumps, his transport, his harbours, his cities and all that makes possible a prolonged war shall be smitten into nuclear dust.

Those who wish to study further the Soviet development of this thesis are advised to read the articles in *Pravda* and *Red Star* devoted to the recent large-scale manoeuvres called 'Dnieper' and 'Dvina'. These, combined with Savkin's work, will give them a good idea of the new theory.[253] Speed is clearly its essence; and interesting points like the provision of mobile pipelines for the supply of petrol to Soviet armoured formations (thus allowing the speed and weight of the attack to be maintained) are further evidence of the extent to which the Soviet authorities are seized of the new theory, and of the extent to which they wish to see it implemented. It would also be wise to recognize that, in the furtherance of this objective, the USSR may well resort to the use of chemical warfare.

It should be pointed out, in passing, that a desire to bypass the long-term factors making for a Western victory is not the only reason why the Soviet forces in Europe are so obsessed with this notion of blitzkrieg. Another must be the vulnerability of their lines of communication in the event of a prolonged war; for they can hardly imagine that they are popular in Poland or in Hungary, Czechoslovakia or Romania. Should they become engaged in a war with the West, their communications would be obviously at risk; and they would be likely to find themselves in serious trouble, if the West should inflict a major defeat on them.

As I have said, they cannot be ignorant of this; and it therefore becomes another factor to urge upon them the adoption of blitzkrieg tactics.

It will be further noted that the above tactics are based upon the seizure of the offensive from the very first moment of the war, and of the maintenance of that offensive till the war is over. It will also be remembered that the seizure and maintenance of the offensive have traditionally been basic doctrine in the Soviet armed forces since the very first days of its inception. Indeed, so far as the communists are concerned, they can trace its parentage to Engels; though 'bourgeois' writers on military affairs may prefer to father it on Gideon.[254]

Since there has always been a remarkable continuity in Soviet strategic, and even tactical, thinking, the fact that the implications of nuclear weapons evoked a return to the old doctrine, after the strategic innovations of Khrushchev, ensured an immediate welcome for the new theory among Soviet military leaders. Indeed, they have seized upon it with enthusiasm, and worked out its practical consequences; and the results are to be seen in those large-scale exercises to which I have already referred above.

I repeat that the purpose of this chapter is to examine the Soviet attitude to war as a social and a political phenomenon; it is not to examine Soviet strategy and tactics. Nevertheless, I foresee a difficulty in gaining any widespread acceptance among Western officers for some of the theories postulated; because those who work at the 'sharp end' are well aware that Soviet military tactics are *offensive* in their conception; and they therefore believe that the policy behind it must necessarily be offensive too.

In my view, this is mistaken. The tactics are offensive because, as we have seen, they offer to the Marxist military mind the sole hope of victory in a war with the West. Tactics based on the defensive would, the Russians believe, be certain to lose such a war.

But this does not mean that the Politburo, the body which takes the decisions on war and peace, is necessarily thinking offensively: in my own view, this is not so. At the present stage in history, the policies propounded by the Kremlin are, I believe, defensive rather than offensive; but, in case those policies fail, the Soviet generals and admirals have worked out strategies and tactics to cope with the situation if the worst comes to the worst. And those strategies and tactics are offensive, as has just been said above.

If it be asked how this can be, how the Soviet military posture can be both defensive and offensive, I would point out that in *any* army the manuals insist that a static defensive position cannot be held without offensive patrolling being carried out in front of the position. A similar blend of the defensive/offensive is to be found, and always has been, in Soviet policy-making; and this is particularly true with regard to nuclear war. This means that, assuming that they are not attacked and that they make no technological breakthrough, they will do all that they can, in my opinion, to avoid taking part in nuclear war or in one that might escalate into one. That is to say, their *policy* will be defensive. And the offensive *tactics* are for use only in those circumstances where the defensive policy has broken down, and the USSR is embroiled in Europe in a war which she almost certainly will not have wanted.

It is, however, important to remember that nuclear rockets are the only weapon available to the Soviet Union which are capable of ravaging the territory of America herself; and that the fact that the United States in both world wars escaped damage to her own territory has always rankled grievously with the leaders of the USSR, who are never tired of referring to this particular circumstance. Therefore, if, despite her wishes, the Soviet Union becomes embroiled in a *major* war with America, here are two important considerations reinforcing those various others which urge that such a war should be thermonuclear; for unless it were, the USSR would be in the position of a pugilist parrying the blows of his opponent, but unable to retaliate effectively with a lead to the chin or the solar plexus.

## Conclusions

Accepting, for the purposes of argument, that what has been written in the preceding sections approximates reasonably closely to the Soviet Union's notion of the nature and purpose of war, the final business of this chapter must be to try and make some assessment of the way in which the attitude of mind of the Russians is likely to be reflected in their present practice, and also in their practice in the future.

We may begin by enunciating a truism. No man will willingly engage in war if he thinks he will be defeated. Since the Soviet rulers believe that even today the USSR would lose a war with the West, obviously they will be most unwilling to become embroiled in one, unless they can manage to circumvent or nullify the factors that make (they think) for an unquestioned Western victory.

Since many of my readers may reasonably be sceptical that the Soviet leaders do indeed believe this, I would like to recall what Isaac Deutscher said to us when he came to lecture at Sandhurst. The date was early in 1958; Suez and the Hungarian Uprising were barely a year away, and the USSR was engaged in threatening Turkey, Norway, Denmark, and West Germany. The Cold War may not have been exactly at its height; but it was still very much a feature of the international landscape. Under those circumstances, it was natural enough for the members of a military academy to want to know whether the lecturer thought that the Russians might decide to attack us. He was therefore asked for his views on this particular matter.

Deutscher replied that he was confident that the Russians would do no such thing. He explained his conviction by giving a résumé of the Marxist view of the factors making for victory, and went on to point out that the Soviet leaders were Marxist. He then continued (and his words have remained engraved upon my memory to this day): 'The Soviet leaders are perfectly well aware that the economic powers of the West, taken as a whole, are still superior to those of the Communist bloc. You may therefore take it for certain then that they will never willingly engage in a war which, *by their own theories, they must lose.*' And he put tremendous emphasis on those last seven words.[255]

Further evidence of the Soviet attitude of mind, at least in the middle 1950s, is to be found in the Khrushchev memoirs. Without re-opening the controversy of whether these memoirs were written by Khrushchev or by someone else, few people doubt that, if Khrushchev himself did not write them, they were written by one who was well acquainted with senior Soviet officialdom. On page 400 of those memoirs, Khrushchev says (or is made to say) that, when he and Bulganin went to Geneva in 1955, they 'were encouraged, realizing now that our enemies [i.e. the enemies of the Soviet Union] probably feared us as much as we feared them'.[256] It will be no news to a Westerner that the West was frightened of the Russians; he may be less well aware that the Russians were also frightened of the West.

Weapons have grown bigger and more deadly since these two opinions were delivered; but there has been no essential change in the military balance. The industrial potential of the West, taken as a whole, is still greater than that of the Communist bloc—from which it follows that, according to Marxist doctrine, victory in war is likely to lie with the West. From which in turn it follows (as I said above) that, so long as these premises hold good, the Soviet leaders will be most unwilling to fight one.

There are three obvious ways of nullifying or circumventing the factors making for a probable Western victory. One is to invent some 'secret weapon' which could neutralize the Western defences. For instance, if the Russians could render inoperative the American rockets while preserving intact their own, the whole of the Western world would lie at their mercy; and they could then, if they wished, indulge in a war against it in the knowledge of certain victory; or they could (as would seem more likely) attain their political objective of the replacement of capitalism with communism purely by nuclear blackmail, without the need to resort to actual hostilities.

The second way of circumventing the difficulty is to find some means of winning the war quickly; so that the long-term factors, which the Russians believe to be the ultimate determinants of victory, will not have time to operate. It is therefore no coincidence that, in recent years, Soviet military thinking has been much preoccupied with notions of some kind of blitzkrieg; nor that Soviet military manoeuvres have been designed to embody these notions and test them out in practice.

However, although it seems not impossible that a Soviet attack on Western Europe might reach the Channel speedily, and even conceivable that an invasion of Britain could be launched without long delay, it appears to be out of the question for the 'krieg' to go so 'blitzly' that the final bastion of imperialism, the United States, could itself be attacked, invaded and conquered before the long-term factors making for a Western victory had had time to make their effects felt. If indeed the United States is to this extent invulnerable, there could be no point in the Soviet leaders ordering a blitzkrieg in the first place.

The third way to circumvent the adverse factors is to split the Western Alliance. If this were done, the Soviet Union would be fighting, not the West as a whole, but just a portion of it. Under these circumstances, the economic potential of that part of the West which was engaged in the war with Russia might actually be less than that of its adversaries. In which case, the long-term factors would favour a Soviet victory.

However, although the behaviour of the French has certainly weakened the cohesion of the West's defences, the latter survive (at the moment) sufficiently intact to prevent this means of circumventing the long-term factors from being at all effective. Nevertheless, the strong encouragement given to de Gaulle by Russia, the Russian opposition to the enlargement of the Common Market, and the notable attention being paid by Soviet writers today to the concept of 'coalition warfare',[257] all show that the potential value of this third method has been fully realized by the Soviet Government, which is doing its best to implement it.

But so far the Soviet leaders have not been more than marginally successful in splitting the Western Alliance. Nor have they yet invented a 'secret weapon'. As for a blitzkrieg, this can never achieve the winning of a war (as distinct from the winning of a battle), so long as the West retains a nuclear deterrent, and also the will to use it.

As things stand today (but as they may not necessarily stand to-morrow), the deterrent, and the will to use it, still exist. Consequently, this remaining method of circumvention or nullification is no more effective than its fellows at the present time. Therefore, for the reasons that have been given in the course of the preceding paragraphs, it seems unlikely that the Soviet Government will willingly resort to war *under present circumstances*. Nor, provided these circumstances still hold good, do they seem at all likely to resort willingly to war in the foreseeable future. A change in these circumstances, however, has only to occur and the very forces that at present impose caution will urge the Russians in the direction of using war as a means of pursuing their policies.

No man will lightly embark on nuclear war, or on war which may possibly go nuclear. Enthroned on a pile of radioactive dust, even victory ceases to be sweet. The Russians recognize the truth of this assertion as much as does any Westerner; and they do not want nuclear war.

So little, indeed, do they want it that it is even possible that the British or French deterrents are in themselves sufficient to deter, save on all but the gravest issues. They are certainly sufficient to prevent an advance to the Weser or the seizure of Hamburg or Hanover; for though these no doubt are attractive prizes for the USSR to win, they are simply not worth the destruction of three or four Soviet cities (Moscow, Leningrad, Kiev and Kharkhov, for instance) which is the price they might have to pay for them. True, the British and the French might not press the nuclear button in order to defend Hamburg; but then again they might. And is the probable gain sufficiently great to offset the possible loss? It seems very likely that the Russians would think it was not, and would act with corresponding caution.

As for the American deterrent, this, if used, would cause unbelievable destruction: it must therefore be expected to deter effectively on all conceivable occasions except for the following three:

(i) An invasion by an 'imperialist' nation of the territory of the USSR or of the 'satellites'.

(ii) A pre-emptive nuclear attack by the West which fails to neutralize the Soviet second-strike capacity.

(iii) A situation in which the Soviet Government comes to believe, whether rightly or wrongly, that the West is planning a pre-emptive nuclear strike, and therefore decides to pre-empt first, so as to make the best of a bad job.

But these three occasions, in my opinion, are none of them likely nowadays to materialize, especially in view of the modern techniques for preventing them. In which case, we are left with the proposition that the Soviet Union does not want nuclear war, and will be very reluctant to embark upon any adventure which might conceivably escalate into one.

We have therefore concluded so far that, in the case of a war against the West, a Soviet victory is deemed unlikely by the doctrines of Marxism-Leninism, and Western nuclear retaliation is considered probable. Therefore, both Soviet ideology and commonsense alike seem to agree in banning a resort to war against the combined forces of imperialism, unless and until the circumstances outlined above change radically in the Russians' favour. This view is reinforced by the consideration which we discussed in a preceding section—namely, that there is really no need to resort to war because history is on the side of the communists (see pp. 134-5).

To some Westerners, however, these comforting deductions may not seem wholly valid. What if Soviet ideology should change, as it has changed several times already? Can, moreover, the Russians' sense be described in any meaningful way as 'commonsense'? If not, might not the Russians' own brand of sense push the USSR, in the last resort, along less comfortable lines of policy? The best way to evaluate these objections is to analyse, starting from different premises, the Soviet Union's approach to war in the conditions of the modern world.

The next set of premises, therefore, from which we shall approach this problem is one which is dear to Soviet politicians and generals, and which asserts that war is an instrument of policy, and consequently subordinate to it. We have discussed the assertion already, of course, in an earlier section of this chapter: we are here concerned solely to evaluate its significance in the context of the world of today.

Since the rulers of Russia are wholly persuaded that war is an instrument of policy, and therefore subordinate to policy, those in the West who wish to discover what use the Soviet Union might make of war should study Soviet policy. In other words, Western observers must seek to establish the *aims* of Soviet policy; and then to enquire to what extent (if any) war would seem to be the most suitable and effective instrument for achieving those policies' ends.

But the policy of states is customarily divided into foreign policy and domestic policy. With which policy, then, are we to concern ourselves? And by what criterion are we to establish its objectives?

As a general rule, war is an instrument of foreign, and not of domestic policy; and it is therefore on Soviet *foreign* policy that we should concentrate our attention. Exceptions to the rule may perhaps be found in such kinds of war as civil war and wars of national liberation; since these, if not the instrument, are at any rate largely the result of the domestic policies of the states in which they occur. But the subject of our concern is the USSR; and civil wars and wars of national liberation would be the products of that country's *domestic* policies only in those instances where they occurred on Soviet territory. Obviously, in the circumstances of today, they would take place (if they ever took place at all), not at the wish, but *despite* the wishes of the rulers of the USSR. Such wars, therefore, are not to our present purpose; for we are concerned here only with those kinds of war to which the Soviet Government might have recourse as an instrument of state policy—that is to say, with wars in which the Soviet state as a whole might become embroiled against other states as a whole, or against certain sections of the populations of other states.

This is not to say that civil wars and wars of national liberation would never be regarded as instruments of policy by the rulers of the Soviet Union. On the contrary, they have said on innumerable occasions that such wars can indeed serve as acceptable political instruments for a communist government to employ; and history shows that in this respect their deeds have matched their words. But wars of these kinds, when used by the Soviet Union as instruments of state policy, have been ignited, not on Soviet territory, but on the territory of other countries. From which it follows that they have been used as instruments of the foreign, not of the domestic, policy of the Government of the USSR.

But it is Leninist doctrine that foreign policy is subordinate to domestic policy, and, furthermore, is determined by it.[258] This is true, said Lenin, of any country, whether 'bourgeois' or 'proletarian'.

Nor is this just a notion of Lenin's which once was fashionable but has now been largely discarded. On the contrary, such powerful bodies as the Soviet Ministry of Defence go to great pains continually to re-emphasize its importance. Thus, in 1958, this Ministry published a book called *Marksizm-Leninizm o Voine i Armii*. This has become a standard work on the subject; and in 1968 a fifth, revised and enlarged edition was published. The doctrine that a country's foreign policy is subordinate to its domestic policy, and furthermore is determined by it, is to be found in both editions.[259]

This being so, it is presumably upon Soviet domestic policy, not upon Soviet foreign policy, that our attention should be focused. But since it is always possible that, under certain circumstances, the USSR might *not* subordinate her foreign policy to the requirements of her domestic policy, it would be only prudent to examine the aims of the former, as well as those of the latter, in our present survey.

The tasks of Soviet domestic policy have been enunciated in many authoritative statements from the time of the October Revolution down to the present day. Since we are here concerned only with the contemporary scene, we may take as the ones most relevant to our purpose those which were formulated by Brezhnev in 1971 at the Twenty-Fourth Party Congress. As it happened, he did not tabulate them in a neat and concise form; but a reading of his report delivered on the first day of the congress allows us to present them as follows:[260]

(i) the complete satisfaction of the material and cultural needs of the population;

(ii) the closure of the gap between the countryside and the towns;

(iii) the furthering of the development of 'socialist democracy';

(iv) the moulding of the new [Soviet] man.

Given that the Soviet Union is indeed engaged in the business of progressing from socialism towards the building of full-scale communism (as is made clear by the reissue in 1974 of the famous Programme which was adopted by the Twenty-Second Congress in 1961), the above four aims are wholly consonant with Leninist ideology on this point;[261] and the first two, at any rate, must be agreeable to any government anywhere. We may therefore take it as a working hypothesis that these are indeed the major aims of Soviet domestic policy at the present time, in fact as well as in theory.

But it is clear that war is a wholly unsuitable instrument for the attainment of any of these goals. A third world war would do little to satisfy the Soviet citizens's cultural and material needs; the gap between town and country would not be closed; such a war would not, one can say with confidence, be a good way of developing 'socialist democracy'; and it would be an equally unsuitable instrument for helping to mould the 'new Soviet man'.

If we turn from the Russians' domestic policy to their foreign policy, then the aims of the latter have similarly been authoritatively enumerated. Once again, they have varied slightly over the fifty-odd years of the USSR's existence; but at the Twenty-Fourth Party Congress Brezhnev formulated them as follows:[262]

(i) Together with the other socialist countries to provide favourable conditions for the building of socialism and communism;

(ii) to strengthen the unity, solidarity, brotherhood, and friendship of the socialist countries;

(iii) to support the national liberation movement and to co-operate in every possible way with the young, developing countries;

(iv) consistently to uphold the principle of peaceful coexistence between States with differing social systems;

(v) to give a decisive rebuff to the aggressive forces of the imperialists, and to save humanity from a new 'world war'.

There can be little doubt but that Brezhnev and Kosygin have been pursuing these aims in deeds, as well as in words. They have worked very hard to establish socialism in various countries of the world; they have tried their utmost to promote cohesion between the USSR and her 'satellites'; and they have given a great deal of support to the 'national liberation movement', in particular to North Vietnam. Furthermore, whatever they may have done in Czechoslovakia (which is a country with the *same* social system as the USSR and to which Brezhnev's fourth aim is therefore by definition not applicable), they have practised 'peaceful coexistence' with countries with *differing* social systems in as full accord with their understanding of that ingenious expression as is decent in public affairs.[263] Finally, whether or not they have 'saved' humanity from a new 'world war' (which in Soviet parlance, it will be remembered, means 'a war which has been launched by the imperialists upon the USSR'), it is undeniably true that no such war has erupted; while it is equally true, for that matter, that the USSR has not launched a war on the imperialists.

Given, then, that these are indeed the aims of contemporary Soviet foreign policy, it is hard to see how an attack on the West would be the best means available of furthering them. In no imaginable circumstances could it 'provide favourable conditions for the building of socialism and communism', because these require for their construction a material abundance which the ravages of large-scale warfare would not permit. It is unlikely to do anything notable 'to strengthen the unity, solidarity, brotherhood and friendship of the socialist countries'; and indeed in the event of a serious Russian defeat, the 'satellite' peoples, many of whom loathe the Russians, might take advantage of the Soviet embarrassment to break free from the Russian grip. Furthermore, an attack on the West will do nothing to help the 'national liberation movement': on the contrary, it will drain away those resources which at present are used to give that movement support. By definition, a war against the West could hardly 'uphold the principle of peaceful coexistence', even admitting that the Soviet understanding of that expression is considerably different from ours. Finally, while an attack on the West would indeed succeed in saving humanity from a new 'world war', this is merely because, with the Russians starting it, it would be a 'revolutionary war', not a 'world war'. This, obviously, is a distinction without a difference, so far as the realities are concerned. Faced with their cities blasted by nuclear explosions, it would be poor consolation for the men in the Kremlin to reflect that the missile exchanges were 'revolutionary' in content rather than 'imperialist'. The Soviet leaders have their faults; but they are not silly.

The above is perhaps too abstract and theoretical an approach to satisfying the more pragmatic among my readers. For instance, those

British Army officers to whom I have expounded it have a strong tendency to question its practicality. They are prepared to concede that it is interesting, viewed purely as an academic exercise; but they tend to doubt its validity as a guide to action.

This is a reasonable attitude. The business of army officers is not with the weaving of subtleties of intellectual analysis, but with what is to be done if the bugle blows and the Russians advance upon the Rhine. This is a fair question—one moreover which is often postulated by civilians as well as by officers.

The only possible answer to it in the context of our discussion is to put another question to them, and to ask: What bugle? That is to say, what war? War does not just break out: someone has got to start it, and (under modern conditions at any rate) start it for a particular purpose.[264] From which it follows that either the West will begin it, or else it must be the Russians who will do so.

The notion that the Western Alliance would attempt the invasion of Russia is so ludicrous to most Westerners that we can dismiss it from our present analysis. The Russians might view it differently, of course, but this book is written for a Western, and not for a Russian, readership. Granted, then, that a Western reader would dismiss as absurd, nowadays, the notion that the West will begin a war against Russia, the only way in which it is possible for a war to break out between East and West is for the Soviet Union to start it. But for what purpose would the Soviet Union do so? For the attainment of what goal?

This is to raise in a significantly different form the questions we raised above concerning Soviet policy. For, those were framed in the context of the Soviet leaders' own formulations of the goals of their various policies. Our new formulation, however, allows thereby to be postulated any hidden aims or ulterior motives that the Western mind may suspect to be lurking camouflaged beneath the Russians' propaganda statements.[265]

But the only such aims or ulterior motives that can conceivably exist are those concerned with 'Russian expansionism' or with the 'worldwide triumph of communism'. Assuming for the purposes of argument that both these things are important, though unspoken, objectives of Soviet policy (as indeed they very well may be), can it seriously be argued that the starting of a third world war is an effective way for the Russians to try and achieve them? What would they in fact achieve except a nuclear desert?

Let us therefore assume for the moment that the USSR will not willingly launch an attack upon the West. This, however, naturally does not mean that she will be equally unwilling to engage in hostilities with other countries; because then the circumstances would be different. For instance, when she invaded Czechoslovakia in 1968, she knew that she would be victorious; and she also knew that Czechoslovakia had no nuclear missles to discharge at her.[266] Under these circumstances, the use of force was an acceptable tool of policy for the Soviet Union; and in the end, as we all know, she decided to employ it.

So the next point to be considered is the attitude likely to be adopted by the Soviet Politburo towards the application of war as a tool of policy in the case of countries other than the Western Alliance.

But to wage war on a country, you have got to get at it. It is, of course, possible to 'get at it' by launching an ICBM at it; and in that sense the USSR could wage war on, say, South Africa, by the simple process of pressing the appropriate button. The consequences of such an action would be so tremendous, so pervasive, and so far-reaching, that it seems to me inconceivable that the Russians would resort to it except in the actual context of a third world war. (I am, here, using 'world war' in the Western, not Soviet, sense of that expression.)

Apart, then, from hurling ballistic missiles across the stratosphere, the only other way for the Soviet Union to wage war on another country is for her armed forces to assail that country's territory. This is doubly true if the purpose of the war is concerned with 'Russian expansionism' or 'the world-wide triumph of communism'; for then that territory must not only be assailed, it must also be seized and occupied.

But unless seaborne or airborne landings are to be employed on a very large scale, any such territory must be contiguous to the Soviet Union or to one of the 'satellite' countries. A glance at the map will show that only the following countries satisfy this condition: Norway, Finland, West Germany, Austria, Yugoslavia, Greece, Turkey, Iran, Afghanistan, Pakistan, India and China.

Of these countries, Norway, West Germany, Greece and Turkey are members of NATO. I have already given reasons for thinking that the Soviet Union does not want to fight a war against the Western Alliance: we may therefore dismiss the likelihood of a Soviet invasion of any of the above four countries, provided the vital conditions are fulfilled which were given in detail above (see pp. 140–2). Iran and Pakistan are members of CENTO; and Pakistan, in addition, enjoys the support of China. Therefore both these countries, under present conditions, are not in any great danger of Russian attack. That leaves Finland, Austria, Yugoslavia, Afghanistan and China as being the only countries open to a Soviet invasion by land.

We shall be dealing with the case of China a little later. Afghanistan has a common frontier with China as well as with Russia, which might make a Soviet invasion of her a risky and unprofitable task. Austria is a 'perpetual neutral'; and there are strong reasons why the USSR should not wish to cause a breach of that neutrality (see chapter 4). Yugoslavia is a doubtful; but if the West should want to support her, it could do so easily via the Adriatic and Greece. An invasion of Yugoslavia, therefore, runs the risk of an East-West confrontation, and so is probably too dangerous for the Russians to contemplate, at any rate under normal circumstances. Finally, there is Finland; and she admittedly could easily be gobbled up at any moment, but then she has always been in that position. And India . . . well, India is India.

So if we leave aside for the moment the question of China, only Finland and India and (questionably) Yugoslavia and Afghanistan are open to a land invasion by the USSR, unless the latter is prepared to hazard a major war with the West.

If the Soviet Union wishes to use force in countries other than these, she needs a fleet. There is no necessity to point out that she has already got one; nor that she is adding to its strength yearly. There is, however, a necessity to point out that particular naval operations demand a particular kind of ship. One cannot, for instance, indulge in commerce-raiding by means of assault craft; while submarines, which are useful for commerce-raiding and marvellous for nuclear deterrence, have almost no part at all to play in a large-scale seaborne landing, such as the Allied invasion of Normandy in 1944.

According to the Institute of Strategic Studies, the Soviet Navy today has about 245 submarines and 100 landing craft.[267] At first sight, therefore, it seems to be well equipped to indulge both in commerce-raiding and in large-scale seaborne landings. In fact, however, large-scale seaborne landings require large-scale escorts for protection and large-scale sea-trains for supply. The landings in Normandy, for instance, required 286 escort vessels, together with 1,213 warships for the assault phase, and 303 landing ships and 4,093 landing craft for the actual landings.[268] The Soviet Union has got nothing approaching these figures, even if she were to withdraw every warship that she is possessed of and allot them to one particular operation (and, in fact, she would obviously be most unwilling to do this, because she would then have to strip bare her maritime defences).

The invasion of Normandy, it is true, was carried out against heavily defended positions. The USSR would not require an armada of this size and complexity if she were thinking of attacking Ceylon, for instance, or Malaysia. But though, in the case of either country, she could certainly get her troops ashore, there is no point whatever in doing this unless she can reinforce and supply them. And this demands a sea-train of a size that she simply has not got.

Of course, the situation may change; and the USSR in the 1970s may build the necessary ships. But she must build not only the necessary numbers, but also the necessary *kinds*; for you cannot use destroyers

and submarines to ferry supplies—not, at least, to an overseas expedi-
tionary force of seven or eight divisions. It therefore follows that those
who are interested in the role of the Soviet Navy as a tool of Soviet
foreign policy, must watch attentively the construction programmes of
the shipyards of the Soviet Union.

A *defensive* role for that navy would seem to be postulated, if the
yards continue to concentrate upon building submarines (whether
nuclear missile launchers or potential commerce-raiders); for the only
really useful employment for vessels of this kind is against powerful
war fleets or substantial merchant marines or for the discharge of
nuclear missiles; that is to say, that their sole real use is against members
of the Western Alliance. Since we have already agreed (I hope) that the
USSR will not willingly become engaged in full-scale war against the
members of this Alliance, it follows that the purpose of the Russians in
acquiring a large number of submarines is not offensive, but is, on the
contrary, essentially defensive.

If, however, the Soviet naval authorities should proceed to embark
upon the building of a whole fleet of assault craft, *together with a
proportionally numerous construction of the ships required to protect such
craft and supply them*, then there may be much more substance in the
proposition that the USSR is adopting an *offensive* naval policy;
though, even then, the world should be reminded that Soviet military
doctrine envisages the use of seaborne landings in a defensive, as well
as in an offensive, role. An admirable example of such a usage was the
Kerch-Feodosiisk operation of 1943.

But if a large-scale Soviet seaborne invasion of some other country
can be virtually ruled out for the present, what about 'gunboat
diplomacy'? Could not a couple of ships, with a company or two of
marines to act as a landing-party, bring force to bear upon a maturing
political crisis in a small country whose capital was near the coast?
Might not, for instance, Nkrumah of Ghana never have been toppled
from the presidency, if the Soviet Navy in 1966 had been the size that
it is today? Could not President Sukarno similarly have retained his
position, if Russian warships had been in strength in the Indian Ocean
at the time that he was deposed? The answer to these three questions is
probably 'No'.

Modern surface warships do not carry the complements the old-
fashioned warships used to. The British cruiser *Glorious*, which was
built in 1916, had a crew of 1,130 officers and men. From such numbers
it would have been possible to have mustered a landing-party of 600–700
men in an emergency. A force of this size, operating against some
coastal African township, and supported by the guns of the *Glorious*,
would have had a good chance of success—a chance which would have
been very materially increased by the scanty numbers and primitive

level of the weapons with which their native opponents would have been armed.

Of the Soviet Navy today, only the cruisers of the *Sverdlov* class carry anything like this number of men aboard. The *Krestas*, the *Kyndas*, the *Kotlins*, the *Krupnys* and the *Skorys*, which numerically form the bulk of the ocean-going surface warships of the Soviet fleet, have complements of 400, 390, 285, 360 and 260 respectively:[269] it would be hard to mount an effective force from the crew of any one of these vessels. And, of course, their probable opponents are no longer the helpless victims that their grandfathers were a hundred years ago. They have got artillery, they have got aircraft, and a number of them have got some missiles: they obviously could not engage in a full-scale war against the forces of the USSR, but they could fight off a Soviet destroyer.

Naturally, it is always possible that, in extremely favourable circumstances (such as in the case of a very small country which had negligible defences), a well-planned *coup* could be effected by the crew of a Soviet warship, and a pro-Western regime be toppled, or a pro-Soviet regime buttressed. But although the Western statesman or the Western strategist must be aware that such a possibility exists, he would be wrong, I think, to make the meeting of this threat the main task of his policy or strategy.

For one thing, such an operation must always carry the risk of the Soviet Union becoming entangled in an open-ended commitment. For another, it is not the aim of Soviet foreign policy to bring a particular country—let us say Mauritius—into the Soviet empire (if you prefer to use that expression), or to see communism triumph in that one particular island (if it is this way of looking at things that you prefer). The aim of Soviet foreign policy is, if it is anything of the kind at all, to spread Soviet influence, or to see communism triumph, *throughout the world*. In this context, gunboat diplomacy may actually prove counterproductive since, although it will bring into the net the sprat of the tiny island, it will without doubt effectively alarm the mackerel of the rest of the world.

We come last to China. And, from the point of view of our analysis, China is a peculiar country. It is the only possible adversary of the Soviet Union which is both nuclear and 'proletarian': on the other hand its industrial strength is much less than that of the Russians. Given, therefore, the attitude to war that has been expounded in the preceding pages, what views on the question of war with China are likely to be prevalent among the members of the Soviet Politburo and the Soviet military?

It goes without saying that, on ideological grounds, such a war must be considered impossible. The 'proletariat', whatever their nationality, have always the same 'class interests'; and thus, since Marxism teaches that war is begotten by *conflict* between 'class interests', it is quite impossible (according to the theory) for war to break out between two 'proletarian' countries.

On the other hand, it is certainly possible (and Czechoslovakia is an example of this) for the government of a genuinely 'proletarian' country to succumb to some form of heresy—or, to put it more accurately, to succumb to something that the Russians *conceive* to be heresy. Whether that heresy be 'revisionism' or whether it be 'dogmatism', a government can obviously become infected with it, and be damned by the Russians accordingly.

But under such circumstances it becomes a mandatory duty for the Russians, according to Brezhnev's doctrine of 'limited sovereignty', to send 'fraternal aid' to the people of the country in question. (For 'wars of fraternal aid' see pp. 56–8). Moreover, in the case of Czechoslovakia in 1968, they did their duty and sent it. But Czechoslovakia was, militarily speaking, an extremely simple operation; by contrast, the invasion of Maoist China would be a very great deal more difficult. And, even if the invasion were successful, the subsequent task of occupying that country and policing its huge population would be formidable indeed.

If, however, there were a 'splinter group' within the Chinese Communist Party, or within the People's Liberation Army, which was engaged in a struggle against Mao, such a circumstance would make the task of the Russians considerably easier; because they could then send 'fraternal aid', not to the amorphous 'people' of China, but to identifiable Chinese communists who were resisting Mao's perversion of the gospel of Lenin. Moreover, such people could reasonably be expected themselves to take up the burden of ruling and policing China, and thus relieve Russia of what would otherwise be an unconscionable amount of trouble.

Up to the present, however, there have been no signs of the existence of any such 'splinter group' (or, at least, not of one that can claim to have any support); and the absence of it must certainly have been one of the factors that the Soviet Government took into account when deciding what to do about China.

We may reasonably assume that what the USSR would *like* to do about China is to see installed there a government that would be more in agreement with Russia. In other words, the fundamental aim of Soviet policy towards China is to bring to power a communist government that would be generally pro-Soviet.

But is war the most suitable instrument for achieving that particular aim? The answer, surely, must be no. The Chinese (or so I am told) dislike and despise Europeans, and in this respect regard the Russians as being as much Europeans as ourselves. Therefore, unless there exists an anti-Mao faction in China which both enjoys a great deal of popular support and is also willing to co-operate with Russia, a war to topple the Maoists from the seats of power in Peking would be a large-scale, costly, protracted war of conquest. Moreover this, even if it were successful, would have to be followed by the stationing in China of an enormous army of occupation for an indefinite period.

Other considerations reinforce the view that, in these particular circumstances, war is not the tool of policy that it would be appropriate to select. It is true that, if it is to be selected at all, it would be better to select it now, while the Chinese forces have only a very small number of nuclear warheads at their disposal, and have no delivery system capable of discharging those warheads upon the major cities of Russia. Nevertheless, it would be better to be cautious, for the reasons advanced above.

Of course it could be urged in favour of war that the long-term factors making for victory would work wholly in the Russians' favour at the present time; because the Chinese economic potential is so markedly inferior to theirs. But that long-term asset might be considerably stultified by a number of other considerations.

One such is that, in Engels' assessment of the factors making for victory, the quantity and quality of the populations are very important. Knowing nothing of China, it is beyond my powers to attempt to assess the 'quality' of the Chinese people, and especially to try and assess it from the viewpoint of Soviet Leninism. As far as the quantity is concerned, however, one can say with confidence that it is more than three times that of the USSR. Such a disparity of numbers must give pause to a Russian general, even if he finally concludes that he can cope with it.

And by means of an all-out nuclear war he probably could. But is an all-out nuclear war the appropriate tool for achieving the basic aim of Soviet policy towards Communist China today, which we assumed to be the replacement of the Maoist Government by one more likely to be sympathetic to the views of the USSR?

Again, the answer to this question can only be no. It is hard to imagine that out of the ashes would arise, like a Leninist phoenix, a Chinese Government willing and eager to co-operate with its country's barbarian destroyer. Nor could the destruction be limited by restricting the nuclear bombardment purely to the major cities. At the present moment, at any rate, the strength of Communist China does not lie in its major cities: to defeat China, the peasants must be defeated; and if the downfall of these is to be encompassed by nuclear weapons, the whole enormous country will have to be devastated. Would the acquisition of a radioactive desert be a sufficient gain to the USSR to offset the

F

losses deriving from it, among which must be included the almost total withdrawal of support for the policies of the Soviet Union by those countries of the Third World whom she is so particularly anxious to please?

If the above analysis is true, the only alternative to peace with China is conventional war. But, in such a big country with so numerous a population, a conventional war would inevitably be protracted. Not only, therefore, would the factors making for victory not be operating wholly in favour of the USSR, but a long, costly, agonizing conflict might wreak upon the fabric of Soviet society those revolutionizing strains and stresses which, according to Leninist doctrine, war imposes on belligerents.

It cannot be doubted that for a month or two, or even for a year or two, the Soviet people would willingly make the sacrifices that so arduous a campaign would demand of them, and would regard the loss of lives and loss of treasure as being needful to sustain their cause. So did the American people regard their sacrifices in the early years of their involvement in Vietnam; and so did the Athenian people, in their long war against Sparta, accept willingly the losses they suffered for the first decade or two. It is prolonged sacrifice without any sight of victory that in the end wears down a nation's resolve; and a conventional war with China is likely to be both costly and uncertain, the more so as very many Soviet divisions must always be stationed in Central and Eastern Europe to hold down the Russian 'satellites' and ward off 'imperialist' aggression.

'War puts nations to the test' (those words of Marx must ring in the ears of the Politburo). 'Just as mummies fall to pieces, the moment that they are exposed to the air, so war pronounces its sentence of death on those social institutions which have become ossified.' And who would care to bet that the Soviet Communist Party has not become an ossified institution? And who also would care to bet that the Soviet communists themselves are not aware of it?

If these sentiments are remarkably close to some of those put forward by Andrei Amalrik, the reason is, not that I have plagiarized him, but that he, being a Soviet citizen, must inevitably have been nurtured on the principles of Marxism-Leninism; and so the fundamentals of his analysis must be based upon Leninist principles.[270] I have based my analysis deliberately upon Leninist principles, in order to arrive at a Soviet view of the matter. It is not surprising, therefore, if some of our results concur.

So there will be no war? The lion and the lamb will lie down together, and we can beat our swords into ploughshares? No, we cannot do that. As has been explained earlier, no communist has ever renounced war, if it seems to him to be likely to serve his cause. Marx never renounced war, Lenin never renounced war, and the Soviet Union today does not renounce it. It is true that she has renounced it *as a means of settling international disputes*;[271] but then it has never been as a means of settling an international dispute that she has begun a war in the past. On every occasion when the USSR has committed aggression on another country (in the Western sense of 'aggression'), she has done so in order to further the 'international class struggle', or to send 'fraternal aid' to the workers of another country, and so forth and so on. In other words, it has been (in her own terminology) a 'class', not a 'national' dispute; and she can therefore declare with a clear conscience, and with perfect truth by her own reckoning, that she has not, does not, and will not resort to war to settle *international* disputes.

The above is true even of the Russo-Finnish War of 1939–40; for, although this was undeniably a war concerned with an international dispute (the dispute between Finland and the Soviet Union over a piece of Finnish territory which, from the Russian point of view, was strategically sensitive)[272] the war in question was begun by the Finns, according to Soviet reckoning.[273]

By this reckoning, therefore, the USSR was completely innocent of any kind of aggression upon the Finnish people; and my remarks contained in the penultimate paragraph are consequently wholly inapplicable to this particular war.

But if the Soviet Union will not resort to war in order to settle international disputes (unless, of course, she is the victim of aggression), she will very willingly employ war as a means of settling 'class' disputes, if she thinks it would be profitable to do so. For us in the West, it must therefore be our purpose to see that it is *not* profitable. This means that the Western world (and I write for the Western reader) must maintain an effective second-strike capacity together with the will to use it if need arises, and also a credible 'trip-wire' of conventional forces. In addition, we must prevent the Russians from acquiring a technological lead over us (i.e. from acquiring a 'secret weapon'), and refrain from unilateral disarmament. 'Trust in God, and keep your powder dry.' It is not, perhaps, a very fashionable maxim today; but in the world of today we need it.

## A summary of the Soviet attitude to war as it stands today

War is essentially an evil. It is caused by the mere existence of 'class' societies, and can therefore only be abolished when a truly 'classless' society (i.e. communism) is established over the whole of our planet. When that happens, war will disappear automatically, because the conditions for its existence will have been removed.

Meanwhile, war has a profoundly revolutionizing effect upon those societies engaged in it. It exerts great stresses and strains upon all combatant countries; and the longer and harder the war, the greater the stresses and strains. Furthermore a defeated country experiences them much more severely than does a victor country. They can therefore reach such a point that an actual revolution can occur, as happened in Russia in 1917, and as nearly happened in Germany a short time afterwards. The stresses and strains experienced in America as a result of her involvement in the Vietnam War are seen by Soviet writers as unchallengeable evidence that the principle still holds good.

Once world history had reached the point where there was a socialist country in existence on this planet in addition to capitalist countries, the Soviet leaders expected that the latter would gang up together to invade Russia, and thereby destroy communism, while the USSR was still militarily weak, and success would be reasonably certain. At that period, therefore, Lenin was right in saying that war between capitalism and communism was inevitable. Now, however, although imperialism is by its very nature still inclined to war, and although the imperialist ruling class would like to see an end to communism as much as ever they did, the military might of the USSR has grown immeasurably greater; so that an imperialist attempt to destroy Russia would be extremely likely to fail. Furthermore, the USSR is adding daily to the power of its armed forces, so that the chances of an imperialist success in such a venture grow slimmer as the years pass by. The imperialist rulers themselves are aware of this, and so are less likely to make the attempt in the first place. Consequently war between capitalism and communism is no longer to be regarded as inevitable. It should be added that the fact that the danger of a third world war has undoubtedly been much reduced recently is seen by the Soviet Union as convincing proof that its theory is correct; and this is probably genuinely one of the reasons (though not, I suspect, the only reason) why the USSR continually increases the strength of its armed forces.

Wars are classified as either 'just' or 'unjust'; and the Soviet Union supports the former, and opposes the latter. The latest Soviet publications declare that 'just' wars are wars waged by the people for liberation from social oppression (i.e. civil wars) or from national oppression (i.e. wars of national liberation), wars waged in defence of national independence (i.e. against foreign attack) and wars waged by socialist states against imperialist aggression; while wars waged by the 'exploiting classes' in order to suppress the struggle for liberty of an 'exploited' class or nation, or to grab other people's territory, or to enslave and rob them are 'unjust' wars.[274] 'Revolutionary wars', in the sense of 'wars waged to spread communism by force of arms', are now no longer discussed in the open literature; though whether this is because the USSR has now rejected the whole concept, or whether because it is felt to be inexpedient to discuss such a subject in public, is open to doubt. It must be said, however, that no change has taken place in the general Soviet thinking on the subject of war that would rule out, even today, the starting of a 'revolutionary war' if the circumstances were favourable. As for 'wars of fraternal aid', these were still being waged by the Russians as late as 1968. All in all, it remains true that the Soviet Union has no objection to committing aggression, in the ordinary Western sense of 'aggression', if the cause is a sufficiently worthy one from the revolutionary viewpoint and the circumstances favour victory.

The USSR today continues to regard war as the continuation of policy by other means, and hence as the tool of policy. In other words, war is regarded as a means of attaining political objectives. Consequently the USSR will select war as a means of achieving its political objectives whenever it feels that it is the most appropriate instrument in the prevailing circumstances. It will not, however, come to that conclusion lightly.

Strategy is another tool of policy. This must be so; because unless policy directs strategy, the strategy employed may well be such as to render impossible of attainment the political objectives for which the war has been begun. An attempt to seize intact the economy of Western Europe, and harness it to work for that of the Soviet Union, would fail dismally if the factories of Western Europe were destroyed by nuclear strikes. In the Soviet view, however, an even more important consideration flows from this particular concept; for the Russians believe that the size of the political objective determines the size of the war. If the war has been undertaken for such a matter of life and death as the abolition of one's enemy's social system and its replacement with a copy of one's own, the enemy will resist to the uttermost of his power, and employ the whole arsenal of weapons at his disposal in an effort to prevent this happening. Similarly the aggressor will exert (and will exert from the outset) the uttermost efforts of which he is capable, if the goal for which he has begun the war is of vital importance to him.

It is for this reason that the Soviet Union has always been of the opinion, at least until very recently, that a third world war must inevitably be nuclear; for, according to Soviet thinking, a third world war would only be begun over issues that were absolutely vital. In other words, the dimensions of the issue dictate the dimensions of the weapons. Recent signs that the USSR is starting to come to a tentative conclusion that a third world war might be non-nuclear can therefore only be due to the Soviet Union having come to a preceding, and equally tentative, conclusion that the United States might start another world war for a purpose which falls short of aiming at the extirpation of communism from the Soviet Union.

But this is almost certainly the wrong way of stating what has been happening. For, what has in fact been happening has been that, as a result of *détente*, and of President Nixon's visit to Moscow and of Mr Brezhnev's to Washington, the Soviet leaders have come to accept that the USA is not hell bent on attempting to wipe out communism in the USSR; from which it follows that, in the Soviet leaders' opinion, a third world war is now no longer probable, though it still remains possible. (The reader will remember that, by Soviet definition, a world war or *mirovaya voina* can only be begun by the imperialists.) It is therefore worthy of note that very recently an article by General Mal'tsev in *Red Star* declared that the danger of a third world war had begun to recede.[275] But the doctrine remains unchanged that if, despite all this, a third world war should happen to break out, strategic nuclear weapons will certainly be employed, though conventional forces may well be employed too.[276]

But what, then, of the opinion of a number of Western sovietologists, that the Russians are now beginning to come to the conclusion that a third world war can be non-nuclear? I can only proffer my own opinion, which is that they have come to a mistaken conclusion as a result of having posed the question incorrectly. To the Soviet mind, it is meaningless to ask whether a third world war can be non-nuclear: if the war is being fought for 'fundamental' objectives, which must surely be true of a third world war, then the weapons will be 'fundamental' too—which does not, of course, preclude the employment of conventional weapons in addition. The evidence on which the Western sovietologists rely is highly tentative, in one important instance is self-contradictory,[277] and in another it depends upon a nice interpretation of the Russian. As time goes on, further evidence will obviously become available; and one side or the other of us will be proved to have been right. Until then, I can only say that it seems to me to be extremely dangerous to say that the Russians are beginning to envisage a world war that is non-nuclear. What to my mind they are beginning to envisage is that a world war is at present not very likely; but they stick to their view that, if it comes, the strategic rockets will fly.[278]

Although the Russians say nothing about the circumstances in which they would start a world war themselves, it seems logical that, if they were to do so (which is surely highly unlikely in view of the present balance of forces), the same considerations would apply. They would only start such a war for absolutely 'fundamental' objectives; and they would therefore resort from the outset to absolutely 'fundamental' weapons. This consideration is reinforced by the fact that only by the use of nuclear rockets could they do significant damage to the territory of the United States.

It remains only to add that the doctrine that policy directs strategy may be powerfully modified, and indeed can be totally reversed, if the military situation deteriorates to such an extent that one's whole effort must be directed to the task of attempting to avoid defeat. But this, once again, in a war between capitalism and communism would be a 'fundamental' political objective that would call for 'fundamental' weapons.

In any case, before beginning a war, the Soviet Union will want to be sure it will win it; and in order to gain this assurance, it will study carefully the factors making for victory. Among these factors, the economic element, which classical Marxism regarded as being overwhelmingly decisive, is still regarded by the Russians as of great importance; and the constant attention that they pay to their military technology and their defence industries is ample proof of this. In addition, however, the Soviet Union today gives a high place to morale as one of the factors making for victory; and they assert that the morale of the USSR is a great deal higher than Western morale. Other factors making for victory which are stressed by the Russians today include surprise, speed, and the size of the combatant countries.

According to Marx, all wars contain within themselves the seeds of another war; and history has shown that the second war can undo the results of the first. The German gains in the Franco-Prussian War of 1870–1 were more than undone by the French gains that resulted from the First World War. The Russians know this. Consequently, if war breaks out, they make, and have always made, provision for the enforced 'bolshevization' of the territory they conquer, thereby making virtually impossible a return to the *status quo*. By this means, the 'seed of another war' will be effectively prevented from germinating.

While this book has been in the press, signs have emerged that the Russians may be contemplating the possibility that a war could be fought between the USSR and America that would *not* be nuclear. This, of course, is unlikely to be true of a war in Central Europe, because that area is of vital importance to the Russians; and we must therefore suppose that a war there would seem to them to call for 'fundamental' weapons, even if the Western Alliance refrained from using them. But they do seem to be genuinely wondering whether a war in, say, the Middle East between Soviet and American forces would have such a 'fundamental' significance for the USSR that the latter would be *compelled* to go nuclear, though they accept that it might ultimately very well do so, if only as the result of escalation. If it is indeed true that this is what they are thinking, there are the possibilities of interesting developments ahead. Unfortunately, however, there is not enough evidence at the moment to be sure about it.

# 3  The Soviet Concept of Peace

In the context of international relations, 'peace' is defined by the *Oxford English Dictionary* as 'freedom from, or cessation of, war or hostilities'; and the Russian word for 'peace' in the same context is defined by the *Slovar' Sovremennogo Russkogo Lityeraturnogo Yazyka* as 'the absence of war or armed conflict between peoples or States'. In this case, therefore, both East and West appear to have the same notion of peace; and consequently it might be thought that there was no need for me to devote a chapter to it.

The need for such a chapter arises, however, because we in the ¡West (or perhaps I should say, we in the English-speaking world)[1] seldom think about 'peace' in this sort of negative sense (i.e. in the sense of it being the *absence* of war or conflict) but tend rather to think of it in a *positive* sense (i.e. in the sense of something which makes a definite, attestable contribution to human happiness). Thus, we are given to talking about 'peace on earth', 'peace and goodwill,' or 'the peace of God, which passeth all understanding'; and it is clear that, when we are using 'peace' in this sense, we are thinking of it as being something actively beneficent, as something which helps to uplift our squalid human condition and irradiate it with the love of our fellows.

It might be objected at this point that all three of the particular phrases about peace which I have quoted in the previous paragraph are couched in the language of religion; and that therefore, though they provide evidence for the view that a convinced Christian envisages peace in the sort of positive way that I have described, it does not at all follow that an agnostic or atheist would understand it in any comparable manner.

However, because a man is an agnostic or even an atheist, this certainly does not mean that he is wholly uninfluenced by religion. Much of the teaching of Christianity is acceptable even to those who deny the existence of God; and few Christian concepts are more universally acceptable than the particular positive notion of peace which is enshrined in the above quotations.

Moreover, modern secular writing has continued in the same tradition; and there are plenty of examples of Westerners, and even of Western politicians, writing or speaking of 'peace' in a manner which, though not identical with the above (naturally enough, since they are talking of politics, not philosophy), is nevertheless quite consonant with it. For instance the preamble to the Charter of the United Nations says that 'We, the peoples of the United Nations, determined to live in peace with one another as good neighbours . . .' while Thomas Jefferson, in his First Inaugural Address, declared that the Americans wanted 'peace, commerce and honest friendship with all nations'. Obviously, neither of these quotations has the same sort of breadth or depth of overtones as 'the peace of God, which passeth all understanding' but all three alike clearly regard peace as being something much more than just a mere absence of fighting.

It is important to note that this *positive* understanding of the word 'peace' depends upon coupling it to another word ('peace and goodwill', 'peace of the Lord', 'peace, commerce and honest friendship'), in the way in which it has been coupled in the preceding paragraphs. For us in the West, this constitutes no difficulty, since we do traditionally couple it in this way; moreover, we do so to such an enormous extent that we now, I feel, subconsciously supply the coupling, even when we come across the word being used entirely on its own. As a result, the word 'peace', in current Western usage, has come to be regarded as being synonymous with 'peace and goodwill'; and if someone were to use it in the exact sense in which the dictionary defines it (that is to say in the sense of it being merely 'an absence of armed conflict') or still more, if he were to use it in what would be no more than a perfectly logical extension of that usage, and write about 'peace and *ill*-will', he would be regarded by almost everyone as extremely perverse. Yet this is exactly the sense in which Soviet diplomacy so often uses it.

For proof of the above, one may cite the period of 1945–55. In international affairs, this period was characterized by an absence of armed conflict between the Russians and the West; and therefore (at least so far as Europe was concerned), what we had was, literally, an era of peace. It was also an era in which relations between East and West were imbued with an extreme acrimony; so that the peace which we then experienced, so far from being the 'peace and goodwill' of conventional Western thinking, was actually the 'peace and ill-will' that I have stigmatized above. It is therefore highly relevant to our theme to notice that the West was quite unable to stomach the coupling of these two words together; and that consequently, in order to avoid having to do so (although 'peace and ill-will' would, in fact, have been an admirable description of the situation), it had to think up a new expression, and emerged with the term 'Cold War'.

It is true, of course, that this expression was taken up by the Russians, who translated it literally into their own tongue (as *kholodnaya voina*) and made considerable use of it from then on. But the communists

F*

adopted it, not because they experienced any revulsion at the thought of peace accompanied by ill-will (as we shall see later on, there are frequent examples of Soviet leaders, even today, urging precisely that), but because by using a term which embodied the word 'war', and then by laying the whole responsibility for it at the door of the West (and in particular, of course, at that of the Americans), the Soviet Government was able to instil into its own people the notion that the old Marxist dogma about capitalist hostility was far from dead; and that there still existed, even in the post-war world, powerful groups in all the capitalist countries who could not restrain themselves from expressing open hostility to the Soviet Union, and who, but for the might of the Soviet armed forces, would have proceeded from verbal hostility to outright attack.

In support of this, one can quote contemporary official Soviet definitions of the expression 'the cold war'. The *Bol'shaya Sovyetskaya Entsiklopediya* (second edition) described it as being 'an aggressive political course taken after the Second World War against the USSR and the Peoples' Democracies by reactionary circles in the imperialist countries, headed by America and Great Britain'. The term 'cold war' is, said the encyclopaedia, of American origin; and it went on to aver that its purpose is to prevent peaceful coexistence, to increase international tension, and to prepare the way for the unleashing of a new world war.

These purposes have been achieved in practice, according to the encyclopaedia, by 'forming aggressive military-political blocs, by indulging in the arms race and war hysteria, and by setting up imperialist bases in other countries'. (Significantly enough, the Berlin blockade of 1948-9 was not even mentioned in the context of the 'cold war' either by the encyclopaedia or by other authoritative Soviet reference books.) The volume of the encyclopaedia which contains the above was published in 1957, but subsequent Soviet definitions of the 'cold war' of comparable official status followed the same line.

For our purposes, it is important to note two things. One is that the Russians agree that the phrase *kholodnaya voina* is a translation of an American expression, and is not of Soviet origin. The second is that they make use of the term only in relation to *Western* actions and policies: when they want to speak of their own, they declare that these are motivated solely by a deep longing for peace; and the adjective that they therefore use to describe them is invariably 'peace-loving'.

It is usual in the West to assume that, when they talk like this, they are merely being thoroughly hypocritical; but in fact what they say is perfectly correct, *given that they are using 'peace' in the communist sense of the word*, a sense which we shall be discussing in a moment. Here it is sufficient to point out that, since there can be no question but that

Soviet actions and policies since the end of the Second World War have frequently been marked by hostility towards the West (e.g. the Berlin blockade and the Cuban crisis) and have contributed their full share towards the high level of international tension, it is obvious that, if the Soviet leaders are able to describe them as 'peace-loving', they find no difficulty in reconciling in their minds the notion of 'peace' coupled with that of 'ill-will'. Which is what I set out to demonstrate.

It may be objected at this point that what has been said so far may well have been true of Soviet thinking up to the death of Stalin, but that the more flexible ideas of his successors (and notably the concept of 'peaceful coexistence') have changed the picture completely.

A careful examination of these ideas, however, lends little support to this objection. For example, the doctrine of 'peaceful coexistence', which was introduced by Khrushchev in 1956 at the Twentieth Party Congress, simply stated that, contrary to what Lenin had maintained, war between capitalism and communism was no longer to be considered to be inevitable.

It is important for the reader to notice that this is the sum total of what it said. It did not, on the one hand, assert that war between capitalism and communism is now *impossible*; it merely said that it is now not absolutely inevitable that war should occur. Nor, on the other hand (and the one more relevant to our argument), did it say that 'peaceful coexistence' implies 'peaceful *co-operation*'. On the contrary, the speeches and writings of the Soviet leaders, both then and since, together with the most important publications of the Soviet Communist Party, have all abounded in examples of meditations on the concept of 'peaceful coexistence' in which it is expressly demonstrated that co-operation with the ' "class" enemy' (i.e. with the West) is *not on any account* to be a feature of it.

But before going on to consider further the communist notion of 'peace', we must first make a small diversion. In what is said here about the 'Soviet' attitude to peace, it must be understood that it is referring solely to the orthodox communist view, and hence to the official view of the Soviet Communist Party and of the Soviet Government. It is, of course, true that many ordinary Russians regard 'peace' in exactly the same way as does the ordinary Westerner; and the many expressions of a desire for 'peace and friendship' or 'peace and co-operation' with the West, with which a Western visitor is likely to be greeted by chance acquaintances in Moscow, can usually be regarded as being genuine (and the more chance the acquaintance, the more genuine the remark is likely to be). Unfortunately, the Soviet people have little influence upon the conduct of their government, and especially in the field of international relations; and the views held by many ordinary Russians are often far from identical with those of the Communist Party.

On the other hand, one must not be too naive about such matters. The view that *all* ordinary Russians are on the side of the angels, and that it is only the Kremlin which is responsible for the Russian contribution to international tension, is one which is very attractive to many Westerners; but it is one which, nevertheless, does not always correspond to reality.

I well remember being taken one day to the Pioneers' Palace in Leningrad, and shown upstairs to a room which was said to be dedicated to peace, international friendship and goodwill. The lady in charge made a little speech in praise of these desirable objectives, and then went on to tell us how her work in that room was designed to contribute to their achievement. Among other things, she kept a card-index of the names and addresses of children all over the world, who had expressed a wish to form a pen-friendship with children in the Soviet Union; and by this means, she said, the spirit of international understanding and co-operation was fostered, to the great advantage of the cause of international peace.

While this idyll was going on, I noticed some drawings lying on a shelf, and stepped over to have a look at them. They were not drawings exactly, so much as cartoons—and some of the most savage and vicious cartoons I have ever seen. In all of them, the theme was the execution of American citizens (sometimes civilians, sometimes American servicemen) by members of the Soviet Army. Sometimes the Americans in question were being hanged, while the Red Army men were guarding the gallows; sometimes they were being bayonetted or machine-gunned; but in all cases the drawings, and the captions that went with them, were calculated to inspire a sense of *hatred* against *all* Americans in the minds of those Soviet children who should happen to see them. (It will be remembered that the incident took place in the Palace of Pioneers, a focal meeting-place for the children of Leningrad.)

I asked the lady, when she had come to the end of her speech, whether she did not perhaps think that the exhibiting of cartoons like these was not a somewhat peculiar way of spreading peace and friendship among all the nations. Her reaction could not have been more violent if I had spat at her. She turned bright scarlet and began to yell at the top of her voice, screaming that imperialists were not to be counted as people, and that no peace could come to the world until all imperialists had been exterminated. She was still yelling and screaming in that vein when I tiptoed away downstairs, reflecting, as I did so, that the expression 'the fostering of international friendship and peace' was clearly capable of some rather remarkable interpretations; and that, insofar as she had any influence on the children, some at least of them were likely to regard peace, when it came to a question of peace with the

Americans, not in any of the positive senses I have mentioned, but at best in the sense of 'an absence of armed conflict', and only too likely in that of 'an absence of armed conflict coupled with an extreme ill-will'.

It may seem to the reader, from what has been written so far, that (according to communist doctrine) 'peace', in the sense of 'peace and co-operation' or 'peace and goodwill', is impossible of attainment on this earth. That is very far from being the truth. By the theories of Marxism-Leninism, however, 'peace' in this sense can be brought about only in a society where there is no 'exploiting' class; since otherwise the material interests of this 'class' will clash with those of the 'exploited' class, and this clash will generate conflict.

If we project this thesis on to that society which consists of the world taken as a whole, then there are two 'contradictory' classes to be found in it; and these are capitalism and communism. Therefore, according to Marxism-Leninism, goodwill and co-operation cannot come to the international scene until *one* of these two 'classes' has disappeared. Moreover, communists believe that this will happen; and they further believe that it is capitalism which is doomed to extinction, and communism which is destined to survive. From which it follows that communists must be convinced (as indeed they are convinced) that the only way of bringing co-operation and goodwill to this troubled planet of ours is by the total victory of communism.

But until that day dawns, not only will any attempt on the part of the Soviet Government to practise 'peace and goodwill' towards the capitalist countries be (in the eyes of the Soviet Government itself) a hindrance to the victory of communism, since it will imply a relaxation of its efforts to secure that victory; but it must also be predestined to total failure. This does not rule out, of course, certain limited agreements and certain prescribed acts of co-operation with the various 'bourgeois' countries; but such agreements and such acts of co-operation will come about only when, in the particular matter in question, it is specifically to the Russian advantage to conclude them.

But if it is true that genuine peace can only come about when all the 'exploiting classes' have been extirpated, then goodwill and co-operation should, even now, be discernible in certain parts of the globe. For today, there is in existence not just one socialist[2] state, the USSR, but a number of them; and these states (so their respective governments say) contain no 'exploiting classes', but are composed entirely of the 'proletariat', together with what is officially described as its 'friendly ally', the peasantry.

Under these circumstances, therefore, 'peace' between the countries mentioned above (in the positive sense of 'peace and co-operation and goodwill') is not merely possible, but, according to Marxist-Leninist theory, it is also inevitable; and the fact that there is not much obvious goodwill existing at the present moment between the Soviet Union and China is explained away by communist theoreticians by saying that the group of men in control of one or the other country has ceased to be genuinely 'proletarian' in outlook, and has become heretical. In other words all communists agree that, if the ruling groups of *both* countries were indeed genuine 'proletarians', harmony *must* prevail between them; and that, since harmony obviously does not prevail at present, then one or other (or both of them) *cannot* be 'proletarians'.

It is not my purpose in this chapter to hold Marxism-Leninism up to ridicule or obloquy for not acknowledging the validity of the concept of 'peace', in the sense of 'peace and goodwill'. Indeed, for all I know, it may be entirely justified in refusing to do so. It is certain that 'peace' of this sort has never yet existed upon this planet, except for brief moments of time in small communities; and whether it will do so in future—whether, indeed, such a concept is even conceivable—can clearly be no more than mere conjecture. And Marxist-Leninist conjecture stands on a par with all other conjectures, and its chances of being right are no less (though certainly also no greater) than are those of the others. I should therefore have been extremely foolish, to put it mildly, to have attempted to hold up to ridicule one conjecture, and allow the others to pass (at least by inference) as being intellectually much more valid.

Therefore let us suppose that Marx's vision has been realized, and that communism has been triumphant over the whole globe. The result should be, as both Marx and Lenin saw it, to introduce among every section of mankind wholehearted co-operation and goodwill. Such goodwill, such co-operation, such an absence of the discordant conflict of interests must surely resemble that positive sense of 'peace' (without, of course, any of its religious overtones) which was, I suggested, the one most naturally congenial to the Western mind.

But whether the communist vision does, or does not, resemble that particular Western notion of the concept of peace, one thing at least is certain: if a communist society, on the lines I have described above, were ever to be brought into being, Marxist-Leninists would never describe the resultant goodwill and co-operation by the word 'peace'.

This is because there is no such thing as 'peace' in this sense in the Marxist-Leninist *Weltanschauung*. The latter envisages an 'absence of the "class struggle" ' in a society in which all 'classes' have been abolished; it also envisages an 'absence of the "class struggle" ' between nations, so soon as the world-wide triumph of communism shall have abolished nations. But 'peace' in the sense of 'the strong peace of the soul', or of Spinoza's view of it as 'a virtue, a state of mind, a disposition for benevolence, confidence, justice', such a notion of 'peace' is not a part of either Marxism or Marxism-Leninism, even if one makes allowances for the fact that the two latter philosophies are based on materialism, not on religion; and that therefore the specifically religious overtones of the two quotations above are clearly inappropriate when discussing Marxism.

Obviously, therefore, in discussing this concept in the context of Marxism-Leninism, we must reject the whole concept of 'the soul', and confine ourselves strictly to the purely material world, which is all that Marxism acknowledges. Nevertheless, even then, even if we do this, we must still acknowledge that it is impossible for Marxism to employ the word 'peace' in any similar sense to that in which we have employed it above; if only because the whole Marxist picture of the world is based upon the notion of the 'dialectic'.

I must make it clear that I am not here concerned with whether that notion of 'the dialectic' is true or false, nor whether it is even possible to speak of 'truth' or 'falsehood' with regard to it. I am concerned here only to establish that 'the dialectic' is regarded by Marxist-Leninists as the basic stuff of Marxism; and that, this being so, a number of consequences follow.

The first consequence is that, as the Soviet authorities testify, 'the dialectic' itself (this whole concept of how change comes about in the world) is itself dependent upon the notion of the 'contradiction'; for 'contradictions' are not only 'the chief category' of the 'dialectic', but they are also its principal motive force and the source of all development.[3] In other words, it is almost entirely as a result of 'contradictions' that change comes about on this planet, and that the world evolves.

But all 'contradictions' are, in essence, a form of conflict. As an authoritative Soviet textbook puts it, they consist of 'opposite, mutually exclusive aspects' of a particular phenomenon; and these aspects enter into a 'struggle' which culminates in the destruction of the old forms and the emergence of new ones.[4] The word 'struggle' is put in inverted commas in the Soviet textbook; because, as it says, it is by no means always possible to speak of 'struggle' in its literal sense when speaking of, for instance, inorganic nature. On the other hand, the 'struggle' of opposites in the direct, literal sense does occur as a feature of living organisms, and therefore occurs as a feature of human society; and indeed, as the textbook goes on to explain, in the case of human societies 'struggle' in this direct and literal sense is to be regarded as a normal feature.[5]

There is no need to enquire more closely into the nature of 'contradictions': the sole point that concerns us here is that they are unmistakably and incontestably a negation of the concept of 'peace' when 'peace' is used in the sense of 'total harmony'. Therefore, those who believe in 'contradictions' cannot also believe in this particular sort of peace.

This consequently means that, for one who subscribes to the Marxist-Leninist *Weltanschauung* (that is to say, for one who believes that 'the dialectic', with its attendant 'contradictions', is an integral part of the make-up of this world), true 'peace', in the Westerner's positive sense of that term, can only come about in a world which has ceased to change; for all change (in the Marxist-Leninist view) is produced by 'contradictions', and all 'contradictions' are some form or other of conflict.

Moreover, this statement is true with regard to *all* kinds of change (and not just with regard to political change and economic change), since 'contradictions' lie at the root of changes of *every* kind. It therefore follows that, even when mankind has arrived at the state of true communism, and even when that particular form of society has been established all over the globe, either changes of one sort or another will continue to take place (in which case there will be 'contradictions', or, in other words, 'conflict'), or else there will be universal stagnation.

And the stagnation in question would have to be 'universal' in the literal sense of that word. All aspects of the universe would have to stagnate. Since both biological change and geological change, for instance, are seen by Marxist-Leninists as being based upon 'contradictions',[6] no such changes could come about in a world from which 'contradictions' had been banished.

From which it follows that communists do *not* picture even their ideal society of true communism as one from which all 'contradictions' have been banished; and consequently they cannot, and do not, picture it as one which is the embodiment of 'peace' (in the sense in which we have just been using that word).

Once this point has been grasped, it is easy enough to understand why the concept of 'peace' in this sense is never discussed by communists. There is nothing to be found on the subject in either the first or the second editions of the *Great Soviet Encyclopaedia*, nothing in the *Dictionary of Philosophy*, nothing in the *Diplomatic Dictionary*, and nothing about it in any of the fifty-six volumes of the *Complete Works of Lenin* (fifth Russian edition). Obviously, it is impossible for me to state that, of the many hundreds of thousands of books which have been published in the Soviet Union during the fifty-odd years of its history, not one has contained a discussion of the subject in question; but I do say that there has been no authoritative publication, produced with the full support of the Soviet Communist Party, which has ever so much as mentioned 'peace' in the sense in which we are discussing it, except to attribute it to one group or another of its various political oppo. and ridicule it as illusory and Utopian.[7]

Nor can it be said that the kind of works I have mentioned are not places in which one should expect to find a discussion of a subject this sort. Lenin discussed an enormous range of subjects, of which many, it is true, are purely economic or political, but of which many others are not. He wrote, for instance, on materialism and empirio-criticism; he wrote on Hegel's logic; and he also wrote on the importance of 'the dialectic'. A man who tackled subjects like these would surely also tackle 'the strong peace of the soul', if he thought that the subject was of even the slightest importance.

Similarly, *A Dictionary of Philosophy*, though it finds no room for 'peace', is happy to expound on 'peaceful coexistence'. It also devotes an article to 'war', another to 'freedom and necessity', and another to 'logical empiricism'. If it regards these, and many other similar subjects, as being proper material for its discussion, it is hard to see what motive it can have for not discussing 'peace', other than that it does not believe in it. Similar remarks can be applied to both editions of the *Great Soviet Encyclopaedia*, neither of which deal with 'peace' except in the sense of 'a peace treaty', and both of which devote plenty of space to concepts equally as recondite as 'peace' and certainly no more important.[8]

Nor can it be maintained that it is not to the Marxist-Leninist element in Soviet thinking, but to the Russian element, that this notion of 'peace' is repugnant. On the contrary, Tolstoy, for instance, devotes a great deal of time to the subject, and so does Dostoyevsky. The final scene of Chekhov's *Uncle Vanya* is a reflection of one aspect of it. Nor among pre-Revolutionary writers is a discussion of the subject confined to literature. At least one famous encyclopaedia, published in Tsarist days, devotes an article to the subject;[9] and if more had survived, no doubt more examples could be found. The fact of the matter is that 'peace', in the sense of 'peace and goodwill', is discussed eagerly wherever the concept is acknowledged; and it is not discussed by authoritative Soviet opinion simply because that opinion does not acknowledge it.

The above, therefore, should always be borne in mind by Westerners when considering any communist statement about peace. If, for instance, the Russians are talking about a 'peace policy', they may be meaning 'a policy of avoiding armed conflict', or they may be meaning 'a policy designed to further a communist takeover'; or they may be using the expression (and frequently are) in both these senses at once. The one thing, however, of which one can be quite certain is that they are *not* using it in the sense of 'peace and goodwill towards the bourgeois world'; since this is, by definition, a concept which it is impossible for a communist to hold. Nor, by the same token, are they using it in the sense of 'a policy which, if carried to a successful conclusion, will result in harmony and lack of friction'; since this is also inconceivable to the communist mind.

The above is the reason why 'peace-loving' can be used quite seriously by communists to describe policies which, to the ordinary Western observer, have little obvious concern for the cause of peace, as he understands that word. Thus, Mr Kosygin, in a speech which he delivered to the Supreme Soviet in August 1966, spoke of the 'peace-loving, anti-imperialist policies of the Soviet Union', thereby equating a love of peace with a desire to wage a struggle against the imperialists.

Contrary to the impression which this phrase is likely to make on most Westerners, it is not self-contradictory in the eyes of a communist. Kosygin here is using 'peace-loving' in the communists' *positive* sense of the term; and he really does mean that Soviet policies are imbued with a genuine desire to see peace and goodwill established throughout the globe. But, as we have seen, the precondition for this is the total victory of communism. No such victory is possible, however, so long as imperialism exists. From which it follows that, for a communist to be genuinely peace-loving, he is bound also to be wholeheartedly anti-imperialist.

The reader may remember from the chapter on war that, although in a perfect world the communists would expect to see war abolished, nevertheless, in our present imperfect one, they have no objection to waging wars when these can be turned to their advantage. If this fact is borne in mind, and superimposed on the notion we have been just discussing (that is, of 'peace-loving' being synonymous with 'anti-imperialist'), it will shed a good deal of light on the frame of mind which lies behind the attitude of, for example, the North Vietnamese communists towards the peace talks designed to put an end to the war in Vietnam (both before they started, and after they had begun in Paris), and which lay behind that of the North Koreans at the time of the Korean War.

For the purpose of the peace talks was to produce a peace treaty; and, from the communist viewpoint, there are only two possible reasons for wanting such a thing. The first is to obtain a breathing-space, a temporary respite from hostilities. It is something to be sought of the enemy when things are going badly, and when it is necessary to buy time in order to regroup and refuel. As Lenin said: 'A peace treaty is a means of gathering strength.'[10]

Brest-Litovsk is the classic example of a treaty of this kind. Lenin never regarded Brest-Litovsk as having ended the fighting permanently: he always believed that the concessions he made to the Germans would be, and should be, retracted the moment that Russia was strong enough.

But he needed time; he needed a breathing-space.[11] The Germans would only grant him this at a price, so he paid that price. But, as he himself said repeatedly, the moment that Russia had recovered her strength, the struggle would be renewed.[12] This was 'peace', as Lenin understood the term; it was a 'temporary, unstable armistice between two wars'.[13]

From talking about Brest-Litovsk in particular, he went on to speak at the Seventh Party Congress about the characteristics of peace treaties in general. On two separate occasions he informed the Congress that 'peace is a means of gathering together one's forces'; and on two separate occasions he informed it that the history of war makes it perfectly obvious that 'the conclusion of a peace treaty after a defeat is a means of gathering strength'. In another passage, he told the same Congress that 'peace is a breathing-space for war, and war is a means of obtaining a somewhat better or a somewhat worse peace'.

The fact of the matter is that, in Lenin's eyes, the whole of life was a never-ending struggle. It might be true that, under communism, there would be peace and co-operation and goodwill; but communism was something which belonged to the distant future, and so, therefore, did that positive kind of peace.

The second reason for a peace treaty that is acknowledged by Marxism-Leninism is the desire or the expediency of making a formal and public register of the gains or losses produced by the actual fighting. The Treaty of Riga in 1921 between Soviet Russia and Poland is an example of a peace treaty in this second sense; because the function of this was to put an end to the fighting (which neither side was in a condition to sustain much longer) and to put on record the gains and losses that had accrued as a result of the war. From the Soviet point of view, the Treaty of Riga recorded a territorial loss, because Poland received a great deal of territory in the border areas which Russia very much coveted, and which indeed she subsequently recovered at the end of the Second World War.

On the other hand, the Soviet treaties with Finland of 1940 and 1947 recorded considerable gains. From both treaties, Russia derived important additions of territory; and from the second she also derived a number of other benefits. The Finnish peace treaties are therefore a record of the advantages *won* for the USSR by the military operations that preceded them. But both the Polish and the Finnish treaties fulfil admirably Lenin's requirement that this other function of a peace treaty is to register the gains and losses produced by the war.

Now this attitude towards peace treaties differs sharply from the one so common in the West, which regards the actual ending of hostilities as a major good in itself. Thus, a slogan which, prior to the cease-fire agreement, used to enjoy great popularity in the West was 'End the war in Vietnam'; and many of the people who chanted it were clearly of the opinion that the putting of an end to fighting is a laudable action *per se*.

No communist has ever been of this opinion. Lenin himself, for instance, repeatedly rejected it, even when faced with the slaughter of the First World War. Works that he wrote during this period make it abundantly clear that he was not in favour of an end to the fighting for its own sake: on the contrary, it was, he said, the duty of every Marxist to direct his efforts to harnessing the chaos of war for the purpose of making the 'proletarian' revolution. In other words, Lenin's main concern was with political objectives, not with the saving of lives.

To return to the Vietnamese War, therefore, it is pertinent to remark that a termination of hostilities had been offered to the North Vietnamese on several previous occasions; but since they did not regard the putting of an end to the killing as being in itself a particularly meritorious action, they were willing to accept 'peace in Vietnam' (in the sense of 'an absence of fighting there') only on their own conditions. And these conditions included an end to the bombing, the withdrawal of all American troops from South Vietnam, and the supervision of elections by the Vietcong.

These conditions would obviously have greatly facilitated the seizure of power in South Vietnam by the Vietnamese Communist Party; but then, as we have seen, it is only when a communist government comes into power in a country, it is only when a country passes from 'bourgeois' to 'proletarian' rule, that (according to communist notions) true peace may be said to have been established in it.

Of course, if the military position of the North Vietnamese had been bad enough, they would no longer have been physically capable of insisting on their conditions, and would have been glad enough then to accept a 'peace' in the sense of 'a cessation of hostilities'. But they would have regarded this peace as merely a temporary truce, as a means of winning for themselves a breathing-space, in order to renew their campaign for establishing a united, communist Vietnam at a later time and under more favourable circumstances. In other words, they might actually have termed this truce a 'peace'; but they would have been using 'peace' in the same sense as Khrushchev did in the phrase that has been quoted earlier (see p. 171). In other words, it would simply have been in their eyes a temporary, unstable armistice between two wars.

The North Koreans and the North Vietnamese are therefore true followers of Lenin. In 1953, the North Koreans were compelled to give up, at least for the time being, their stated objective of bringing the whole of Korea under communist rule, when they were forced to sign an armistice at Panmunjom. But this was merely the North Korean equivalent of the Treaty of Brest-Litovsk. The North Koreans had need of time in order to regroup and replenish; and they bought this time by means of the Panmunjom armistice. Once they had done so, it was their firm intention to renew the struggle, so soon as circumstances were favourable.

As things have turned out, circumstances have never been favourable for the North Koreans to resume their attack on the South Korean Government by means of a formal attack across the land frontier: the defences erected along the 38th Parallel by United Nations troops have been too strong. Nevertheless, the North Koreans have never lost sight of their objective; and, although they have been unable to make use of a conventional land offensive, they have tried outflanking the defences on the 38th Parallel by means of seaborne landings to the rear of it (the operations in 1968 are a good example of this); and they have also tried to bring down the South Korean Government by means of guerrilla-type terrorist attacks launched from inside South Korea itself.

The North Vietnamese continue in the same tradition. For a long time, the peace talks in Paris between themselves and the Americans made little headway. This was because the North Vietnamese had not suffered sufficiently severely on the battlefield to see the need for a 'breathing-space'; and therefore the only peace that they would sign was one which would effectively hand over the whole of South Vietnam to communist rule, as we saw earlier. The agreement signed in Paris in January 1973, between the North Vietnamese and the Americans, promises to do just that. (There is a brief analysis of this agreement in the final chapter of this book.)

The reader, however, should not suppose that there is some particular virtue in the North Vietnamese which has caused their struggle to be more successful (so far, at least) than that of the North Koreans. Geography has been the decisive factor. Korea is a peninsula: it is therefore possible to draw a line across it, build intensive fortifications along that line, and thus prevent an incursion to the south of it being made by any state which does not possess the mastery of the local sea and air. The North Koreans do not possess such mastery; and therefore the seaborne landings that they have since made, have been more in the nature of small-scale commando raids than an all-out seaborne invasion, and consequently have not been big enough to threaten seriously the existence of South Korea.

The situation with regard to Vietnam is very different. The country was in fact divided into two by the Geneva Agreement of 1954; but a glance at the map will show why it has never been possible for the South Vietnamese and the Americans to keep their enemy the other side of the dividing line. That huge, meandering frontier with Laos and Cambodia (which the North Vietnamese use as a transit route) runs for over 1,500 miles; to build a Maginot Line that could protect it may not be technically impossible (it would be foolish to say what is impossible nowadays); but it would certainly be unbelievably expensive, and it has certainly not been built.

The North Vietnamese have therefore always been able to find at least one point at any particular moment through which they can pour reinforcements of men and munitions. And the Americans have not been able to kill enough of them to make this course unprofitable. Therefore, the North Vietnamese have had no need of a 'breathing-space'; and therefore they have felt no need of a peace treaty in the first of those meanings of a peace treaty which we have just been discussing.

Nor did they have any need of one in the second of those meanings. It appeared to them neither desirable nor expedient formally to register the gains and losses produced by the Vietnam War. As we have seen, they did not reckon their military situation to be bad enough to force them to register a loss. As for the gains, the gains that the Americans were offering were nowhere near sufficient. The North Vietnamese were convinced that, provided the war continued, sooner or later South Vietnam would pass into communist control. Why, then, should they settle for less favourable terms than these? Or rather, to put it more accurately, why should they settle for any conditions other than those that would make it easy for them, once the Americans had withdrawn, to stage a communist takeover in South Vietnam? Marxism-Leninism recognizes no other reasons; and though many Westerners might think the stopping of the killing to be reason enough, this, as we have seen, is not an argument which has much appeal for communism. In this context, it is interesting to note that, during the twelve months subsequent to the signing of the Paris Agreement, no less than 60,000 South Vietnamese and communists were killed in South Vietnam.[14]

There is one final aspect of 'peace' which ought to be discussed here. That is, 'peace' when used in the sense of a 'peace campaign'. The 'Peace Campaign' of 1949–51 is well documented, and provides an excellent illustration of the way in which 'campaigns' of this kind work, and of the ends they are intended to serve.

The Peace Campaign of 1949–51 was based originally upon the organization called 'The Partisans of Peace', which was set up under the auspices of the Cominform in August 1948, at Wroclaw in the Polish People's Republic. The highlight of the campaign was a World Peace Congress in Warsaw in November 1950.[15]

At this Congress, nine resolutions were passed, which may be conveniently summarized as follows:[16]

(i) An end to the Korean War, on the basis of the withdrawal of foreign troops from Korea and the conflict settled by 'the representatives of the Korean people'. (It should be remembered that this was three years before the Korean armistice was signed.)

Communist China to have a seat on the Security Council of the United Nations. American troops to leave Formosa, and to cease hostilities against North Vietnam.

(ii) Germany and Japan to remain demilitarized, and all occupation forces to be withdrawn from these two countries.

(iii) A condemnation of forcible attempts to 'hold peoples in a state of dependence and colonial oppression'. All colonies to have a right to freedom and independence. No racial discrimination anywhere.

(iv) No aggression. That state which is the first to use force against another state, under no matter what pretext, is guilty of aggression. 'No political or economic consideration, no reason arising from the internal situation or any internal conflict in a State can justify armed intervention by another State.'

(v) All who conduct propaganda for a new war of any kind whatsoever to be made liable to criminal prosecution.

(vi) The war crimes in Korea to be investigated, and especially 'the question of the responsibility of General MacArthur'.

(vii) A ban on all atomic, bacteriological and chemical weapons of all sorts. A progressive reduction of the armed forces of the Great Powers. A supervisory body, working under the Security Council, to supervise the above. These proposals 'would result in no military advantage to any country'.

(viii) Restoration of normal trading relations between all the various countries of the world.

(ix) Improvement of cultural relations between the various countries.

Although, of course, the Russians played upon the emotive overtones of the word 'peace', in order to attract as much support as possible from a world which had not yet really recovered from a conventional war, and was terrified at the thought of an atomic one, nevertheless a careful examination of the proposals adopted at the Peace Congress will show that most of them really *were* designed to further 'peace', in either the one or the other of the ways in which the communists use that word.

One of these is, as we have seen, 'an absence of fighting'. At the time of the Warsaw Peace Congress, fighting was going on in the world in a number of places, of which the following were the most important: the war in Korea; the war being waged against the French in Indo-China; and the communist insurrection in Malaya.

It is therefore highly relevant to note that the proposals put forward at Warsaw for ending these particular conflicts would, if implemented, have greatly increased the chances of communist takeovers. In particular, the withdrawal from Korea of 'foreign armies' would have left the South Koreans almost defenceless; and it must not be forgotten that the war started with an outright invasion of South Korea by the armies of North Korea; nor that the invasion was so blatant and so indefensible that the 'foreign armies' mentioned in the proposals were in fact armies of the United Nations, sent to Korea on the orders of the United Nations, in pursuance of a resolution of the Security Council.

Of the other proposals, a few seem to have been designed, not so much to further the cause of peace (whether in the 'bourgeois' or the communist sense), but to act as a sop to those attending the Congress who were neither communists nor 'fellow-travellers'. A certain number of people in this category were invited by the communist organizers in order to lend an air of impartiality to the Congress; but the reception accorded to Mr John O. Rogge, for example, when he attempted to speak impartially on the resolutions, will prove to anyone who cares to investigate the incident that an impartial study of the policies of the communist bloc (or, for that matter, of the capitalist bloc) was not at all what the Congress had in mind.

The remaining proposals are genuine 'peace proposals', in the sense that they were designed to further 'peace' as the communists understand that word. That is to say that, if these proposals had been implemented, they would have greatly increased Soviet power and influence, and would have facilitated communist takeovers in a number of countries. (In this connection, it must be remembered that, at the time of the Peace Congress, the USSR was still the only real source of communist strength in the world, for the Chinese People's Republic was barely a year old. It could still reasonably be claimed, therefore, that an increase in Soviet power was synonymous with an increase in the power of communism as a whole.)

Thus, if the Russians had succeeded in creating a unified, but demilitarized, Germany within easy distance of the huge conventional forces of the Red Army; and if, in addition, atomic weapons had been banned and all occupation forces had been withdrawn—which would have meant the Americans leaving the continent of Europe—how long would it have been before not only Berlin, but also the whole of what we now call West Germany, had been swept into the Soviet orbit? That this was the Russian intention, at any rate as regards Berlin, is evident from the whole episode of the 'Berlin airlift', which immediately preceded the launching of the 'Peace Campaign', and which makes no sense, except when viewed as an attempt to grab the whole of Berlin and incorporate it in the Soviet bloc.

Furthermore, the Congress was quite wrong in saying in section (vii) that the 'unconditional prohibition of all manner of atomic weapons', even if accompanied by reductions in the powers' armed forces, would 'result in no military advantage to any country'. By the end of 1950, the Western conventional armies in Europe were reduced from their wartime level to only about fifteen divisions, as compared with the Soviet Union's 150. No force reduction conceivably acceptable to the Russians would have reduced this enormous disparity; so a ban on atomic weapons would have left the Western forces bereft of their nuclear shield and faced with a Russian army of about ten times their number. Despite what the Congress had to say on the matter, this situation, if it had materialized, could only have been described as conferring on the Soviet Union a military advantage of quite overwhelming proportions.

Finally, the statement on aggression, given in section (iv), was also clearly intended to benefit the communist cause. Some of the greatest successes of post-war communism came from the use of subversion from within coupled with a threat from the Soviet Army without; and this technique led to the communist seizure of Czechoslovakia, and nearly led to a communist seizure of Greece. The only counter to tactics of this sort was for the West to send in troops, which it failed to do in the case of Czechoslovakia, but which it did do in the case of Greece. Under section (iv) of the 'peace proposals', however, any such action would clearly be prohibited; and if the Western governments had been forced by their electorates to accept this (and the other) sections, it is obvious that the freedom of action of the communists would have been very greatly increased. It is perhaps worth noting that the *Daily Worker*, the organ of the British Communist Party,[17] thought this fourth section of such particular importance that, as well as printing it in its proper place along with the other proposals, it also gave prominent display to a condensed version of it, which it put in heavy black type in the centre of the page under the heading 'Aggression Defined'.

These, then, were the proposals of the Peace Congress; and I hope I have demonstrated sufficiently how, if the world as a whole had been persuaded to accept them, they would have enormously strengthened the power of the Soviet Union, and would, in addition, have almost certainly led to the appearance of communist governments in a number of places (and notably in West Berlin, Malaya and South Korea). In other words, they would have significantly strengthened 'peace', in the communist notion of that word.

As it happened, however, the West rejected these proposals; and therefore, as its enemies aver, it rejected peace. This may be true; but if it is, the peace that it rejected was a peace that would have entailed the almost total surrender of the Western position, and one that would have transferred into communist hands the political, strategic and economic mastery over vast stretches of the globe. This is not peace in the ordinary sense of the word; though it is a kind of peace with which the old Romans were well acquainted, and the kind to which Cicero was referring when he said: 'Peace is to be produced by victory, not by negotiation.'

Communist statesmen would say 'Amen' to that.

# 4    The Soviet Concept of Neutrality

Essentially, the whole concept of neutrality is foreign both to Marxism and Marxism-Leninism. According to these theories, the historical process evolves through the medium of the dialectic, the clash of opposites; and the notion of a neutral position, unaffected by any such clash, and in its turn exercising no influence upon it, is not one which can possibly be fitted into the dialectical scheme. Furthermore, if we abandon the abstract, and confine ourselves to the concrete (in this case, the concrete conditions of human existence), all human beings are bound, so Marxists believe, to give support to one side or the other in the 'class struggle'.

For our present purposes, there is no need to consider *why* the Marxists should hold this particular belief: it is quite sufficient to realize that they do; and that this belief is one which is held by Marxist-Leninists as well as by Marxists. As a result, the Soviet Communist Party is firmly convinced that all men and all women must play some part in the 'class struggle', however small; and that therefore no human being can properly be said to be 'neutral'.

Nor can a man make himself neutral by deciding to opt out of the 'class war' altogether. Not to give aid to the 'proletariat' in its fight against the 'bourgeois' is, objectively speaking, to help the latter: 'He who is not with me is against me'. On this point at least, the Christian view coincides exactly with the Marxist one; and the effect of it is to deny that there is (or, indeed, that there can be, or should be) any such thing as neutrality in ideological or religious commitment.

Nevertheless, in the actual world in which the Soviet Union finds (and has found) itself, there are certain circumstances and certain situations where the use of the terms 'neutrality' and 'neutral' are inescapable. For instance, when war is raging, not all the nations of the world may be engaged in it; and it is essential to have a word to describe those countries which are not.

The words which the USSR uses on these occasions are *nyeitral'nyi* and *nyeitralityet* ('neutral' and 'neutrality'). Both these words are clearly derived from the Western ones; and both East and West understand their respective words for this particular kind of neutrality in exactly the same sense.

If anything, indeed, the Soviet usage tends towards a rather more strict interpretation of 'neutrality' than is often the case in the West; and the Russian word *nyeitralityet* would, in this connection, be better translated as 'absolute neutrality' or 'perfect neutrality' (the two terms used by Western international lawyers to describe 'neutrality' in the strict interpretation of the word) instead of just by the one word 'neutrality' on its own.[1] For, in Western parlance, countries are often said to be neutral simply because they are not engaged in the actual fighting, although they may be busily employed in furnishing arms, munitions, and supplies to one or the other side.[2] The United States, for instance, in 1940 described herself as neutral, even though she was sending supplies to Britain and none to Germany. In the language of conventional diplomatic parlance, she was still a neutral; by Soviet reckoning she was not.[3]

Nor is war the only occasion on which Soviet statesmen are obliged to speak of 'neutrality'. They accept that a country can fairly be said to be 'neutral' with regard to a particular international dispute in time of peace. When in 1959, for instance, Khrushchev proposed to solve the Berlin question by turning it into a 'free city', he said that the USSR was prepared, if necessary, to see installed in it a small garrison of troops to be drawn from 'neutral' countries, i.e. from states which, unlike Britain, France, America, and the Soviet Union, were not interested parties to the Berlin dispute. Similar instances abound in Soviet official utterances; and it is therefore plain that the Russians accept that a country can fairly be said to be 'neutral' in such a context; that the concept of 'neutrality' is useful in such circumstances; and that therefore the Soviet lexicon should contain the word.

Of course, the Russians will not be prepared to accept that, in a given dispute, all those countries are automatically to be considered 'neutral', which are not an actual party to the issue. Belgium is not directly concerned with the Berlin question; Belgium has no troops there; but the USSR would still not regard the Belgians as 'neutral' in any dispute over Berlin, because Belgium is a member of NATO. This, however, is obvious commonsense: the West holds the same view of 'neutrality'; and therefore the West would clearly not consider some such country as Poland, for instance, to be 'neutral' on the Berlin question either.

We turn now to the sort of neutrality which is neutral both in peace and in war. This is called, in English, 'permanent neutrality' or 'perpetual neutrality';[4] and, in Russian, *postoyannyi nyeitralityet*. The Russian expression is a literal translation of the English; but the two meanings do not exactly coincide, as will be explained below.

Nevertheless, in their *broad* outlines the Eastern and Western definitions of 'perpetual neutrality' do certainly agree. A country is said to be 'perpetually neutral' by both East and West alike, if it not only refrains from taking part in a war, but also refrains in peacetime from such actions as might, in the event of war, draw it into the conflict. Consequently, it must not take part in any military alliance; nor allow its territory to be used for bases for foreign troops; nor for storage depots for foreign arms and equipment. Furthermore, although a 'perpetually neutral' country has the right to self-defence (and hence to the maintenance of armed forces, and to the building of fortifications along its frontier), nevertheless, according to an authoritative Soviet definition of the Khrushchev era,[5] no country has any claim to be accredited with 'perpetual neutrality' if it equips its forces with nuclear or atomic weapons.

This last point, of course, is one which distinguishes (or, at least, distinguished) the Soviet concept of 'perpetual neutrality' from that of the West. So, too, does the fact that the USSR does not regard membership of UNO as being incompatible with such neutrality; although the Charter of the United Nations, to which all members are bound to adhere, obliges those who subscribe to it to 'take such action by air, sea or land forces as may be necessary to maintain international peace and security', when such action has been decided upon by the Security Council.[6]

It is the Soviet Union's declared view that this is no obstacle to the practice of 'perpetual neutrality'; and the same authority specifically states that Switzerland is wrong in refraining from applying for UN membership because of it.[7]

There are only nine countries which, according to the Soviet Union, have ever actually enjoyed the status of 'perpetual neutrality'; and the Russians reckon, as we shall see in a minute, that at least five of these can no longer be said to do so. It should be added, however, that, in 1920, the Soviet Union would have liked to have seen both Lithuania and Estonia recognized as 'perpetual neutrals'; and that it was only the fact that the co-operation of the other powers was not forthcoming which prevented this from happening, Lithuania and Estonia themselves being eager for it.[8] There were good, solid, practical reasons why the USSR should have wished for the 'perpetual neutrality' of these countries, as there also were in 1958, when she suggested the same status for Japan. This, however, is not an appropriate moment at which to discuss these reasons; and a detailed examination of the Soviet motives for making such proposals must therefore wait until later in this chapter (see pp. 182–8).

The nine 'perpetually neutral' countries which are given in the Soviet reference books as having actually existed are: Switzerland, Sweden,

Belgium, Luxembourg, Honduras (1907), Albania(1913),Iceland(1918), Austria (1955), and Cambodia (1957). By now, of course, Belgium and Luxembourg have forfeited their status by joining NATO; and Albania ceased to be 'perpetually neutral' when she entered the Communist bloc. It was the granting of permission to NATO to station troops on her territory which deprived Iceland of her title, while similar permission with regard to American troops robbed Honduras of hers. That leaves Switzerland, Sweden, Austria, and Cambodia as the only ones with any pretensions to 'perpetual neutrality' at the moment.

In fact, in the late 1950s and early 1960s, both Sweden and Switzerland considered acquiring atomic weapons for their forces; and this, as the Russians then saw it, 'gravely compromised' their status as 'perpetual neutrals'.[9] To the best of my knowledge, however, no Soviet official has ever declared that they forfeited that status completely; and there are a number of passages in recent Soviet writing where both countries are classified as 'neutral' without any qualification whatever.

On the other hand, it remains true that, until the recent events in Cambodia, the only two countries which were, in Soviet official eyes, *unquestionably* 'perpetually neutral' were that country and Austria; and it is Austria and Cambodia, therefore, which exemplify the concept of neutrality in Soviet official thinking in much the same sort of way that Switzerland does in the political thinking of the West.[10]

Nevertheless, a country can be genuinely 'perpetually neutral' in Soviet eyes, and still not be regarded by the USSR as neutral on every question. For the Marxism-Leninism which moulds Soviet thinking sees to it that the Russian leaders can never entirely forget the 'class' structure of the particular country concerned. In other words, Austria may be 'perpetual neutrality' personified, but she is also capitalist.

In some circumstances, this may not matter. The Soviet Union and America, for example, may be engaged in a dispute; and they may be in search of neutral territory on which to hold a conference. In this respect, Austria would be very suitable. Indeed, in 1961, it may be remembered, it was Austria which was chosen as the site for a meeting between Kennedy and Khrushchev; and it was also Austria which, in the same year, was officially asked by the Soviet Union if she would be prepared to provide the United Nations with a permanent headquarters in Vienna, since New York was considered by the Russians (and especially by Khrushchev) to be too unneutral to serve any longer as a base for the impartial international organization which UNO was intended to be.

On the other hand, if it were not just a question of playing host to a summit conference, but of acting as mediator in a dispute, then the fact that Austria is capitalist could easily mean that the Soviet Union would *not* regard her as neutral on a given issue. For instance, let us suppose that a dispute arose concerning the future of one of the trust territories of the United Nations. The territory in question, we will imagine, was on the verge of being granted its independence; and, just at that moment, some of its inhabitants demanded that the new State should be socialist in character; and that it should start by 'nationalizing' its industry, its agriculture, its banking, and its foreign trade. Such a move would be opposed by a number of the members of UNO, especially America, but would almost certainly be supported by the Soviet Union. In the debate that followed, suggestions might be made that a 'neutral' nation should be appointed as a mediator; but in a dispute of this nature, which concerns a choice between a 'bourgeois' and a 'socialist' form of society, capitalist Austria would not be considered neutral by the USSR, although her general status of 'perpetual neutrality' would, even in Soviet eyes, remain unquestioned.

But, in order to acquire a more complete understanding of the Soviet concept of neutrality, we must now turn from a consideration of the status which Austria at present enjoys, and enquire into why and how she came to acquire that status.

Austria's 'perpetual neutrality' dates from 1955; for it was in that year that the Soviet Union quite unexpectedly announced that it was ready to sign a peace treaty with the Austrian Republic. The Second World War had ended ten years previously; but, owing to disagreements among the victorious Allies, by 1955 it had still proved impossible to formulate a treaty which they all were prepared to accept. In the West, it was generally believed that the chief reason for this unfortunate state of affairs was the Soviet Union's obstructiveness; but whether this was true or not, the fact remained that, until 1955, there was no peace treaty, and that Austria therefore continued to be occupied by the troops of Britain, France, America, and the Soviet Union.

From the military point of view, this particular situation was extremely advantageous to the West. A glance at the map will show that, with the western half of Austria in the occupation of the British, the French, and the Americans, it was easy for NATO to move its troops from West Germany to Italy and *vice versa*. The Soviet Union, however, derived no corresponding advantage; for, with Yugoslavia out of the Soviet orbit, there was no territory south of Austria which needed reinforcement by the Red Army, and therefore no call for the USSR to have transit routes across Lower Austria. Troop movements between Czechoslovakia and Hungary were easy enough, even if Austrian territory should be denied to the Soviet Union. But if, by some means, Austrian territory could be denied to the West, considerable problems of supply and reinforcement would at once be created for the latter, as they would no longer be able to use the excellent road and rail links between Munich, Innsbruck and Verona (where a NATO headquarters had been set up).

Moreover, as it so happened, the state immediately to the west of Austria was 'perpetually neutral' Switzerland; and Swiss neutrality isolated, militarily speaking, a great deal of the northern frontier of Italy. If Austria were to become 'perpetually neutral' too, NATO troops would have to make a very considerable detour, if they needed to move from Germany to Italy, or from Italy to Germany.

It is therefore no wonder that, as the Soviet Union saw it, the essential precondition for the signing of any peace treaty was that Austria in future would have to accept the status of 'perpetual neutrality'; nor that, when once the Austrian Government had given assurances that it would do so, the Russians were ready to sign.

And sign they did—on 15 May 1955. And the net result of it all (at least, from the purely military point of view) was a considerable weakening of the Western position, and a considerable strengthening of the Soviet.

The lesson to be drawn from a study of this particular episode is that, while neutrality itself, viewed as a Hegelian abstract, may well be perfectly neutral, nevertheless the *effect* of neutrality can be, as the Russians see it, greatly to the benefit of one side or another, and hence to be *un*neutral.[11]

This view of neutrality (or, rather, of its effects) is by no means a new one, so far as the USSR is concerned. The Soviet Union did not suddenly acquire it in the Malenkov or Khrushchev period, nor even in Stalin's time. On the contrary, a careful examination of Soviet foreign policy, right from the very beginning of the Soviet state, will show that the Soviet leaders have always believed that neutrality could be made to produce effects which would be 'unneutral' in their favour,[12] and that they have frequently taken practical steps to achieve this. A consideration of these various episodes of Soviet foreign policy must therefore form the next part of our enquiry.

But, before doing so, it is essential to point out to the reader that the particular episodes in question can only be properly understood, if he approaches them in the light of one particular belief; and if he realizes that this particular belief has lain at the roots of Soviet political thinking from the October Revolution right up to the present day. The belief in question is that the USSR, from the very first moment of its foundation, has never been militarily superior to the West taken as a whole; that, at best, it has achieved military parity with it; but that usually its military potential has been markedly *inferior* to the West's, except, of course, in certain local areas at certain periods of time. Furthermore, the reader must bear in mind that the USSR, as a result of its Marxism-Leninism, believed that the capitalist nations (which, with their colonies and dependencies, hemmed in the Soviet Union on all the four points of the compass) would sooner or later gang up together, in order to crush the world's sole communist state.

I must repeat here, at the risk of wearying the reader, that, when one is dealing with a belief (or, rather, with the results of a belief) it is really scarcely material whether the belief is true or false. If a man firmly believes that something is true, he will act as though it *were* true: it may, in reality, be false; but, unless you can convince him that this is so, he will not alter his behaviour. A friend of mine committed suicide because he believed that he had cancer. It transpired at the autopsy that, in fact, he had no such thing; but his life was extinguished just the same.

So, too, in the case of the Soviet leaders. The fact that they may have been wrong to have believed in their own military weakness, and in the aggressive tendencies of the West, has nothing to do with whether they did, or do, believe in it; nor with the actions that they have taken, and will take, as a result of these particular beliefs. Some of these actions, as I hope to show, have been concerned with the concept of neutrality and, in particular, with certain advantages which this concept could be made to bring them; and it is such actions which it must now be our business to discuss.

It may be remembered that we have already come across instances of the Soviet liking for neutrality as early as 1920, in connection with the Soviet peace treaties with Lithuania and Estonia. The latter two countries, which had only recently achieved their independence, wanted a status of 'perpetual neutrality', which would, they thought, be the best possible means of ensuring that their new-found independence should endure. As we have seen, 'perpetual neutrality' normally requires those powers which are most concerned with the prospective neutral, to enter into solemn guarantees that they will respect its 'perpetual neutrality'; and that, in addition, they will do all that they can to see that it is respected by others.

In the situation of 1920, such a proposal suited the Russians well. If Lithuania and Estonia were indeed recognized as 'perpetual neutrals' by the capitalist powers, this would automatically prevent those powers from setting up bases, or manoeuvring troops, in the two countries in question. Since both of those countries had a common frontier with Russia, this meant, in effect, that two neutralized buffer zones would be created in a region which was within easy striking distance of such major cities of the USSR as Leningrad and Smolensk. It would certainly have been extremely advantageous to the Bolsheviks, if Latvia too had desired 'perpetual neutrality'; since Latvia separates Lithuania and Estonia, and Latvia's acceptance of the same status as the others would have automatically brought into being a continuous strip of 'perpetually neutral' territory about seven hundred miles long and, on an average, approximately two hundred miles deep, in what was, for the Soviet Union, an extremely sensitive area.

As things turned out, Latvia was not interested in 'perpetual neutrality'; while, in the case of the two countries which were eager for it (Lithuania and Estonia), the capitalist powers were not prepared to join in the required guarantees. The project therefore lapsed.

But the lapse was only temporary. The USSR had come to appreciate keenly the very real advantage which neutrality could bring (in the particular sense in which 'neutrality' was interpreted), and a wish to secure them underlay a great deal of Soviet diplomatic activity throughout the 'twenties and 'thirties. These efforts were, in general, directed to persuading as many states as possible, and especially all those which had a common frontier with Russia, to sign a treaty of non-aggression and neutrality with the USSR.

The countries with which these particular pacts were signed were: Afghanistan; China; Finland; Iran; Latvia; Lithuania; Estonia;[13] Poland; and Turkey (all countries which border the Soviet Union); Germany, who was a friend at the time of signing,[14] as well as being a past (and potential) aggressor; France, with whom the original 'non-aggression treaty' was soon to be extended into a 'treaty of mutual assistance'; Italy, who in 1933 (the date of the signing of the treaty) was the only established fascist state in the world, and whose military might at that time impressed all Europe.

These treaties have usually been the subject of rather contemptuous comment by Western writers, who indeed frequently completely ignore the element of neutrality contained in them, and then refer to them somewhat disparagingly as 'a series of non-aggression pacts'. Indeed, the general tone of the comments of such writers clearly implies that no sane man would value a non-aggression pact at more than that of the paper on which it is written; and that, furthermore, the fact that Soviet diplomats worked so eagerly over so many years in order to get such agreements is merely a proof that the Soviet diplomacy of the time was very inept.

But a look at the actual texts of these agreements should dispel this particular illusion. The main practical purpose of the treaties was not to pledge non-aggression; nor even to get each party to the treaty to promise to stay neutral (in the strict sense of 'absolute neutrality') if either of them were attacked by someone else. Their main purpose was very much more than that: it was to get both parties to agree that they would not join any political or military alliance, nor take part in any financial or commercial boycott, which might be organized against either one of them by a third party. The Soviet Union, in other words,

G

might not have been able to persuade these various countries to opt for 'perpetual neutrality' in general; but she was able to persuade them to promise to be 'perpetually neutral' so far as the USSR was concerned.

And these promises were not without their value. For, although a pledge not to commit aggression against another country can be torn up (if it is thought worth bothering to tear it up) two seconds before one's tanks cross over into the other country's territory; and although a pledge to observe neutrality if the other country should be attacked by a third party (that is, a pledge not to help the attacker) can always be abrogated at any particular moment at which it is thought expedient to do so; nevertheless a pledge not to join in a political or military alliance aimed at the other country, though it can certainly be disowned every bit as easily as the other promises, acts as a kind of strategic trip-wire, in a way that the others do not.

For, even supposing that Estonia, for example, had violated her pact, and had joined a military alliance aimed against Russia, no immediate harm would have come to the Soviet Union. Actual harm comes from an actual invasion; and though an invasion may result from such an alliance, it cannot occur simultaneously with the formation of it. Between the signing of the alliance and the launching of an invasion there must be an interval of weeks, probably of months; and this will serve to alert the threatened party, and give him time to take the necessary counter-measures.

Of course, in actual fact the Soviet leaders never seriously imagined that Estonia would go mad and, with a population of just over 1,000,000, would attack the 153,000,000 of the Soviet Union (the population of the USSR at that time). They did, however, think it a distinct possibility that the capitalist powers, yearning to destroy communism, might try to use the territory of Estonia as a convenient base for the invasion of the USSR. But before any actual invasion could be launched, Estonia would first have to agree: in other words, Estonia would first have to join some kind of military and political alliance. But this would give a warning to the Soviet Union; and the USSR could promptly inform Estonia that such an alliance was a breach of her treaty of neutrality; and, if the warning were unheeded, could invade and seize Estonia before her capitalist allies could come to her aid. (It will be remembered that this was, in essence, exactly the sequence of events in 1939.)[15] Furthermore, the knowledge that the Russians could easily do this would act as a powerful restraint on Estonian statesmen, supposing that they ever should find themselves tempted to assist the capitalists in the way described above (which, so far as we know, they did not).

But one of the effects of Hitler's invasion of Russia was to put an end to Soviet experiments with neutrality, such as have been described above. If the word was ever on Russian lips during the war years, it was only in connection with 'neutrality in wartime', that concept which we considered at the beginning of this chapter; and it was usually in connection with some country (Sweden, for example) whose practice of it did not accord with Soviet notions of what neutrality should be.

After the war, however, the USSR reverted to her former practice; and, on three important occasions, she tried to arrange for 'perpetual neutrality' to be imposed on various countries. The countries concerned were Austria, Germany and Japan. We have already considered the case of Austria, and seen the advantages for the USSR which followed from the acceptance of these proposals. Considerable advantages, too, would have accrued to the Soviet Union, if she had been able to persuade Japan and Germany to follow the Austrian example.

The Soviet plan for the neutralization of Germany was put forward in 1952, when the question of the rearming of the German Federal Republic, and of her incorporation into NATO, was beginning to be discussed in the West. In the case of Japan, it was the proposed revision of the American-Japanese Treaty of Mutual Co-operation and Security which lay behind the Soviet 'neutralization' proposals; because if the revision of the treaty were brought to a successful conclusion, American troops could stay in Japan, which would otherwise have had to leave.[16]

There would therefore have been considerable advantages accruing to the Soviet Union, if in either case her proposal had been accepted. For, in the case of Japan, American forces would have had to evacuate that country, and would no longer have been able to threaten the Soviet Far East from a distance of a mere three hundred miles or so. In the case of Germany, not merely would German territory have had to be evacuated, but the use of the twelve divisions proposed for the Bundeswehr would have been denied to NATO Headquarters. It is worth observing that, in both instances, when once the desired advantages were no longer obtainable,[17] Soviet interest in the 'perpetual neutrality' of these countries 'withered away', and has never been heard of again.

And this, indeed, is the nub of the Soviet position. Since the USSR does not consider neutrality to be a valid intellectual concept (and the fact that it has, or can have, effects which are quite unneutral is seen by the Russians as proof that their view of the matter is correct), the Soviet Union has never shown any enthusiasm for neutrality as such, but only for any advantages which it can bring. And these advantages are, at best, secondary. Neutrality can do no more than deny territory to an opponent; it cannot bring that territory within the orbit of the Soviet Union, which is the primary long-term advantage, so far as the USSR is concerned. The Russians have therefore always regarded proposals for 'perpetual neutrality' as a *pis aller*, and have put them forward only when they themselves were negotiating from a position of weakness. There was no Soviet proposal for the 'neutralization' of Poland, Romania, Hungary, or Bulgaria at the end of the Second World War, nor for that of Georgia at the end of the First World War, when the USSR was in a strong position with regard to these particular countries. On the other hand, the middle 1920s and the early 1930s saw the lowest ebb of Soviet military potential; and it was those years that witnessed the signature of the bulk of the so-called 'non-aggression pacts'. Similarly, the Russian proposals for the 'perpetual neutrality' of Japan and Germany were put forward only in an attempt to prevent the accretion to the Western military strength of the war potential of those two powerful states, and only because the USSR was in no position to prevent this happening by other means.

It is an obvious corollary from what has been said in the two preceding paragraphs that the USSR will have nothing to do with any form of neutrality that does *not* confer an advantage on the Soviet Union. In 1956, for instance, at the time of the Hungarian Uprising, Imre Nagy, the head of the new government, put forward proposals that Hungary should be neutralized, and should leave the Warsaw Pact. It is generally agreed that it was the formulation of these proposals which caused the Soviet Government to send in troops. A neutral Hungary would have meant a weakening of the Soviet position; and this the Soviet Union would not accept.

The reader, who has been kind enough to follow carefully this somewhat lengthy disquisition on the Soviet attitudes towards neutrality and neutralization, will at any rate have his reward in this final section, when we come to consider the Soviet view of 'the neutrals'. This is the phrase used frequently in the West to describe those countries which belong (or were belonging at the moment of which one is writing or speaking) neither to the Communist nor to the Western bloc. Thus, Yugoslavia, Egypt, India, Ghana, and Ethiopia have all at various times been described as 'neutrals' by Western writers, because, during the period in question, they were trying to avoid giving active support either to the West or to the Soviet Union.

The USSR, however, did not follow this usage, at least until very recently.[18] Soviet writers did not describe such countries as being 'neutral' (except when addressing a non-communist audience—a point which will be considered below) because it was the USSR's profound belief (for reasons which we have sufficiently considered above) that they were not neutral at all. Thus, in the case of the five examples given in the preceding paragraph, the first of them, Yugoslavia, is (and was) regarded by the Soviet Union as being a socialist country; and therefore, in Russian eyes, so far from being neutral, it is basically pro-communist, despite the occasional disagreements which have arisen over matters of policy.[19] The other four countries are classified by Soviet thinking as belonging to the National Liberation Movement,[20] and therefore as being (whether consciously or unconsciously) in transit from their former state, which was one of subjugation to the imperialists, to their future, final, and inevitable state of membership of the 'socialist camp'. Consequently, Soviet terminology could not possibly describe their outlook as being neutral; and, in fact, until very recently, it has never done so.

By the end of the 1950s, however, the Soviet Union began to take serious interest in a new movement in international politics which, in English, is termed 'neutralism'.[21]

The chief points about 'neutralism' of which the reader should be aware is that it is not the same as 'neutrality'; nor is a 'neutralist' country a 'neutral'. When it comes to deciding what 'neutralism' *is*, however (as distinct from what it is *not*), considerable difficulties arise, because not even the 'neutralist' countries themselves can agree on an exact definition. However, it appears to be the general view of the experts that there are four main strands in 'neutralist' foreign policy, and that these can be summarized as follows:

(i) a refusal to support either side in the Cold War, and consequently a refusal to grant facilities to either side for military bases on their territories;

(ii) anti-colonialism;

(iii) support for world disarmament;

(iv) a demand for greater 'neutralist' representation on the various policy-making bodies of the UN.

By the logic of Soviet thinking, all these policies, to the extent to which they can be implemented, are believed to work to the advantage of the 'socialist camp', and to the grave disadvantage of the West. For, to take them in the reverse order to that in which they are given above, if a 'neutralist' country is allotted a seat on a UN organization, the former member whom it thereby displaces is bound to be (as the Russians see it) either one of the major imperialist nations or else one of their stooges. In either case, Western influence at the United Nations is seriously weakened as a result.

In the case of (iii), a call for world disarmament is almost always a prominent feature of any important Soviet statement on international affairs. The reasons for this have been authoritatively discussed in a number of Western publications; so here it is only necessary to point out that this particular point of 'neutralist' policy closely resembles a point of Soviet policy; and that therefore it is obviously welcome to the Soviet Union.

Anti-colonialism, the second of the 'neutralist' policies, is also clearly agreeable to the USSR. Ever since Lenin, it has been a cardinal principle of belief for the Soviet leadership that the colonies form the 'Achilles heel' of the West; that the loss of the colonies would cripple the West industrially, by depriving it of its sources of cheap labour and raw materials; and that the colonies themselves, once they had been freed from the yoke of the imperialists, were historically destined to continue to evolve until they attained socialism (the Marxist-Leninist form of socialism, that is), thereby tilting the balance of power still more pronouncedly in the communists' direction.

As for the first of the 'neutralist' policies, as given in the summary above (which consists of their declared intention not to give support to either side in the Cold War, and not to allow their territories to be used as bases by either the capitalists or communists), this policy, which seems to the 'neutralists' themselves to be the one specifically neutral element in their programme, seems to the Soviet Union, on the other hand, to be totally unneutral—and, as luck would have it, to be totally unneutral in favour of the USSR.

For the objective result of refusing to allow either East or West to maintain military bases on 'neutralist' territory is, as the Soviet Union sees it, gravely to weaken the West. This is because the USSR has never had bases in any of the 'neutralist' countries, except possibly one.[22] Three of the other 'neutralists' have never had either Eastern or Western bases, though they have been much under Western influence; but all the remaining twenty-one of the twenty-five countries which took part in the 'neutralist' Summit Conference at Belgrade in 1961 (and which may therefore be taken to be the bulk of the 'neutralist' movement) had all had Western military bases on their territory for the greater part of the hundred years which preceded the Belgrade Conference, and all of them were occupied by Western troops at the end of the Second World War.[23]

But once these countries agreed to deny their territories to the armies of both East and West, the only actual losers of the scheme must necessarily be the West. And, in the early days of 'neutralism', the loss was particularly important, since the Soviet Union at that time had the lead in long-range rockets, while the West's strength lay in medium- and short-range missiles. But such missiles obviously had to be launched from comparatively near their targets, and one effect of 'neutralism' was to make it less easy to do so.

It took some time before the true significance of 'neutralism' penetrated the Soviet consciousness. There is no entry for it to be found, for instance, in any of the standard Soviet reference books published before 1961. Until such time as the new movement was accorded recognition by the Party, therefore, those countries which did not belong either to the 'imperialist bloc' or to the 'socialist camp' had to be described by Soviet writers as 'members of the National Liberation Movement', with the phrases 'the young independent states' or 'the Afro-Asian countries' as occasional alternatives. Western writers of the time often described them, as we have seen, as 'the neutrals'; but that phrase, as we have also seen, was ideologically repugnant to the communists, and consequently was never used by them.

The above statement needs to be qualified a little. It is true that, when writing for non-communist audiences, Soviet publicists of the time employed the word 'neutral' much as we Westerners do, simply because the only alternative expression available to them, 'the National Liberation Movement', would not have been readily intelligible to a non-communist. Thus, L. Modjoryan, writing in 1956 in the *New Times*, uses the word 'neutral' as freely as a Westerner would, and with exactly the same connotation; but then *New Times* is a Soviet publication which is printed in many languages, and expressly designed for an international readership.[24] The same sort of thing can be said about E. A. Korovin's article which appeared in *International Affairs* in 1958. Here again was a Soviet publicist writing specifically for an international audience; and here again 'neutral' was frequently used in its non-communist meaning.[25]

Moreover, it sometimes happened that a Soviet writer used the word 'neutral' in the particular Western sense we are now discussing, even though he was writing exclusively for the attention of a Soviet audience. V. P. Nikhamin's contributions to *Myezhdunarodniye Otnoshyeniya; Vnyeshnyaya Politika SSSR 1950–1959* are a good example of this. But then V. P. Nikhamin is a highly sophisticated Russian, with a cosmopolitan outlook and vocabulary. Not only does he use other Russian words (e.g. *kontrol'*) in their Western, not in their Russian, sense; but he is also sufficiently eccentric, from the Soviet point of view, to quote repeatedly *Keesing's Contemporary Archives* as a primary source. One must therefore clearly regard his use of 'neutral' as being the officially tolerated aberration of an ideologically impeccable writer, and not as a sign of a general acceptance of his usage by the Party leadership. Indeed, the Soviet leadership, it should be noted, *never* used 'neutral' in this sense during the period in question; nor has it ever done so since, to the best of my knowledge, apart from an occasional example to be found in some of Khrushchev's outbursts. In the whole of Brezhnev's long speech to the Twenty-Third Party Congress, for instance, there was no mention made of the word 'neutral'; while Kosygin, in his speech to the Supreme Soviet of the same year, used it once only, and then with reference to Austria. Both men's speeches at the Twenty-Fourth Party Congress similarly eschewed 'neutral'.

But, by about 1960, the Soviet leaders had come to believe that the effects of 'neutralism' were likely to be extremely beneficial to the communist bloc, for reasons that have been outlined above. They had also come to realize that (contrary to the Marxist-Leninists' original assumption) the independence which had been granted to the new nations by the imperialists was completely genuine; and that, if such nations wanted to turn 'neutralist', they were perfectly free to do so.

The USSR, once it had realized this, welcomed the new concept with enthusiasm; and 'neutralist' and 'neutralism' are therefore to be found scattered with a free hand in any Soviet writing after this date. So, too, are their internationally accepted synonyms, 'positive neutrality' and 'non-alignment'.

It is true that most of the 'neutralists' themselves prefer to use either of the two latter terms (which they regard as being completely synonymous), and to relegate to the background the word 'neutralism' (which they regard as somehow less appropriate than the other two); but Soviet practice follows them in this, and prefers most of all the term 'positive neutrality', then 'non-alignment', and places third the original term 'neutralism'. When it comes to the choice of an adjective, however, then 'neutralist' is the greatest favourite (Khrushchev indeed made frequent use of it); but that is perhaps because the Russian equivalents for 'non-aligned' and 'positively neutral' are extremely cumbersome expressions.[26]

The result of this Soviet enthusiasm has been that Soviet writers now know what 'neutralism' means. Moreover, when writing for Soviet audiences, they now *always* put 'neutralist' when they mean 'neutralist', and they usually put 'neutral' when they mean 'neutral'. It is true that they very occasionally put 'neutral' when they mean 'neutralist'; but they never fall into the opposite error, and put 'neutralist' when they mean 'neutral'. How indeed could they do so? It would be to deny their Marxism-Leninism.[27]

The West, too, for its part, has begun to appreciate that there is a real distinction between 'neutralist' and 'neutral'; and serious Western writers nowadays are, like the Russians, also usually scrupulous about observing it.

Furthermore, they are usually a great deal more scholarly in their approach to it. By contrast, Soviet writers, until very recently, invariably portrayed the 'neutralists' as being, on every issue, in complete accord with the Russians; and in those instances where, in fact, this was not true, and where it was not possible to give the contrary impression by only a minor reshuffle of the material, the desired effect was made on the Soviet reader by the simple process of leaving the incident out. This is good propaganda, but it is not scholarship.

It remains only to note that the expressions 'neutralist' and 'positive neutrality' have not yet found their way into the most formal of Soviet political pronouncements (into those, that is to say, where the Soviet communist leaders are speaking to their fellow-communists). Neither Khrushchev's speech to the Twenty-Second Party Congress in 1961, for instance, nor the highly important *Programme of the Communist Party of the Soviet Union*, also published in that year, contain so much as a single instance of these neologisms; although Khrushchev in the same year, but on less formal occasions, was using them with enthusiasm. They are not to be found, either, in Brezhnev's speech at the Twenty-Third Party Congress in 1966, nor in Kosygin's speech which followed, nor in the speeches of either man at the Twenty-Fourth Party Congress. At all three congresses, the orthodox term 'the National Liberation Movement' was invariably used instead.

Just recently, however, as the Brezhnev and Kosygin era approaches the end of the first decade of its existence, there are signs that its attitude towards neutrality and neutralism is very slightly changing. What appears to be happening, on the somewhat scanty evidence so far available, is not a reformulation of the classical Leninist definition of what neutrality means to a communist, so much as a loss of interest by the Party in the whole subject.

This is particularly true of 'neutralism'. Indeed when, in 1970, the 'non-aligned' (or 'neutralist') countries held their summit conference in Lusaka, *Pravda* gave it only the most scanty coverage. Despite the fact that fifty-four countries took part, that sixteen of them were represented by their Heads of State and another twelve by their Vice-Presidents or Prime Ministers (so that the countries themselves clearly thought it important), *Pravda* devoted less than half a column to it on each of the three days when it was in session. Yet the countries taking part were typical 'neutralists' of the kind which *Pravda* has in the past so lavishly supported.

The year 1971 saw the publication of a new edition of *Diplomaticheskii Slovar'* (*A Dictionary of Diplomacy*). In it the space allotted to neutrality proper has been cut by about 70 per cent; and there is no entry for 'neutralism' at all. 'Non-alignment' now has an entry to itself, but the space allotted to 'positive neutrality' has been very sharply reduced. Interestingly enough, the two definitions are no longer completely synonymous: 'positive neutrality' is depicted as confining itself to abstention from joining any military bloc, and to active struggle to avert war; while 'non-alignment' is portrayed as being, in addition to the above, anti-colonialist, anti-racist, in favour of general and complete disarmament, and in favour of the abolition of all forms of nuclear weapons. This, no doubt, explains why it is allotted more space in the dictionary than 'positive neutrality'.

If this might appear to indicate a shift of emphasis by the Soviet Communist Party, the sponsors of the dictionary, away from 'positive neutrality' towards 'non-alignment', and a desire to inject the latter with

G*

a different meaning, I can only say that the position is reversed if one turns to consult *Kratkii Politicheskii Slovar'* (*A Short Dictionary of Politics*), which was also published under Party sponsorship in the same month of the same year as the other dictionary.

Here there is no entry at all for 'non-alignment', nor for 'positive neutrality', despite a statement that an entry for the latter has been given a place in the dictionary.[28] There is, however, a fairly full entry for 'neutralism', which describes it as meaning abstention from military blocs and alliances, strong opposition to imperialist aggression, and support for peace, international security and disarmament.[29] Both dictionaries were passed for printing within a few days of each other, so that there can be little question of a change in events giving rise to a change in interpretation.

Of course, there is no doubt that, of the two, the *Dictionary of Diplomacy* is by far the more authoritative. Not only does it run to three volumes of approximately 600 pages each, as compared to the one volume of 295 pages which makes up the *Dictionary of Politics*, but its editor-in-chief is A. A. Gromyko, the Soviet Foreign Minister. Nevertheless, in the old days such divergencies of treatment on the then important subject of neutrality would never have been tolerated, nor would the editorial slackness which has manifested itself in those two references to articles which do not exist.

What seems to have happened is that, by the early 1970s, the Politburo had come to the conclusion that the 'neutralist' movement was not going to effect those radical, pro-Soviet changes in international affairs which the Politburo of the 1960s had expected of it. Consequently, interest slackened. Nor, today, are there areas of the world in which the USSR shows signs of wishing to implant 'perpetual neutrality', or indeed neutrality of any kind. Consequently, neutrality, perpetual neutrality, neutralism and non-alignment are all somewhat at a discount at the moment as a tool for promoting Soviet foreign policy; and this is reflected in the smaller space allotted to them in the Soviet dictionaries, and in the lack of concern which the editors of those dictionaries display towards these particular concepts. At some time in the future, they may revert to an importance as a tool of Soviet foreign policy comparable to that which they enjoyed in the Khrushchev era; and if they do, they will be allotted a comparable coverage in future editions of the dictionaries. Meanwhile, all one can say is that the essential meanings of these words have remained unchanged, but that the emphasis placed upon them has considerably lessened.

# 5    Theory and Practice

Theories should be tested against facts. The last stage in our enquiry must therefore be to test the theories outlined in the preceding chapters against the facts of Soviet history; and such a testing consequently forms the substance of this final chapter.

The theories enunciated may be conveniently summarized as follows:

(i) Until such time as communism is established over the whole globe, of which event the total abolition of war will be a desirable and an inevitable concomitant, war will continue to be regarded by the Soviet Union as a useful tool of Soviet foreign policy and as a valuable agent of the world-wide revolutionary process. (War in this connection naturally means civil war and wars of national liberation as well as the 'normal' wars between independent sovereign states.)

But although valuable as a tool, war will only be selected by the Kremlin leaders for solving a particular problem of international relations if it seems to be the tool best adapted for securing the objective they desire. Implicit in this is the premiss that war will only be deliberately begun if victory seems to be certain: a defeat in war would *not* allow the Russians to attain their desired aim. But if victory seems certain, and if in addition, having regard to all the circumstances in question, war seems the tool best adapted for securing the Russians' goal, and if moreover that goal is important enough and profitable enough, the Soviet leaders will not be restrained by any considerations of morality (whether 'bourgeois' morality or 'proletarian' morality) from indulging in aggression against other countries, in the Western sense of 'aggression'.

Notwithstanding the above, the Soviet Union will do all that she can to avoid becoming embroiled in a *nuclear* war; because then, whether or not she emerged victorious, she would herself have received hideously unacceptable damage. (This conclusion would not apply, of course, and the whole of this paragraph would no longer necessarily be valid, if she discovered a 'secret weapon' of such a sort that in some way or other it could prevent her from suffering this damage.)

Finally, if the USSR were to be attacked by another country, she would prosecute the resulting war with the utmost vigour, whether or not it turned into nuclear war, and whether or not she believed she would be victorious.

(ii) In the Soviet view, there can be no such thing as 'peace', in the sense of 'peace and goodwill' or 'peace and co-operation', between socialist and capitalist countries. Between such countries, 'peace' can be no more than 'an absence of fighting'. The Soviet Union will resort to peace with the capitalist countries either when, for one reason or another, an open struggle seems likely to be unprofitable; or when it has become desirable for the Soviet Union to break off a struggle in which she is already engaged, and to use the resulting 'peace' as an opportunity to regroup, replenish and reinforce her armies.

She will also engage in 'peace' with capitalist countries whenever she thinks that to refrain from fighting them is the best means of attaining her long-term ends in the particular circumstances of the time; and during such periods of 'peace', she may well devote much effort to promoting trade, scientific co-operation and other such forms of contact. In Soviet eyes, human society is a function of economics; and excellence in economic performance is an essential precondition for human beings to rise from the miseries of capitalism to the joys of communism. The Soviet Union has not yet attained true communism and does not claim to have done so: furthermore, just at the moment, Soviet economic performance is in many respects inferior to that of the capitalists. Trade, therefore, with capitalist countries and exchanges of scientific information with them are obvious means of improving the Soviet performance.

(iii) Neutrality is not a concept that is recognized by Marxist theory: 'He who is not with me, is against me'. Nevertheless, in practice (as distinct from theory) several sorts of neutrality are acknowledged by the Soviet Foreign Ministry.

Only two of these are relevant to this present chapter. The first is the one that we Westerners ordinarily mean by neutrality: a war is raging, and a particular country has decided to take no part in it; such a country is neutral. The USSR makes use of this kind of neutrality when it suits her purpose, as in the case of the Vietnam War; but when, on the contrary, it suits her purpose to take part in a war (as it did for instance in 1945 in the case of the war against Japan), she then rejects neutrality as a tool of her foreign policy and turns to war instead.

The second kind of neutrality which is relevant to this present chapter is 'perpetual neutrality'. The Soviet Union has never herself adopted 'perpetual neutrality'; but from time to time she has been prepared—indeed she has been positively anxious—for certain other countries to adopt it. This, however, has only happened in those areas where the USSR has had no hope in the then foreseeable future of acquiring significant influence; and where at the same time there was considerable risk, if 'perpetual neutrality' were *not* adopted, of the country in question entering the orbit of the West. In other words, 'perpetual neutrality' from the Soviet point of view is always a last resort.

If we now proceed to compare these theories with the realities of Soviet history from the October Revolution to the Soviet invasion of Finland in November 1939, we shall see that from the end of 1920 until the end of 1939 there were only three occasions during that whole period when the Soviet Union deliberately embarked upon a war. The first was when in February 1921 the Red Army invaded and conquered Georgia, which at that time was an independent Menshevik republic whose existence *de jure* as well as *de facto* had been recognized by the Entente Powers.

In this operation were present all the elements which, in our theoretical exposition, we agreed were necessary before the USSR would be willing to go to war as a means of attaining her objectives. First, victory was certain: the tiny forces of the Menshevik Georgian government could be no match for the hordes of the Red Army. Second, foreign intervention in support of the Georgian Republic could be dismissed as virtually impossible. The German and Turkish forces which had been occupying Transcaucasia had been withdrawn to their own homelands as a result of the collapse of the Central Powers in November 1918; British troops, which had replaced them, had left by 1920. By February 1921, there was no armed force of any significance in the immediate area of Georgia; and no likelihood of any such force being sent by the Western governments.

Militarily, therefore, the task set by the Bolsheviks to the commanders of the Red Army was extremely easy of accomplishment. Furthermore, to the Bolshevik mind the prize was well worth the having. The benefits to be expected from the incorporation into Soviet Russia of the erstwhile independent Georgia were such as to gratify both the 'Marxist zealots' and also the 'Soviet nationalists': a further tract of territory with its attendant population would be won for the communist cause; the oil refineries of Batumi, which in normal times provided fuel for the industrial complexes of the Southern Ukraine, would continue to be preserved for Russia; the railway link with Soviet Armenia would not have to pass through potentially unfriendly territory; and last, but perhaps not least, the wines, the tea, the tobacco and the oranges of Georgia would be a welcome addition to a Soviet Russia which was gripped by a terrible food shortage.

To sum up, therefore, we may assert that, in the case of the Soviet invasion of the Georgian Republic, the prize to be won was considerable; victory over the local forces could be guaranteed in advance; and there was no possibility of 'bourgeois' intervention arriving before the country had been conquered. Under these circumstances, war was an acceptable, and also the most expedient, tool for attaining Bolshevik objectives; and war was accordingly embarked upon.

The second occasion on which the Soviet Union deliberately began a war during the period under discussion was when, in 1929, she attacked in China. The Chinese had attempted compulsorily to nationalize the Chinese Eastern Railway which ran for the bulk of its length through Chinese territory to connect the Trans-Siberian Railway with Harbin and Vladivostock. It was at that time predominantly under Russian management, and re-emerging Chinese national pride seems to have been a principal motive in prompting the latter to nationalize it; but since it provided the shortest route between Moscow and the great Russian naval base in the Far East, its importance to the Soviet Union was also obviously considerable.[1]

Moreover, it was clear that, if the USSR should resort to force, victory was certain. The ill-armed horde, which was all that the Chinese Government could muster in the way of an army, was no match for the Russian forces which the Soviet Government had been building up and re-equipping for years in that part of the world.[2] Furthermore, the British, French and American Governments had no troops within hundreds of miles of the area, and those that they had were scanty: even the Japanese had no real possibility of intervention.

All the elements were therefore present which our theoretical analysis has indicated to be necessary before the Soviet Union will initiate military operations; but since they were present, and since moreover the Soviet objective could be obtained more easily by war than by other means in the circumstances prevailing at the time, war was accordingly selected as the tool for implementing Soviet policy.

The next occasion on which the USSR deliberately resorted to armed force as an instrument of her foreign policy was the Russo-Finnish War of 1939–40. The Russians, of course, assert that the Finns began it; but apart from the absurdity of supposing that a country of roughly 4,000,000 inhabitants would start a war against a country whose population at that period was approximately 171,000,000,[3] the Russians' own version of the story lends little support to their assertion.

For the Russians say that on 26 November 1939 Finnish artillery opened fire on Soviet frontier guards, killing and wounding 'several'. At the same time, some detachments of Finnish troops 'tried' to cross the Soviet-Finnish frontier.[4] Even if one assumes that this is what happened (and there is plenty of evidence to suggest that it is not), it is an extraordinary comment on Soviet political thinking that it should require so small a provocation to be answered with a full-scale devastating war.

In the case of this war, the value of the objective was very high indeed. As it was, Leningrad was nearly captured by the Germans in the course of the Second World War; and if the Russians had not secured from the Finns the territory they sought and fought for, it is very probable that Leningrad would have fallen. Nevertheless, they did their best to get it by non-violent means (though with any amount of heavy diplomatic and other pressures); but when these means had failed, they turned to war.

As to the prospects of victory, it must have seemed to Stalin, as it seemed to the world, that the campaign would be a walkover. Why it was not is an interesting question, but one outside the limits of this present argument. Here, we are concerned only with the question of whether the Russians did or did not believe *before the war began* that they would win easily; and there can be no doubt but that they *did* believe it. Intervention by foreign governments on behalf of the Finns was certainly a distinct possibility, and we know that the Russians were worried by it: it was, indeed, an important reason why they chose negotiation to begin with, as a means of attaining their objective. Moreover, if that objective had not been of such enormous value to Stalin and his ministers, it is very likely that the fear of foreign intervention (in Soviet eyes, of *renewed* foreign intervention) would have been sufficient to stop them from going to war. The value being, however, as great as it was, and victory seeming certain, foreign intervention would have to be risked in order to secure it. In the event, as we know, the threatened foreign intervention failed to materialize.

In addition to these three instances of the USSR being willing to start a war in furtherance of its political objectives, there is yet another. This is the case of Afghanistan in 1934. But since, as things turned out, the pro-Soviet Emir's regime, in support of which the Red Army had been ordered to intervene, collapsed before the Russian troops could get to it, the orders were revoked before any fighting had occurred; and consequently it may be thought that this particular incident should not be numbered among the occasions where the USSR has initiated the use of force.[5]

In any case, even if this instance be included, and if we include, too, the military aid given to the Governor of Sinkiang in the mid-1930s and the subjugation of Eastern Poland in 1939 and of the Baltic States in 1940, nevertheless the total number of occasions on which the Soviet Government was the aggressor during the whole period from 1917 to 1944 is only about half a dozen. This compares very favourably with the record of other countries over similar periods.

One is therefore next led to ask whether this was due to some special virtue on the part of the Soviet Government, as the Russians themselves naturally claim that it is, or whether the particular circumstances of the time had something to do with their restraint.

In support of the latter hypothesis one may cite a good deal of evidence. First, from early 1921 (after the end of the Russo-Polish War and the civil war) until approximately 1939, the Red Army was too weak to be used for serious fighting. According to the then Head of the Russian Section of the Romanian General Staff, the Soviet infantry in July 1921 amounted to somewhere between 300,000 and 350,000, while the Soviet cavalry was 50,000–60,000.[6] Moreover, according to the Romanian officer, experience had taught the Russian leaders that the Red Army of that period could not stand up to regularly organized troops; and ten Romanian divisions could, he said, take on the thirty-two Soviet divisions of the Kiev Command and the Reserve.[7]

There is important confirmatory evidence that the Soviet High Command was worried about the strength of the Romanian Army, as it also was about the Japanese Army.

In 1922, Lebedev, the Chief of Staff of the Red Army, was present as a delegate at the Moscow conference on disarmament. The official Soviet account of the conference has him on record as saying that the geographical situation of Soviet Russia and 'her aims' forced her to think of Romania 'with her 200,000 bayonets' and also of the East, and especially the Far East, 'where the threat is very real'.[8]

In view of this and of the food shortage, and of the unreliability of the lines of communication in Russia where armed bands of marauding demobilized soldiers were roaming across the Ukraine,[9] it is easy to see that the Bolshevik Government would refrain from engaging in military operations whenever it could manage to do so.

The second reason for supposing that the Soviet Government's reluctance to engage in war in the 1920s and 1930s might be due as much to military weakness as to any moral virtue, lies in the fact that by the time that the civil war was ended in December 1920, the Soviet economy was in ruins. Lenin, in his speech to the Tenth Party Congress, and Trotsky, in his *The Revolution Betrayed* (trans. Max Eastman, Faber & Faber, 1937), bear eloquent testimony to the dire straits in which Russia found herself in 1921, that year of starvation in which, according to official Soviet data, approximately 5,000,000 people died of famine and its after-effects.[10] Nor was industrial production any better than agricultural production: the output of the metallurgical industry, for instance, amounted to less than one-tenth of the pre-war level.[11] Under such circumstances, military adventures on any scale were clearly out of the question, the conquest of Georgia that same year being made possible purely by the fact that a force of less than 25,000 men was necessary to accomplish it.[12] Indeed, the greatest need of Soviet Russia was unquestionably an absence of any sort of fighting: in other words, she desperately needed peace.

Consequently, one of the first operations conducted by Soviet diplomacy was to make peace treaties with those countries with which Russia had been at war. Between 1917 and the end of 1921, treaties of peace with the following countries had been signed: Germany, Estonia, Lithuania, Latvia, Finland and Poland. As a result, Soviet Russia was afforded what Lenin had claimed she very badly needed, to wit, a breathing-space, a respite to allow her to get her strength back and to replenish and refurnish her forces.

But this was to be a long process: even by 1941 it cannot be said that the Red Army was entirely ready to face a well-armed adversary; and from 1921 to around 1936, the defences of the Soviet Union were extremely weak.

Of course, there would be no need for any defences if the peace that had materialized by the middle of 1921 was indeed that 'peace and goodwill' or 'peace and co-operation' of which some 'bourgeois' idealists were dreaming. But the Leninist cast of mind of the Bolshevik leaders, fortified by their recent experiences at the time of the civil war, convinced them that no 'bourgeois' government had, or could have, any goodwill for Bolshevism, a point of view which was probably correct. While Lenin had made it plain that Bolshevist Russia had no goodwill for the 'bourgeois'.[13]

The peace that emerged in 1921 was therefore seen by the Bolshevik leaders as 'peace' in the Soviet, not in the 'bourgeois', sense—in other words, it was merely an 'absence of fighting'. But 'peace' in this sense was clearly not sufficient, if the capitalist powers were indeed to deliver a second onslaught on Soviet Russia, as the Bolsheviks were convinced that they intended to. Consequently, the strength of the Russian armed forces would have to be increased.

Nevertheless, it was recognized that the armies of the 'bourgeois' governments were at that moment of time comparatively small, and that they were not maintained on a war footing.[14] To enlarge them sufficiently to launch an invasion of Russia would be a long-term business; and the first signs of an attempt at such an enlargement would put the Soviet leaders on the alert. It was therefore felt possible to reorganize the Red Army on what was essentially a defensive basis: in 1925 its size was fixed at 562,000 men, of whom three-quarters were not regulars, but were enrolled on the militia system.[15] Its sole real *offensive* capability lay in a mobile striking force of ten cavalry divisions which Frunze introduced.[16] A similar defensively-orientated policy was applied to the reorganization of the Soviet Navy.[17] As a result, the maximum number of Soviet citizens were made available for work in industry and agriculture, and a considerable impetus was thereby given to the rebuilding of the country's economy. At the same time the corollary was plain: the Soviet armed forces of the late 1920s were in no condition to start wars against any but the weakest of opponents.

The skills of Soviet diplomacy were also enrolled to do what they could to strengthen the country's defences. Throughout the 1920s and 1930s, the People's Commissariat for Foreign Affairs was extremely busy in trying to get neighbouring countries to sign pacts of non-aggression and neutrality with the Bolshevik Government. The purpose was to help to make a capitalist invasion more difficult, as has been explained earlier in the chapter on neutrality; and by the middle of the 1930s a considerable proportion of the land frontiers of Russia had been afforded the protection of these treaties (see pp. 185–6 above). Not that the degree of protection was very high; but Russian statesmen have usually been willing to recognize that half a loaf is better than no bread.

Moreover, some of the schemes, notably those of 1920 for the 'perpetual neutrality' of Lithuania and Estonia, would have given the Russians something much nearer three-quarters of the loaf, when viewed against the background of the time. In 1920, the Soviet Government's greatest concern was protection against capitalist invasion; and history had proved how the territory of the Baltic States, and especially their coastline, could be used by Western governments as springboards for an assault on Russia. For the Soviet leaders to deny themselves the facilities of the port of Riga, for example, in exchange for a similar denial on the part of the capitalist governments made good strategic sense at that particular moment; though naturally, when the Red Army had sufficiently increased its strength, there was greater advantage in seizing these countries than in renewing the neutrality proposals.

The attitude of the Soviet Government towards war, peace and neutrality during the period under discussion may therefore be summed up as follows: During the whole of this time, it desperately needed an absence of fighting (or 'peace' in the Soviet sense). It could also probably have done with 'peace and goodwill' and 'peace and co-operation'; but peace of this sort was simply not forthcoming. More-over, it should be made quite clear that the blame for this must be laid at the door of the capitalists at least as much as, if not more than, at that of Lenin and his followers. It may be, therefore, that the communists are perfectly correct when they say that peace of this sort is *inherently impossible* between a capitalist and a communist regime.

As to war, Soviet Russia was in no condition to fight a war against any but the weakest enemy until about the early 1930s; and even by the middle of the 1930s, it could only take on a properly equipped opponent if the hostilities were limited in scale. In the fighting against the Japanese in the Far East in 1938, for instance, the Russian forces numbered no more than 15,000 men;[18] it was the Japanese who started it, and the Russians were extremely cautious in the way they exploited their victory.

In the following year, at the Battle of Khalkin-Gol, the size of the armies had increased to 75,000 on the Japanese side, and to 112,500 on that of the Russians.[19] Even so, it was again the Japanese who started it; and again, the use that the Russians made of their very considerable victory was extremely restrained. It is noteworthy, however, that Soviet sources themselves suggest that the cause of this restraint was the growing threat of war with Germany on their western frontier—which menaced them, if the fighting in Mongolia persisted, with the calamitous possibility of having a war in both the east and the west at once. Indeed, the suggestion is even made that it was this threat which was chiefly responsible for persuading the Soviet Government to sign the Nazi-Soviet Pact.[20]

Perhaps the chief point to be made with regard to those particular operations is that it demonstrates clearly the Russian determination to resist any form of aggression, even under circumstances that are not very favourable to them: *Nemo me impune lacessit*. It is, I seem to remember, Agesilaus to whom this saying is attributed; and the circumstances under which he said it were not altogether dissimilar from those under which the Russians were operating in 1938–9.[21]

As to the war against Finland, we have already discussed it. It seems clear that the Russians would never have waged it, if they had not felt that they desperately needed the territory that they subsequently obtained, and that the Finns were incapable of offering serious resistance. But since they did feel both these things, they did, as we know, embark on the Finnish War.

This underlying military weakness must always be borne in mind, therefore, when trying to assess the Soviet attitude to war in the 1920s and 1930s. It may be that even if the USSR's armed forces had been stronger than those of all the capitalist countries combined, it would still have been reluctant to make use of them; on the other hand, it is also possible that increased strength would have brought an increased intransigence, and even perhaps a readiness to resort to arms as a means of converting to the doctrines of Marxism-Leninism those countries and those peoples who would otherwise have rejected them.[22] Certainly, there are instances in this period which prove beyond doubt that the USSR is not pacifist; but further than that one cannot really go.

From 1941 to 1945, the USSR was engaged in repelling the German armies which had wantonly attacked her. As we argued earlier, the Soviet Union will always defend herself vigorously if others attack her; and her war record in the Second World War is ample proof of the truth of this assertion.

At the end of the war, however, she was exhausted. Her total dead numbered about 20,000,000; a large part of European Russia was devastated to a degree that is simply indescribable; and her huge armies were in poor condition for fighting another war.

This last statement may sound odd to many in the West today; but I was myself in Berlin in 1945, and I have no doubt of the truth of it. To begin with, the Red Army's losses incurred merely in the one operation of capturing the German capital had been appalling: in just the twenty-three days from 16 April to 8 May 1945, the killed, wounded and missing on the Russian side amounted to more than 304,000 men.[23] In addition, 2,156 Soviet tanks and self-propelled guns, 1,220 guns and mortars, and 527 aeroplanes had been destroyed by the enemy in that brief space of time.[24]

But the real weakness of the Red Army in 1945 was shortage of mechanical transport. Many competent authorities have agreed in saying that the trucks and lorries supplied to Russia by the Americans were among the most valuable items of aid that the Western allies provided.[25] In 1945, the Soviet Union's own production of such vehicles amounted to no more than 69,662,[26] while the total supplied by the USA between 1941 and 1945 was 427,386 (including jeeps).[27] And in the autumn of 1945, American aid to Russia was stopped, so that thenceforth the latter was dependent on her own resources for supplying her armed forces. And the 665,000 motor vehicles which she possessed 'towards the end of the war' was by no means sufficient for her military needs, as Soviet sources agree. They agree, too, that the Red Army was compelled to make use of horse-drawn transport; and that its rear echelons were 'to a significant degree tied down to the railway network'.[28]

Nor was this the only serious difficulty which the Soviet Union would have had to face in the event of another war. For if a war involving the USSR had actually broken out in the years immediately following the end of the Second World War, the United States (with or without some allies) was bound to have been the enemy. But in those immediate post-war years, the USA was virtually unassailable so far as the Soviet Union was concerned, because the Soviet Union had neither the long-range bombers nor a strong enough navy to attack the American homeland. By contrast, the USSR was extremely vulnerable to attacks by the United States, which at that time, it will be remembered, had the monopoly of the atomic bomb.[29] Furthermore, these difficulties would be operative, irrespective of whether it was the USSR or the USA which started the war in question.

As a result, Soviet foreign policy in those years was in general extremely cautious. All the countries of Eastern Europe lay in the Russians' hands, and the Red Army was present in every one of them with the exception of Yugoslavia. Yet, despite these advantages, it was

three years before communist regimes were operating as open dictator-
ships there, and the countries in question 'communized'. Fear of
Western (and particularly American) reaction was the chief reason, it is
generally agreed, why the Russians took so long over enthroning their
protégés. It was only when the Soviet leaders discovered that there
would be *no* effective Western reaction to any policy for Eastern Europe
that the Russians might care to implement, that they set about in
earnest on the task of 'communization'.

A similarly cautious policy, again stemming largely from Soviet
military weakness when measured against the strength of the United
States, led to the abandonment of plans for Western Europe in 1944–5
that Stalin had hoped to mature. It was his intention, as we have seen,
to make use of the advance of the Soviet armed forces to install communist or communist-type governments in the various countries they
liberated. In the case of Eastern Europe, this was actually done; but
there is firm evidence to suggest that, *if circumstances had permitted*, it
would also have been done in Western Europe, particularly in West
Germany and France and Italy.

With regard to France, the clearest evidence is probably to be found
in a letter that Stalin wrote to the Yugoslav Communist Party in May
1948, in which he said that the chief reason why there was a communist
government in Yugoslavia, but none in France and Italy, was because
'Unfortunately, the Soviet Army did not and could not render such
assistance to the French and Italian Communist Parties' as it had
rendered to the communists of Yugoslavia.'[30]

Nor is this the only piece of evidence to be found in support of this
thesis. Recent Soviet writing on the history of the Second World War is
fond of discussing what it terms the 'liberating mission of the Soviet
Armed Forces'. This 'liberation' is not regarded by them as being
confined to the freeing of this or that country from the tyranny of Nazi
Germany; it is also seen as a mission to liberate the workers and
peasants of *as many countries as possible* from 'reactionary' (i.e. capitalist)
regimes, and subsequently to 'democratize' them.

Seen from this viewpoint, the Allied landings in Normandy can be
(and are) regarded as a move by the Western 'bourgeois' governments
to prevent the spread of communism. For the real purpose of the landings, so the Soviet version runs, was to seize the territory of Western
Europe, including a number of districts of Western Germany; to
prevent the victory of 'democratic' forces in the countries of Western
Europe; to set up in those countries reactionary regimes, and block the
Soviet Army's way to the West.[31]

The latest edition of the *Great Soviet Encyclopaedia* puts the matter
thus: 'The international and military situation in the spring and
summer of 1944 was such that a further delay in the opening of the

Second Front would have led to the liberation of *all* Europe by the Soviet Armed Forces' (italics mine).[32] The earlier edition moreover makes a point of saying that France, in particular, would have been liberated by the Russians, if no Second Front had occurred.[33]

And if the Soviet armed forces had indeed liberated the whole of Europe including France, what would have happened then? It is clear that there would have been no restoration of the 'pre-war capitalist form of society'; because the encyclopaedia goes on to denounce the British and American 'ruling circles' for aiming at such a thing. We have some idea of what would have happened in the case of France, not only because of Stalin's letter, but also because of other passages in authoritative Soviet writing, which describe the role and policies of the French Communist Party in 1943-4, and regret that the presence of the Western armies prevented these policies from being implemented.[34]

Where Soviet forces occupied a country, moreover, we know as a matter of historical fact that the 'pre-war capitalist form of society' was *not* allowed to be restored; and that 'genuinely democratic' (i.e. communist) regimes were installed in the seat of government. This happened throughout Central and Eastern Europe in the years just after the war. We therefore have good reason to suppose, particularly in view of the contents of Stalin's letter, that, had the Red Army managed to liberate France, France today would be a communist, not a 'bourgeois', country.

But, as we have seen, in actual fact it was troops from the Western European countries which liberated France; and in these circumstances the French communists were unable to realize their plans. Stalin would have been very grateful if they had succeeded in doing so; but in order to give them the necessary help, he would have had to have gone to war against America and Britain. His army, as we have seen, was simply not capable of starting a new war against such powerful opponents: the Leninist conditions for starting a new war therefore did not exist, and the 'reactionary ruling circles' of Britain and America consequently had to be allowed to restore the 'pre-war capitalist form of society' in liberated France.

In subsequent years, the same military weakness (or, to put it more accurately, the same lack of decisive military superiority) gave rise to the same caution. Even when the Russians were prepared to gamble a little, as in the case of the blockade of Berlin in 1948, they took the greatest care to prevent the outbreak of actual fighting. If they could get the Allies to quit Berlin by a mixture of threats and bluff, they would willingly do so; but they were not prepared to evict them by resorting to war.

In 1948, Stalin broke with Tito. Reliable reports show that he was furious with him, and that he was determined to put an end to his existence as ruler of Yugoslavia. 'I shall shake my little finger', he is quoted as saying, 'and there will be no Tito.'[35]

One way of achieving his objective was to order the invasion of Yugoslavia; but, as we know, he did not do this. The question then arises why he did not; because the Soviet Army would have unquestion-ably been victorious; and the reward of victory would have been the ending of Titoism, that attitude of mind which Stalin found so pernicious, and the crushing of which he evidently so greatly prized. Why, then, did Stalin refrain from ordering his troops to march?

The answer seems to be that, although a Soviet victory was ultimately certain, there were good grounds for believing that it might not be very quick. The northern part of the country could indeed be overrun speedily, because it consists of a long, flat plain across which the Soviet armour could move with complete freedom. This area then, which contains Belgrade and Zagreb, could be quickly subjugated, as the Germans had subjugated it seven years before when they invaded the country. But between that area and the sea lies a mountainous region which presents a formidable obstacle. It was these mountains where, during the war, Tito with his partisans had managed to hold out. If they had held out once, could they not hold out again?

The answer to this question is probably not, if they were to remain wholly alone and wholly unsupported. But behind the mountains lies the Adriatic; and at that time the Adriatic, and indeed the whole Mediterranean Sea, was dominated by the American and British navies, which held undisputed mastery. The Soviet Navy in 1948 was small and technically backward; and its Black Sea Fleet, in any case, could be bottled up in its ports. As a result, the Western world could, if it chose, give prompt and effective assistance to Tito's army.

Whether the West would in fact have given such assistance is open to doubt. Ulam, in his thorough examination of the question, thinks that it probably would not.[36] But Ulam, as well as writing in 1968 with all the advantages of hindsight, was also himself a Westerner: Stalin was not. Unlike Lenin and Trotsky and so many of the other old Bolsheviks, Stalin had hardly ever been abroad; and his whole cast of mind was extremely provincial. He had little understanding of Western politicians and of Western political pressures; he did not even properly understand the Marxist conceptions of them. His Marxism was crude, vulgar Marxism, and he applied the theory, itself not noted for subtlety in those parts which deal with international relations, in a crude and vulgar fashion. Here was a quarrel between one set of communists and another. Would not the 'bourgeoisie', eager to weaken in any way that citadel of communism, the USSR, leap at the chance of doing this by sending help to Tito? Perhaps they would not, but the risk was undeniably present; and that risk had been considerably increased by the Yugoslavs' action in July the same year (about the time, in other words, that the Stalin-Tito crisis was coming to a head) in agreeing to settle outstanding financial problems with the USA. To a suspicious mind (and all agree that Stalin's mind was inordinately suspicious) the talks in Washington might have covered military, as well as purely financial, matters. In which case the risk of American intervention was not just possible; it might even be considered probable.

There is another reason why Stalin should have refrained from war against Tito. In an attempt to counter the Americans' atomic bomb, he had started the 'World Peace Movement' and he had started it, more-over, in 1948, the year of his quarrel with Tito. The two points about it that are relevant here is that a main objective of the movement was to outlaw atomic weapons; and that another was to build up an image of Soviet Russia as being inherently and invariably peace-loving, in contrast to the Western countries which were depicted as invariably bellicose.

But if now that same peace-loving Russia should suddenly invade another country, if the Soviet Army should turn its guns upon the people and government of another nation merely in order to secure its adherence to Soviet precept and practice, what effect would this have on the credibility of the Soviet claim to be peace-loving?

This line of reasoning was reinforced by another. In 1948, the Soviet Union's sole support among the citizens of Western countries was to be found, naturally enough, among those of the Left. And these supporters were, and had always been, of the very greatest assistance to the USSR. Such people might possibly be persuaded that the armed invasion of a capitalist country was necessary in the interests of com-munism; and furthermore that, being in those interests, it could fairly be described as 'peace-loving'. But if the victim were not a capitalist, but a fraternal socialist, country, would not even such people's loyalty to the USSR and its policies be severely strained?

However, despite such arguments for caution, there can be no assurance that, if war had been the only instrument available to attain his purpose, Stalin might not have used it. As it so happened, however, he thought that there were others.

When considering these, one must bear in mind that Stalin was accustomed to absolute obedience from the rulers of his 'satellite' empire. He shook his little finger at Rajk of Hungary; and Rajk, who in 1948 had been Minister of the Interior in Hungary and a member of the Hungarian Politburo, in 1949 was arrested, tried and executed. Kostov, the Vice-Premier of Bulgaria in April 1949, had died on the scaffold, similarly on Stalin's orders, by December of that same year. Gomulka of Poland and Slanksy of Czechoslovakia were also toppled from power; though the former, unlike the latter, contrived to live.

Events have proved that Stalin's little finger was unquestionably a force to be reckoned with: he can hardly be blamed for supposing that it would be effective when it came to dealing with Tito.[37]

There were, moreover, other grounds to strengthen him in this belief. A number of officers in the Yugoslav Army and police had been recruited by the Soviet Secret Service to be Soviet agents, and would therefore (so Stalin hoped) help to isolate Tito and his close associates from the Yugoslav people as a whole.[38] To increase the pressure on the latter, the USSR imposed an economic blockade on Yugoslavia, which was intended to make the lot of the average citizen, already hard, a very great deal harder, so that in the extremity of despair he would rise up against the government, and Tito would be swept away by the Yugoslavs themselves—with a little 'fraternal aid' from the Soviet Army if necessary, once the uprising had reached the pitch of neutralizing the Yugoslav Army. Nor was it only the uprising that was intended to neutralize that army. The suborned Yugoslav officers, to whom reference has been made above, were expected to play their part, as well as the people.

All in all, therefore, Stalin believed that he could attain his end without resorting to war, and that the alternative means would be just as effective and even more efficient. Under these circumstances, war was *not* the most suitable instrument of policy for Stalin; and accordingly he rejected it. The fact that, in the event, the views he held on the power of his little finger were proved to be wrong, in no way proves that he did not actually hold them. And since he held them, he acted according to the logic of them; and their logic, as demonstrated by Stalin's actions, corresponds faithfully to the theory of war that has been described in an earlier chapter.

In 1950, the Korean War broke out. An important effect was to make the West rearm. As a result, the use of force by the Soviet Union as an instrument of its foreign policy was likely to seem even less expedient than it had been in the preceding years. And by the time that the Korean War had ended, Stalin was dead; and his successors were faced with a number of internal problems of sufficient difficulty to make them regard the military instrument, viewed as a tool of foreign policy, with even greater wariness than Stalin had done. Certainly they used it in Hungary, but even then with reluctance, despite the fact that Hungary was one of their satrapies. Moreover they only used it when no other choice was left to them than using it or quitting.

It is also true that they threatened to use it over Suez. But threats are one thing, carrying them out is another; and this particular threat was not carried out. Nor, indeed, was it probable that it would be. To the serious student of the communist attitude to war, it was clear that the likely profit accruing to the Soviet Union by actually embarking on hostilities would not be great, and that the risks involved were considerable. Nor could the chances of a quick and decisive victory be reckoned high. The nearest Soviet troops were a very long way from Suez; and although London and Paris could be destroyed by nuclear missiles, the use of these missiles on America's allies might evoke retaliation from America. There was as much advantage to be gained by the Soviet Union among Arab countries from the propaganda effect of threatening the French and British in the Egyptian cause as ever there was by making those threats good.

And by the time that the Hungarian Uprising and the Suez crisis were over, international affairs had become dominated by the proliferation of nuclear weapons. Both East and West possessed so many, and so many means of delivery, that no profit was to be seen in resorting to war (that is to say, to any sort of war that might conceivably escalate to nuclear). The use of war, in communist thinking, is to further the cause of communism. That cause is in no way served, so the Russians reckon, if the cradle of communism, the Soviet Union itself, gets turned into a nuclear desert, even supposing the United States, the fountainhead of imperialism, were also to perish. Khrushchev himself on a number of occasions said as much.

This attitude to war was given its clearest practical demonstration in the course of the Cuban crisis of 1962. The United States was militarily capable of invading and conquering Cuba and also, if she was compelled to, of waging nuclear war against Russia. By contrast, the sole capability possessed by the Soviet Union was of waging nuclear war against America: she had no conventional forces stationed in Cuba, and no means of getting them there in time. So the choice confronting the Kremlin leaders was nuclear war or nothing; and they chose nothing— a choice made easier for them because President Kennedy promised them that, if they chose it, he would refrain from invading Cuba.

Even so, the choice was not as easy as I have made it appear above. The Soviet climb-down cost the Russians a good deal of prestige among the Third World countries, and infuriated Castro; and Khrushchev and his colleagues must have known that this would be so. Yet rather than engage in nuclear war for no perceptible profit, they chose to lose face.

And the 'no perceptible profit' is the crux of the matter. The gains to be had from the Cuban adventure were useful, but by no means vital, for the Soviet Union. They were hardly even big enough to justify fighting a large-scale conventional war; they did not begin to be big enough to justify fighting a nuclear. Khrushchev ought to have known this before he put his missiles in Cuba, as he ought to have known that their presence offered such a serious threat to America as to justify her in resorting to war as a last resort. Indeed, one of the causes of

Khrushchev's subsequent dismissal was precisely this 'voluntarism' of his (or, in other words, the embarking on schemes that had never been thought through properly). It should be noted, however, that, though the Soviet involvement in the Cuban crisis began as a result of 'voluntarism' (that is to say, as a result of *not* obeying the precepts of Marxism-Leninism), the disengagement from it, which permitted the Soviet Union to cut its losses to the minimum, stemmed from obeying them implicitly.

In 1968, the Soviet Army invaded Czechoslovakia. Here victory was certain; and, in addition, as the Russians saw things, the gain was huge. For the USSR had convinced itself that, if the Czech reforms continued, genuinely alternative political parties would be allowed to be created, and genuinely free elections would be held. In which case it was probable, given the social structure of Czech society, that the communists would lose, and Czechoslovakia would cease to be a member of the Communist bloc.

In this context it is no use pointing to the declarations to the contrary uttered not only by Dubček but also by others of the Czech leaders and by many thousands of ordinary Czechs besides. These declarations were no doubt wholly sincere; but just as in Hungary, in 1956, Imre Nagy's ability to control events was swept away by the effervescence that bubbled up from below, so too in Czechoslovakia in 1968 it seemed highly likely that, if the reforms were allowed to go further, public enthusiasm would sweep away from the tiller the would-be guiding hand of Dubček and his colleagues. By Soviet reckoning, a large element of the Czechoslovak people was 'petty bourgeois' in outlook; and by their votes they would see to it that their country became 'petty bourgeois' in fact. Or in other words, as the Soviet leaders expressed it, 'counter-revolution would triumph'.

Since it was unthinkable that the Kremlin leaders should allow 'counter-revolution' to triumph in a country that was a member of the Communist bloc, if they could possibly prevent it, the question they had to determine was how to suppress it. Peaceful means were tried. At one confrontation after another, Brezhnev and Kosygin attempted to persuade the Czechs to toe the line. But Dubček was both unwilling and unable to annul the reforms which the 'Prague Spring' had bestowed on the Czech people. The people themselves would have decisively rejected any leader of theirs who tried to do such a thing; and Czechoslovakia by then, it must be remembered, had become a comparatively free country.

Since ordinary diplomatic negotiations proved unavailing, even when accompanied by quite un-ordinary military manoeuvres by Soviet troops both inside Czechoslovakia and along its frontiers, there remained to Brezhnev and Kosygin, as instruments for attaining their objective, either economic blockade or armed invasion. But economic blockade was unlikely to be effective. Czechoslovakia has a common frontier both with West Germany and with Austria. The Czechoslovak economy, by comparision with the economies of most of the other socialist countries, was comparatively highly developed. Czechoslovakia already ran a successful, if limited, export trade to the non-communist world which could no doubt be expanded, just as the Yugoslavs expanded their trade with the non-communist world when Stalin imposed his economic blockade in 1948. An economic blockade on Czechoslovakia, therefore, was unlikely to be successful; and if it were, it would certainly take a very long time to be so. But, given the liberating effervescence that was bubbling in Czech society in 1968, time was of the essence from the Soviet viewpoint.

There remained, therefore, only war as a tool for attaining the Russians' policy objective. If they shrank from war, they would be unable to attain that objective; and it was their considered view that, in that event, 'counter-revolution' would triumph. Of course, there was no need to shrink from war because of any fear of losing it: in a war between Russia and Czechoslovakia, victory for the Russians was certain.

But supposing the Czechs received support from countries *outside* the Communist bloc? Supposing America in particular should send military aid to the Czechs? There are various signs that this possibility seriously worried the Politburo and was a major factor in causing them to delay so long. (The other, of course, was the effect that the invasion would have on world opinion.)

The Soviet Government therefore took precautions, before the order to invade was actually given. As a result, the Soviet Ambassadors in the most important Western countries (notably, of course, in America) were sent to call on those countries' governments in the middle of the night of Tuesday/Wednesday, and explain to those governments that what had just been done in Czechoslovakia was in no way directed at Western countries or Western spheres of influence; it was merely an internal matter of the Communist bloc.[39]

Since that time, the USSR has not employed the military instrument as a tool of her foreign policy. Nor, so far as we know, has she contemplated doing so.

With regard to such military operations conducted by other countries as the American and British landings in the Lebanon and Jordan in 1958, or the American landing in the Dominican Republic in 1965, geography and the lack of suitable naval units made it impossible for the Soviet Government to get itself involved in them, whether it would have liked to or not. It is perhaps worth noting that, though the factor of geography is more or less invariable, that of the lack of suitable naval units can be, and is being, modified; and that the process of modification started in approximately 1957.

With regard to the Korean and Vietnam Wars, there was (as seen from the Soviet point of view) no significantly greater gain to be had from direct participation than could be had by confining Soviet support to the supply of arms and military advisers. The dangers and possible losses were, on the other hand, considered to be very much larger.

In the case of the Korean War, for instance, direct Soviet participation was almost bound to have led to a war with America; and in 1950, as has already been explained above, the USSR was very ill-placed to fight one. America could have bombed the Soviet Union (with atomic bombs, if necessary), while the USSR was totally without the means of dropping bombs of any kind on to the territory of the United States.

The Vietnam War presented somewhat different dangers, but of a similar order of magnitude. North Vietnam, unlike North Korea, at no point enjoys a common frontier with Russia. The despatch of units of the Soviet armed forces to Vietnam, and their subsequent supply and reinforcement, would therefore have to depend upon the goodwill of this, that or the other country through which they would have to pass; and the country in question would probably have to be China. Alternatively, to send them by sea would put them at the mercy of the immeasurably more powerful fleets of the United States, well equipped as the latter are with bases in that part of the world. Direct involvement with conventional forces on the part of the Soviet Union would therefore be courting disaster; and it would in addition give a strong incentive to the Americans to invade and conquer the whole of North Vietnam, thereby inflicting a serious loss on the Communist cause as a whole.

The only alternative means for the Soviet Union to participate directly in the Vietnam War would be to launch ballistic missiles at America. But this would mean the start of a nuclear war, which would involve (whatever its outcome) an inevitably tremendous destruction of Soviet lives and property. The North Vietnamese might just conceivably benefit as a result of this proceeding; but the Soviet view of war refuses to countenance the winning of benefits for other people, however ideologically congenial, at the expense of heavy damage to the USSR.

All in all, therefore, one is justified in asserting that the Soviet attitude to war, as laid down in the theory, corresponds with remarkable fidelity to the facts of Soviet history from the October Revolution down to the present day. This is therefore important empirical evidence that the theory itself has been correctly stated; and that it exerts, and has always exerted, a profound effect upon Soviet political practice. That being so, we must now turn to consider the subject of peace, and see whether we can detect a similar correspondence there between Soviet theory and practice.

The whole period from 1917 to 1973 can show few examples of direct armed clashes between the Soviet Union and the 'bourgeois' countries; though such as have occurred (the Second World War in particular) have been of a remarkable ferocity. On the whole, though, the period in question can fairly be described as a period of 'absence of fighting', so far as concerns the relations between the USSR and the capitalist countries, and therefore a period of 'peace'.

By no stretch of the imagination, however, can it possibly be described as an era of 'peace and goodwill' or 'peace and co-operation'. Right from the very beginning of the Bolshevik rule in Russia, neither Lenin and his colleagues nor the 'bourgeois' governments were at all ready to co-operate with each other. Obviously, when the area of potential co-operation offered large immediate benefits without any commensurate losses to offset them, both sides, Bolshevik and 'bourgeois', had much to gain and very little to lose by agreeing to co-operate. But such areas were, and are to this day, comparatively small. The International Geophysical Year, for instance, offered significant advantages in the scientific field, if both sides would agree to co-operate in it. Since, moreover, both sides stood to gain by a similar order of magnitude, the International Geophysical Year became official policy, and was given official recognition and official support by both the communist and the 'bourgeois' governments.

Other acts of co-operation have occurred in the economic field. The Fiat company of Italy did a deal with Russia, whereby it was to install in the Soviet Union a complete factory for the manufacture of cars. Here again both sides obviously benefited: Fiat made some money, while the USSR received a slice of Western productive technology. Moreover, this kind of business deal is likely to continue: there is much talk, for instance, of agreements between Russia and America, whereby the United States would get access to Russian raw materials, which she badly needs, while the USSR would receive in exchange some advanced US technology, which is badly needed by the Russians.

But this is not 'co-operation and goodwill'; it is the result of a cold appraisal by both sides of the merits and demerits of a particular deal. Indeed, so little does goodwill normally enter into trade relations between the USSR and America, that there has been for years a lengthy list of items of goods made in the United States which the American Government will not allow to be sold to the USSR. Among such items have been large-diameter pipes suitable for pipelines, tankers, ball bearings and rolling-mill equipment.[40]

If, therefore, the proposed agreements come off, it will only be because the United States sees more to be gained by getting those raw materials than it would lose by letting the Russians acquire a particular piece of technology. This may be good business judgment; it is certainly not goodwill. An equal lack of goodwill towards the West could easily be shown to be operative among the Russians.

It seems, therefore, that we are justified in saying that the first part of the theory that lies behind the Soviet attitude to peace has been shown to be valid in practice. The Soviet Union and the West have *not* co-operated in the various crises that have beset our world since the October Revolution. Between the wars, there was indeed talk of co-operating over 'collective security'; but when it came to the test of action, nothing was done. After the war, in crisis after crisis, the USSR has pursued policies that have been in no way correlated with Western policies; while Western policies have been in no way correlated with the Russian. This seems to confirm the Leninist dictum that there can be no such thing as 'peace and goodwill' or 'peace and co-operation' between capitalism and communism, and hence the first part of my thesis.

A second part of my thesis was that the USSR will accept a peace if the preceding war has given her what she wants. But this is standard practice with every country, whether capitalist or communist: it is so self-evident that further comment seems needless. An obvious example from Soviet practice is the Treaty of Moscow of 1940, which was signed by the Russians precisely because the fighting that preceded it had compelled the Finns to accept terms that they had previously rejected, but on which the Russians insisted. Once the latter had got what they wanted, they granted the Finns a peace treaty.

But a third part of my thesis with regard to peace between capitalist and communist societies was that the Soviet Union will resort to it when she thinks that an open struggle is likely to be unprofitable; or when she feels compelled to break off a struggle in which she is already engaged, and to use the resulting 'peace' as an opportunity to regroup, reinforce and replenish. How, then, does this third part of the thesis stand up to a comparison with the facts of Soviet history?

Here, it seems, the verdict must be 'not proven'. We have Lenin's own words to indicate to us that, from his point of view, the whole purpose of the Treaty of Brest-Litovsk was precisely to obtain such a breathing-space; and that it was his firm intention to renew the struggle, as soon as his forces should have been sufficiently replenished (see pp. 170–1). The peace treaties with Latvia, Lithuania and Estonia were also designed to put an end to fighting which at that particular moment of time the Russians were ill placed to conduct (see pp. 200–1). Twenty years later, however, when circumstances were considerably more favourable, the Red Army was employed to nullify the provisions contained in them. *Mutatis mutandis,* the same sort of thing may be said about the Treaty of Riga, which put an end to the Russo-Polish War of 1920 (see p. 171); for if the Treaty of Riga put an end to that particular war, the Soviet occupation of Poland after 1945 effectively put an end to the Treaty of Riga.

So far, so good. When one comes to the post-war era, however, the trouble is that the Soviet armed forces have not been engaged in armed conflict during the whole of that period with the exception of such incidents as the suppression of the Hungarian Uprising, the invasion of Czechoslovakia, and the fighting along the Sino-Soviet frontier. In none of these was there the slightest likelihood of the Russians being beaten; so in none of these was there even the possibility of their being forced to accept the type of peace that is the subject of our present discussion.

However, if one turns from military to diplomatic offensives, the picture looks somewhat different. Here, of course, the 'peace' that we shall be discussing will not be the formal peace treaty that puts an end to fighting, but a slackening of tension in international relationships, a significant *détente,* a lull in the Cold War that serves the Russians the purpose of allowing them to accumulate more diplomatic ammunition, to acquire more allies, to work out new lines of advance; and then to end the *détente,* to heighten the tension in international relationships, to 'hot up' the Cold War, and thereby hope, by undermining the will to resist of the 'bourgeois' governments, to attain those aims of their foreign policy which they have temporarily had to forego. These are the Leninist principles underlying the Brest-Litovsk Treaty transferred to a peacetime environment, but they are the same Leninist principles.

An authoritative description of the workings of this Soviet manoeuvre can be found in Malcolm Mackintosh's *Strategy and Tactics of Soviet Foreign Policy,* to which interested readers are referred. Here, there is room to mention only one instance of it; and of all the instances the most notable is surely Berlin.

By the very nature of its precarious position, Berlin is ideally suited, from the Russian point of view, to the stage-managing of a crisis whenever Soviet interests require. And for a great many years Soviet interests required that the Western allies should be made to leave Berlin as soon as possible: it was only after the Berlin Wall had cut off the flight to the German Federal Republic of the hundreds upon hundreds of skilled East German workers and highly qualified East German professional men who each year had fled to the West via West Berlin, that the East German economy began to acquire a certain degree of stability. Five or six years later, one could speak of it as stable. This in turn made it less necessary for the East Germans (and hence at one remove the Russians) to turn West Berlin into a communist-dominated area.[41]

But until 1967 or so, the fact that West Berlin was *not* dominated by the communists made it urgently necessary for the Russians to try to dominate it. The efforts they made were spasmodic: they would begin for no discernible reason at a particular point in time; they would continue vigorously until it became evident to the Russians that the West was not going to quit; they then subsided, and the Soviet diplomatic offensive switched to some new target (the Polaris bases in Scotland, for instance, or colonial regimes in Africa); while at the same time the Soviet diplomatic apparatus pondered new tactics, sought new allies, accumulated new stores of political and economic ammunition in readiness for the day when it should renew its assault on Berlin. The list of Soviet 'initiatives' over the Berlin question—the blockade of 1948, Khrushchev's ultimatum of 1958, the building of the Wall in 1961 —demonstrate clearly this sequence of peaks and troughs, where the peaks are the Soviet efforts to dominate West Berlin, and the troughs are their 'Brest-Litovsk tactics' (i.e. their acceptance of temporary defeat, their continuing intention ultimately to gain their objective, and their concentration meanwhile on the preparations necessary before a new assault could be attempted).

However, as we have seen, the improving situation in East Germany made it no longer necessary after 1963 or so for the USSR to regard the eviction of the West from Berlin as an urgent political objective; and the Four-Power Agreement of 1971 may well mark the end of communist harassment of the West's position in that city, though only time will tell.

If one turns from regarding *minutiae*, and looks instead at the whole grand sweep of Soviet foreign policy from 1917 to 1941 with regard to the great capitalist powers, the basic fact on which it was built was Soviet military weakness. The Soviet leaders themselves admitted this over and over again (see pp. 133–4). Therefore an open struggle was not likely to be profitable, and therefore it was avoided. In other words there was 'peace', an 'absence of fighting'. As a corollary, during the greater part of this period the USSR made determined efforts to build up its armed forces (in other words, to regroup, reinforce and replenish); and these efforts resulted, as we all know, in the re-creation of the Soviet Navy and the rebirth of the Red Army.

We cannot, of course, tell whether the Soviet Government, if given the time to complete the work of rebuilding and modernizing its forces, would have passed over to an open offensive, and launched on the principal bastions of Western capitalism that 'revolutionary war' of which Lenin had dreamed; because Hitler invaded Russia before that moment came.[42]

H

What, however, we *can* say is that, when the opportunity presented itself at the end of the Second World War to 'liquidate' those bastions (admittedly, minor bastions) of Western capitalism which found themselves in the grip of the Red Army, that opportunity was taken; and the 'bourgeoisie' of Poland, Hungary, Romania, Bulgaria, East Germany and Czechoslovakia ceased to exist as a 'class', just as those of Russia, Latvia, Lithuania, Estonia, Georgia and half a dozen other countries had ceased to exist before them.

We are also entitled to say as a matter of sheer historical fact that the USSR has been busily engaged in regrouping, replenishing and building up her forces in the years since the Second World War; and that this could be interpreted as being the first phase of Lenin's concept of *nakopleniye sil*.

Nevertheless, we cannot leave it like that. We are bound to take into serious consideration the very real possibility that the Soviet amassing of troops and equipment, which has gone on now for almost half a century, is not a Leninist *nakopleniye sil* at all, but a straightforward reaction to threatening Western responses.

It may be so. The trouble is that it is quite impossible to determine. To make things still more difficult, the reaction itself (if it was indeed a reaction) provoked a counter-reaction among Western governments, and this in turn was the cause of a further reaction from the Soviet Union. Which came first, the hen or the egg? And which was the hen, and which the egg, in the circumstances of Central Europe in 1945?

All that we can truthfully say is that, as between the USSR and the Western powers, there has been an 'absence of fighting' for a great many years; that the USSR has used those years to build up her armed forces; but that we do not know the *real* purpose, as distinct from the *declared* purpose, that lies behind this build-up. Nor can we tell whether today's real purpose might not change, if circumstances changed; so that, for instance, a significant reduction in NATO might not lead to today's real purpose, which is (we will assume) to react to Western armament increases, being replaced by tomorrow's real purpose, which is (we will equally imagine) to seek to profit by Western weakness to further the expansion of communism. Contrariwise, a change of circumstances that led to a strengthening of NATO might also lead to the abandonment of today's real purpose of waging 'revolutionary war' against Western Europe (if that is what today's real purpose of the Soviet leaders is), and its replacement by tomorrow's real purpose of seeking to do no more than react to Western initiatives.

There is one more point to be discussed. The North Vietnamese are, it goes without saying, a different breed of men from Soviet Russians; and their brand of Marxism-Leninism is not, at all points, the same as that of Moscow. Nevertheless their views on peace and those of the rulers of the Kremlin coincide to a remarkable degree, as has been already indicated above. In which connection, the peace terms agreed between the North Vietnamese and the Americans for the ending of the Vietnam War deserve especial study. They were printed in full in *The Times* on 25 January 1973; and it is on this version that the following analysis is based. First, the USA made enormous concessions, but North Vietnam made none of any substance. The United States, for instance, agreed to withdraw within sixty days its troops, military advisers and military personnel, including technical military personnel and military personnel associated with the pacification programme, armaments, munitions and war material (Article 5); North Vietnam gave no undertaking whatsoever as to what would happen to its own troops. It should be observed that the ban on 'foreign' troops is not applicable to the North Vietnamese, who do not regard themselves as foreigners in South Vietnam, because the whole of Vietnam, both North and South, is, they say, just one country that happens to be temporarily divided (see Article 15).

Second, the implementation of many of the major Articles of the settlement was to be effected as a result of decisions agreed between 'the two South Vietnamese parties' that signed the treaty in Paris. These two parties are, according to the text, 'the Government of the Republic of Vietnam' (i.e. President Thieu's Government) and 'the Provisional Revolutionary Government of the Republic of South Vietnam' (i.e. the Vietcong). What are the chances of 'agreed decisions' being arrived at between those two bodies? And what will happen if they do not reach an agreement? What will happen, too, if no agreement is reached between *all four* parties signatory to the treaty (the other two being the USA and North Vietnam), whose concurrence is said to be necessary for the implementation of the other major decisions?

For this is the heart of the matter. Any violation of the Agreement is to be investigated by the International Commission (Article 2 of the Protocol on Supervision and Control); and whenever the Commission is unable to correct this, it is to report the matter to the four signatories (Article 3 of the same protocol), so that they can hold consultations to find a solution. But what happens if they do not succeed in finding one? The violation will then continue unchecked; because there is no means provided in the Agreement for arbitration over a disputed point, still less for the enforcement of the arbitrator's award. To any party determined to pursue its aims, possessed of the means to do so, and indifferent to the methods by which they are pursued, this is giving *carte blanche* to sabotage the Agreement, so that it can attain its goals by other methods. In the context of South Vietnam, such a party might be either the Thieu regime or the Vietcong; but it is a fair bet that it will be the Vietcong, because of its greater efficiency. There can, in any case, be no doubt but that the Agreement is being sabotaged, and on a very large scale. In the twelve months subsequent to the signing of the Paris Agreement, 60,000 people, both South Vietnamese and communists, have been killed in South Vietnam.[43]

If, now, the reader will kindly turn back to what has been said on the subject of the Vietnam War in the chapter on 'Peace', he will find that it stated that the Vietnam communists would never sign a peace treaty until either they needed a breathing-space to reinforce and replenish, or else had beaten the Americans. Those words were written nearly seven years ago; they remain good to this day.

Finally, there is the question of neutrality. The chapter on the Soviet view of neutrality indicated that, in the Marxist view, there was no such thing as neutrality, properly speaking; and that therefore the uses made of neutrality by Soviet diplomacy were a policy of the second best, or of even the third best, operating from a position of weakness with regard to the area concerned. If, now, one starts to compare this theory with the realities of Soviet history, one finds a startling correlation between theory and practice.

The first Soviet proposals for 'perpetual neutrality' were made in 1920, and with reference to Lithuania and Estonia. As already indicated, the USSR at that moment was militarily extremely weak, and the territory of these two states could afford, and had previously afforded, a ready means of access into Russian territory for the armies of the Western 'bourgeois'. At that moment, Soviet Russia was quite unable to defend the whole of her sprawling frontier against foreign attack; so any proposal that might lead to the 'putting in baulk' of any section of it (especially one of a considerable strategic importance) was bound to be advantageous for the Russian communists. This, no doubt, is why they made the proposal; but it is important to note that they did so only because they were weak. Once they had recovered their strength, there were no further suggestions that the two Baltic States be 'perpetually neutralized'.

The Soviet proposals of 1958 for the 'perpetual neutrality' of Japan follow a similar pattern (see pp. 187–8); and the reasons why the Russians suggested the 'perpetual neutrality' of Austria, and the advantages this would confer on them, have also been discussed above (see pp. 182–3). There seems little point in proceeding further with what can be no more than a recapitulation of a previous chapter of this book; it will suffice, I hope, if I assert roundly that no proposal for the 'perpetual neutrality' of another country has ever been made by the USSR, except in conformity with the principles enunciated at the beginning of the penultimate paragraph.

These remarks also apply to the Antarctic Treaty of 1959 and the

Treaty on Outer Space of 1967, both of which in effect confer the status of 'perpetual neutrality' upon the areas in question. The principles behind the Russian willingness to sign these particular treaties can be shown operating most clearly in the case of the Antarctic Treaty.

For the simple fact is that Antarctica is a long, long way from Russia. Nor could Russia easily get total possession of it, in view of the presence of other powers in that region; nor would Russia's strategic position be noticeably improved if she could. On the other hand, Antarctica is really not very far away from the Western defensive positions based upon Australia and also (as the Russians believe) on South Africa. To agree not to seek what one does not want, on the strict understanding that one's potential enemies will decline to seek what they might *possibly* want, is good business from anybody's point of view: one loses nothing, and one gains a lot. In this particular instance, the Russians gain relief from the heavy expenditure that they would surely have had to incur, if they had felt obliged to put military installations into Antarctica.

Soviet proposals for the mere 'neutrality' of a country, as distinct from 'perpetual neutrality', are a different kettle of fish. The sole function of these is to try and ensure that, if war were to break out between the USSR and a third party, the 'neutral' country would remain neutral, and would not swell the ranks of the Russians' enemies. It is clear that this is a compromise between the wholly unacceptable position of seeing the country in quesion enrolled among the enemies of the USSR and the position the Kremlin aims at, where it is enrolled among its friends. It is clear also that it is a compromise negotiated from a position of weakness. If the USSR were strong enough with regard to the country in question and also with regard to its potential capitalist supporters, it could compel it to become its ally, as it has done in the case of Poland, which, left to itself, would turn to the West and not to the Soviet Union. In those cases where the Soviet leadership is clearly not going to be able to achieve the latter (the ideal) goal, it prefers to aim at neutrality, which is neither the one thing nor the other, rather than see the particular country entering the ranks of its foes.

This, too, is a policy of the second best. The ideal solution would be for the country in question to be an ally of the Soviet Union, if not an actual part of the Communist bloc; the worst solution would be for that country to become an ally of the imperialists. If the former solution is unobtainable, and the latter seems to be possible, the best solution obtainable by the Soviet Union is the neutrality of that particular country.

It is worth noting that, although in this kind of treaty the USSR naturally has to bind herself to observing the same principles of neutrality and non-aggression towards the other signatory as the latter has done towards her, this has never restrained the Russians from indulging in every form of aggression against the other signatory, whenever it has suited her book. The relevant treaties with Latvia, Lithuania, Estonia and Finland were all in full force at the time of the Soviet invasion; though the usual sophistry was produced to camouflage this.

# Notes

While this book has been in the press, the UN General Assembly has passed unopposed a motion defining aggression. It retains the rider which the most recent edition of the *Diplomatic Dictionary* had dropped (see p. 79); and it makes the Security Council the final arbiter of whether aggression has, or has not, been committed. The full text can be found in *The Times* of 16 December 1974.

Alternative dates, when given, are to allow for the change in the Russian calendar.

## Chapter 1    Whose View?

1   They exist, too, for Soviet internal policy, but to try to cram into one book the basic principles of both Soviet foreign policy and Soviet domestic policy seemed to me to be too bulky an undertaking.
2   *A Dictionary of Philosophy* (Progress Publishers, Moscow, 1967), p. 75.
3   The fact that there was a division in the Party on the wisdom, or otherwise, of publishing Solzhenitsyn's novel does not affect the issue. It was Khrushchev who was the leader of the Party; Khrushchev who was the keen de-Stalinizer; and Khrushchev who gave permission to publish.

## Chapter 2    The Soviet View of War

1   See, for instance, the views on the causes of the First World War expressed in such works as A. J. P. Taylor's *The Struggle for the Mastery in Europe, 1848–1918* (Oxford University Press, 1971) and J. A. Spender's *Fifty Years of Europe*.
2   For Lenin's view of the origins of the First World War, see his *Socialism and War* (1915) or pages 34–8 of this book.
3   Speech at the Second Congress of the Communist International.
4   See the account in *Bol'shaya Sovietskaya Entsiklopediya* (hereafter shown as *BSE*), 3rd ed., vol. 5, p. 340.
5   *BSE*, 1st ed., vol. 12, pp. 573–4.
6   Henry McLeavy, *The Modern History of China* (Weidenfeld & Nicolson, 1967), p. 260.
7   For the first set of demands see Tanner, *The Winter War* (Stanford University Press, 1957), pp. 28–30; for the text of the Treaty of Moscow, see pp. 263–7 of the same work.
8   Djilas, *Conversations with Stalin* (Hart-Davis, 1962), p. 140.
9   Lenin, *Bourgeois Pacifism and Socialist Pacifism* (March 1916).
10   Raymond L. Garthoff, *How Russia Makes War* (Allen & Unwin, 1954), p. 11.
11   *Leninskii Sbornik XII*, pp. 398–9.
12   See Marx's *Critique of the Gotha Programme* (May 1875).
13   See the Introduction to *F. Engels: Izbranniye Voenniye Proiz-vedeniya* (Voenizdat, Moscow, 1957). See Select Bibliography.

14 See, for instance, his letter of 7 July 1866.
15 See, for instance, the Appendix to *Anti-Dühring* entitled 'Infantry Tactics Derived from Material Causes' (FLPH, Moscow, 1959).
16 He returned to Russia in November 1905; but that was after the war with Japan had ended.
17 Though not his first mention of Clausewitz. This occurs in *The Collapse of the Second International*, which was written in late May and early June of 1915.
18 See, for instance, *Voennaya Istoriya: Uchebnik* (Voenizdat, 1971), p. 112.
19 It should further be noted that this Soviet emphasis on speed, mobility and the attack was in notable contrast to the strategic thinking of the French and British at the outbreak of the Second World War. There, the concept of the static defence—the Maginot Line mentality—was greatly favoured; though this in turn was mostly a reflection of the kind of war that the Western generals had experienced in the years between 1914–18.
20 Marx-Engels, *Sochineniya* (hereafter shown as *ME*), 1st Russian edition (Moscow, 1953), vol. 10, p. 535.
21 *Socialism and War* (1915).
22 *Malaya Sovietskaya Entsiklopediya* (Moscow, 1931), 1st ed., vol. 2.
23 See, for instance, the article entitled 'Voina' in the latest edition of *BSE*.
24 See, for instance, *BSE*, 1st ed., vol. 12, pp. 573–4.
25 *The Military Programme of the Proletarian Revolution* (1916).
26 These rules are scattered over a wide range of his writings. He was, being Lenin, naturally particularly concerned with the *political* aspects of the waging of them, but military advice is also sometimes included.
27 This statement was true for all armies until quite recent times. In the case of the British Army, it was true until the nineteenth century, apart from those few fortunate enough to be accepted by the Chelsea Hospital.
28 For examples of Marx revelling in war, see his comments on the Russo-Turkish War of 1876–7, and also those on the American Civil War. For Engels, see his *Debate on the Polish Question in Frankfurt* (1848).
29 I am gratified to have the support of Professor E. H. Carr on this point. See *The Bolshevik Revolution* (3 vols, London, 1950–3), vol. 3, note E, 'The Marxist Attitude to War'.
30 J. V. Stalin, *Works* (Moscow, 1953), vol. 11, p. 208.
31 Speech of 6 January 1961 to the Moscow Conference of Communist Parties.
32 *Istoriya Vsesoyuznoy Kommunisticheskoi Partii (Bol'shevikov); Kratkii Kurs* (Moscow, 1950), p. 161. The second edition of the *BSE* says the same (vol. 8, pp. 572–3). The phrasing of the third edition of the *BSE* is much less gratingly Stalinist, but its content is essentially the same as that of the second.
33 *Ibid.*
34 Speech at the First All-Russia Congress on Adult Education (1919).
35 *Ibid.*
36 *A Caricature of Marxism* (October, 1916).
37 From the article 'A Revolutionary Army and a Revolutionary Government' (27 June/10 July 1905).

38   *Ibid.*

39   Speech at the First All-Russia Congress on Adult Education.

40   See, in addition to the works already quoted, the subject-index to the fifth edition of Lenin's works.

41   *ME*, 1st Russian ed., vol. 10, p. 726.

42   *BSE*, 1st ed., vol. 49, p. 58.

43   For a Leninist view of the wars of Louis XIV, see *BSE*, 2nd ed., vol. 45, p. 468. For Lenin's own view of the effect of the First World War, see, for instance, the first of the *Letters From Afar* (7/20 March 1917).

44   *ME*, 1st Russian ed., vol. 9, p. 386.

45   *Marx-Engels: Selected Correspondence* (Lawrence & Wishart, 1956), p. 374.

46   Lenin, *The Fall of Port Arthur* (1905).

47   Letter of Marx to Engels, 7 July 1866.

48   *The Civil War in France.*

49   Letter to F. Lasalle, 4 February 1859.

50   *ME*, 2nd Russian ed., vol. 36, pp. 329–31.

51   *The Fundamentals of Marxism-Leninism* (FLPH, Moscow, 1965, 2nd ed.).

52   *Ibid.*

53   *Ausserordentlicher Internationaler Sozialisten-Kongress zu Basel am 24 und 25 November 1912* (Buchhandlung Vorwärts Paul Singer, Berlin, 1912).

54   Lenin's attitude in 1914 can be found expounded in his *The Tasks of Revolutionary Social Democracy in the European War* (not later than 24 August/6 September 1914) and *The War and Russian Social-Democracy* (not later than 28 September/11 October 1914). Its subsequent development can be traced in such works as *Under a False Flag* (February 1915), *The Collapse of the Second International* (May-June 1915), *Socialism and War* (July-August 1915) etc., etc.

55   *Socialism and War.*

56   *The Question of Peace* (July-August 1915).

57   *Socialism and War.*

58   *The Discussion on Self-Determination Summed Up* (Autumn 1916).

59   *The Junius Pamphlet* (1916).

60   *Socialism and War.*

61   *Under a False Flag.*

62   *The Draft Resolution Proposed by the Left Wing at Zimmerwald* (August 1915).

63   *Programma KPSS* (Politizdat, Moscow, 1961). See also *Diplomaticheskii Slovar'*, 2nd ed., vol. 3, p. 216. Brezhnev, speaking to the Twenty-Third Party Congress, used a similar, though not identical, expression. Other examples abound.

64   *Slovar' Sovremennogo Russkogo Literaturnogo Yazyka* states it is the noun from *predotvrashchat'*; and it defines the meaning of the latter as *nie dopuskat' nastupleniya, osushchestvleniya chego-libo niepriyatnogo, plokhogo* (Akademiya Nauk, Moscow, 1961), vol. 11, p. 146.

65   I do not see how any edition of Sokolovsky can be understood in any sense other than that outlined here. Other authorities too may be cited in support of this contention. The point is discussed in detail later in this book.

I

66  See, for instance, Admiral Gorshkov's article in *Morskoi Sbornik*, February 1973.
67  *ME*, 1st Russian ed., vol. 21, p. 211.
68  Lenin's views on colonial wars can be found set out in detail in his *The War in China* (written September-October 1900; published in *Iskra*, no. 1, December 1900). This is an early work; but on this particular subject his views underwent no change throughout his life.
69  *Politicheskii Slovar'* (Politizdat, 1958), pp. 330-1.
70  For an authoritative discussion of this point, see E. H. Carr, *op. cit.*, vol. 1, note B, 'The Bolshevik Doctrine of Self-Determination'.
71  For a brief summary of the reasons why, see my *A Guide To Marxism* (Faber, 1966), pp. 148-9.
72  E.g. *Marksizm-Leninizm o Voine i Armii* (Voenizdat, Moscow, 1958), pp. 85-6.
73  Sokolovsky, *Military Strategy* (Praeger, 1963), p. 178. For the convenience of my readers, I am quoting from the English translation.
74  Sokolovsky, *Voennaya Strategiya* (Voenizdat, 1968), 3rd ed., p. 222.
75  *Voennaya Istoriya: Uchebnik* (Voenizdat, 1971), pp. 318-26.
76  *Ibid.*, p. 318.
77  *BSE*, 3rd ed., vol. 5, p. 283.
78  Halperin, *Limited War in the Nuclear Age* (Wiley, New York, 1963), pp. 2-3.
79  *Ibid.*
80  *Concise Oxford Dictionary*, 5th ed., p. 228. The Russian word *koalitsiya* is defined by an impeccable Soviet source as 'a voluntary alliance of states or parties for the attainment of common aims' (*Slovar' Sovremennogo Literaturnogo Russkogo Yazyka*, vol. 5, p. 1082).
81  George F. Kennan, *The Decision To Intervene* (Faber, 1958), p. 82.
82  Speech at Moscow Guberniya Party Conference, 20 November 1920.
83  *ME*, 2nd Russian ed., vol. 15, pp. 337-47.
84  See *A Caricature of Marxism*.
85  *Message of Greetings to the Bavarian Soviet Republic*.
86  *BSE*, 2nd ed., vol. 8, p. 583. The third edition (vol. 5, pp. 282-3) is less outspoken; but what it says agrees, in essence, with the doctrine preached by the second edition.
87  See, for instance, *Statements about the War Made by our Party before the Revolution* (May 1917) and *The Tasks of the Proletariat in the Present Revolution* (April 1917).
88  *Farewell Letter to the Swiss Workers* (26 March/8 April 1917), also *Several Theses* (1915).
89  Speech at the First All-Russia Congress of Soviets (June 1917).
90  *O Tezisakh po Agrarnomy Voprosy K.P.F.* (March 1922).
91  The text of the letter can be found in the fifth Russian edition of Lenin's works, vol. 49, pp. 287-8.
92  See, for instance, *BSE*, 2nd ed., vol. 8, p. 573. The third edition expresses itself more cautiously on this subject, for the reasons already given; but readers are referred to vol. 5, p. 283 for an insight into its real view of the matter.

93 It is no rebuttal of my contention to say that Stalin's purpose in seizing the Baltic States was purely strategic. If the *sole* purpose of grabbing these three countries had been to improve the defensive position of Leningrad, there was no need to have thrust upon their inhabitants a Soviet polity and economy which few of them wanted.

94 When I say that the encyclopaedia was published in 1928, I mean that it was in that year that the volume containing the article 'Voina' ('war') appeared.

95 *Ibid.*

96 *Op. cit.*, vol. 5, pp. 282–3. Interestingly enough, it distinguishes between 'revolutionary wars' and 'wars fought in defence of the Soviet Fatherland'.

97 Sokolovsky, *op. cit.*, p. 178.

98 See the discussion on this point in the article entitled 'Voina' in *BSE* (1st ed.).

99 *BSE* (Moscow, 1928), 1st ed., vol. 12, pp. 569–76.

100 See Khrushchev's speech of 6 January 1961 to the Moscow Conference of Communist Parties.

101 For confirmation of the presence of Red Army units in Finland, see for instance Lenin's *Speech at a Meeting in the Polytechnic Museum* of 23 August 1918. For his general attitude towards the state of affairs in Finland see his speech at the Seventh Party Congress.

102 Stalin, *Works*, vol. 4, p. 5.

103 For some details on the 'bolshevization' of the occupied areas of Poland, see the articles entitled 'Pol'sha' and 'Pol'skii Revolyut-sionnyi Komitet' in *BSE*, 2nd ed.

104 *Speech Delivered at a Congress of Leather Industry Workers* (2 October 1920).

105 *BSE*, 1st ed., vol. 49, p. 58.

106 *Leninskii Sbornik XII*, p. 417.

107 *The Civil War in France.*

108 See, for instance, their writings on the subject of the Indian Mutiny.

109 *ME*, 1st Russian ed., vol. 9, p. 386.

110 *The Civil War in France.*

111 *Ibid.*

112 For an authoritative discussion on this point, see Carr, *op. cit.*, vol. 3, note E, 'The Marxist Attitude to War'.

113 Thucydides, *The Peloponnesian War*, book VII, ch. 23.

114 The definition in the encyclopaedia is based upon a number of resolutions tabled by the Soviet Government on the subject of aggression, of which that presented to the League of Nations in 1933, and that to the United Nations in 1954, were probably the most important. In 1950, the communist-dominated World Peace Congress defined aggression as being the first use of force by one state against another state; and it went on to explain that 'no political or economic consideration, no reason arising from the internal situation or any internal conflict in a State can justify armed intervention by another State' (see p. 177 of this book).

115 The reasons for their attitude are given succinctly in Sir Isaiah Berlin's *Karl Marx: His Life and Environment* (London: Oxford University Press, 1960), 2nd ed., pp. 164–6.

116 Marx's and Engels' attitude towards this war was complicated by the fact that Napoleon III was a participant. And he had become involved in it for what they regarded as completely the wrong reasons. But

that did not affect their view that it was a 'war of national liberation' so far as Italy was concerned.

117  *Bellicose Militarism and the Anti-Militarist Tactics of Social Democracy* (23 July/5 August 1908).

118  *Ibid.*

119  Lecture on 'The Proletariat and the War'.

120  *The Russian Brand of Südekum* (19 January/1 February 1915).

121  *Ibid.*

122  *Socialism and War in Lenin: Collected Works* (Progress Publishers, 1964), vol. 21, p. 300.

123  The passage quoted comes from the section of *The Proletarian Revolution and the Renegade Kautsky* entitled 'What is internationalism?' and the whole was written in October-November 1918.

124  For a fuller, but still concise, explanation of 'class' and the 'class struggle', see *A Guide to Marxism*, pp. 31-42.

125  Lecture on 'The Proletariat and the War'.

126  First All-Russia Congress on Adult Education.

127  *Draft Programme of the RCP(b)*, the section entitled 'Preamble to the Military Section of the Programme'. The word 'such' in the passage quoted refers to civil wars, revolutionary wars, and wars in general between the 'bourgeois' and the 'proletariat', which Lenin had just been discussing.

128  *Marksizm-Leninizm o Voine i Armii* (Voenizdat, Moscow, 1968), 5th ed., p. 79.

129  *Slovar' Sovremennogo Russkogo Literaturnogo Yazyka* (Akademiya Nauk SSSR, 1950), vol. 1, pp. 47-8.

130  *Diplomaticheskii Slovar'* (Moscow, 1960), vol. 1, p. 16.

131  *Ibid.*, vol. 1, p. 16.

132  *BSE*, 2nd ed., vol. 1, p. 350.

133  *BSE*, 3rd ed., vol. 1, p. 576.

134  *Ibid.*, p. 577.

135  *Ibid.*, p. 582.

136  See, for instance, *Diplomaticheskii Slovar'* (Moscow, 1961), vol. 2, p. 127.

137  *Ibid.*, vol. 1, p. 12. The 1971 edition says the same.

138  *BSE*, 1st ed., vol. 12, p. 574.

139  *BSE*, 3rd ed., vol. 7, p. 368.

140  See, for instance, *BSE*, 2nd ed., vol. 39, p. 511.

141  *Pravda*, 4 November 1956.

142  *Ibid.*

143  *Ibid.*

144  *Pravda*, 21 August 1968.

145  *Ibid.*

146  Compare *Diplomaticheskii Slovar'*, vol. 1, p. 16, para. 3 of the 1960 edition, with vol. 1, p. 15, para. 1 of the 1971 edition.

147  *Op. cit.*, p. 6.

148  Of course, those who prefer the modern Soviet account of the events in Georgia to the 1928 version, will obviously conclude that aggression was not committed. So great an authority as E. H. Carr, however, has no hesitation in saying that the sovietization of Georgia was 'enforced' (*The Bolshevik Revolution*, vol. 1, p. 349).

149  In the original German, the word is *Politik*, which can mean either 'politics' or 'policy'. The Russian word *politika*, which was used by

Lenin to translate it, also bears the double meaning. In English, however, one cannot sit on the fence; and therefore, each time that one quotes the dictum of Clausewitz or his many variants of it, one has to plump for either 'policy' or 'politics'. I have made my choice dependent upon the context.

150 *Leninskii Sbornik XII*, pp. 440-1.
151 *Ibid.*, pp. 436-7. Colonel Graham's famous translation of Clausewitz prefers to say, 'for policy has declared the war'; but the original German is 'die Politik hat den Krieg *erzeugt*' (italics mine). Lenin certainly understood this in my sense, and not in Colonel Graham's; because, having copied out the original German, he put against it a note which runs 'politika *rodila* voiny' (italics mine).
152 The same line of reasoning is expressed in *A Caricature of Marxism* and elsewhere.
153 *The Military Programme of the Proletarian Revolution.*
154 For details, see *The Times*, 6 April 1968.
155 *Leninskii Sbornik XII*, pp. 408-9.
156 See, for instance, *Two Tactics of Social Democracy* (1905).
157 For the same sentiment expressed later on in his life, see *Prophetic Words* (June 1918).
158 His most important writings on the subject of the Paris Commune are: *Plan of Reading about the Paris Commune* (1906); *Lessons of the Commune* (March, 1908); *Memories of the Paris Commune* (1911); *Marxism on the State* (1917); and *The Proletarian Revolution and the Renegade Kautsky* (1918). The latter is perhaps the most important of all, because in it Lenin explains the reasons why the young Soviet Government was adopting the policies that it did. One of the most important of these reasons, according to Lenin, was that the Bolshevik leaders had learnt the lessons of the Paris Commune.
159 *Lessons of the Commune.* See also *The Proletarian Revolution and the Renegade Kautsky.*
160 *The Proletarian Revolution and the Renegade Kautsky* in the section entitled 'Can There Be Equality Between the Exploited and the Exploiter?'
161 *Ibid.*
162 *Two Tactics of Social-Democracy* (1905).
163 For instance, in *The 'Disarmament' Slogan* (1916).
164 One instance of Clausewitz's use of this expression is to be found in book I, ch. I, section 27 of *On War*; another is in the heading to the sixth chapter of book VIII. They, together with Lenin's notes and comments, can be found in *Leninskii Sbornik XII*, pp. 398-9 and 431-3. There are several others.
165 Once again, Graham's translation is defective. For Lenin's version see *Leninskii Sbornik XII*, pp. 396-7.
166 *Ibid.*, pp. 436-7. Graham's translation runs: 'The subordination of the military point of view to the political is therefore the only thing which is possible.' The Soviet version in Russian is a poor rendering of the German.
167 *Ibid.*, pp. 432-3. Graham translates the final clause as 'a rapier to exchange thrusts and feints and parries'; and one assumes he means 'to exchange thrusts and feints and parries with an enemy'. But the German here is *und mit dem sie [die Politik] Stösse, Finten und*

*Paraden abwechseln lässt*; and ¡the last two words can only mean 'alternates between', 'rings the changes on'.

168   Lenin's attachment to the overall primacy of *politika* was so great that he went so far as to declare that it had primacy even over economics, which in classical Marxism is the ultimate determinant. See his *Once Again on the Trade Unions* (25 January 1921), the section entitled 'Politics and Economics. Dialectics and Eclecticism'.

169   *Bourgeois Pacifism and Socialist Pacifism* (March 1916).

170   Sokolovsky, *op. cit.*, p. 24.

171   *The Peace Programme* (March 1916). The English translation in the *Collected Works* renders *politika*, by 'politics', which I think inappropriate in this context. I have also preferred 'relationships' to 'relation' as a translation of *otnosheniya*. Finally, I have elaborated on *s zapis'yu*, and produced 'with the record written into it' instead of just 'with the record'.

172   *Leninskii Sbornik XII*, p. 429, and elsewhere.

173   The name of Clausewitz was constantly being invoked as late as 1943. See, for instance, *Politika i Voennaya Strategiya* (Gospolitizdat, 1943).

174   *BSE*, 3rd ed., vol; 8, p. 285.

175   See, for instance, Sokolovsky's *Voennaya Strategiya*, 3rd ed., p. 28.

176   First All-Russia Congress on Adult Education (May 1919).

177   *Goryuchii Material v Mirovoi Politike* (August 1906).

178   For Lenin on the inevitability of war between capitalism and communism, see his speech at the Eighth Party Congress. There are many other similar passages.

179   The gist of the above is expressed clearly and authoritatively by Engels in his letter to J. Bloch of 21–2 September 1890, and in another letter of 25 January 1894, addressed to H. Starkenburg. Both these letters can be found in an English translation in *Karl Marx and Frederick Engels: Selected Correspondence* (FLPH, Moscow, 1956).

180   The argument is developed in full in part II, ch. 3, of *Anti-Dühring*, as well as in the Appendix to that work, entitled 'Infantry Tactics Derived From Material Causes'.

181   Letter to Engels of 7 July 1866.

182   *Anti-Dühring*, part II, ch. 3.

183   For a discussion of this point in Soviet military writing, see E. A. Razin, *Istoriya Voennogo Iskusstva* (Voenizdat, 1955), vol. 1, pp. 219–21.

184   In his poem 'Fuzzy-Wuzzy'.

185   Soviet military writing terms this 'failure of Hitler *niereal'nost'* ('a lack of a sense of actuality') and censures him severely for it. See, for instance, Colonel M. P. Skirdo, *Narod, Armiya, Polkovodets* (Voenizdat, 1970).

186   See, for instance, *Lessons of the Moscow Uprising* (August 1906).

187   *Leninskii Sbornik XII*, pp. 422–3.

188   The 'permanently operating factors' can be found quoted and expounded in the *BSE*, 2nd ed., under the heading 'Postoyanno Deistvuyushchiye Faktory Voiny' (vol. 34, pp. 255–6). The encyclopaedia says that they were formulated by Stalin in a People's Commissariat of Defence Order No. 55 of 23 February 1942; but Professor Raymond Garthoff, in his admirable book *How Russia*

*Makes War* (Allen & Unwin, 1954), says that Stalin first formulated them in 1918, and repeated them in 1941. Faced with such Titans, a minnow like me does best to refrain from comment. I should perhaps add, however, that though the Soviet encyclopaedia *implies* that they were first formulated in the Order of 23 February 1942, it does not actually say so.

189 When Garthoff wrote his book, only one of these 'transitory factors' had actually been formulated; and that was 'surprise'. The *BSE* article, however, which was published subsequently, lists two more: 'superiority in military preparedness' and 'superiority in military experience' (*BSE*, 2nd ed., vol. 34, p. 257).

190 M. V. Taranchuk, *O Postoyanno Deistvuyushchikh Faktorakh Reshayushchikh Sud'bu Voiny* (Voenizdat, Moscow, 1952). The author's words are really only a re-hash of those of Stalin, but since the book was published in Stalin's lifetime, this is not very surprising.

191 *Ibid.*, pp. 24–45.

192 *Ibid.*, p. 27.

193 E.g. Taranchuk, *op. cit.*, pp. 78–90. It should be pointed out that Taranchuk's work is cited as an authority on the 'permanently operating factors' by the *BSE* (2nd ed.), in its bibliography at the end of its article on the subject.

194 S. N. Kozlov, M. V. Smirnov, I. S. Baz', and P. A. Sidorov, *O Sovietskoi Voennoi Nauke* (Voenizdat, Moscow, 1964), pp. 292–332.

195 See, for instance, V. E. Savkin, *Osnovniye Printsipy Operativnogo Iskusstva i Taktiki* (Voenizdat, 1972), pp. 302–15.

196 For a discussion of this in English, see *Marxism-Leninism on War and Army* (Progress Publishers, Moscow, 1972), pp. 392–3.

197 *Ibid.*

198 Many may think that it would never have taken root in Alsatian consciousness; but this, whether true or not, is irrelevant to the present argument.

199 The quotation is from *The Civil War in France*.

200 Major-General P. I. Sergeev (ed.), *Vooruzhenniye Sily Kapitalisticheskikh Gosudarstv* (Voenizdat, 1971), p. 3.

201 Major-General M. A. Mil'shtein and Colonel A. K. Slobodenko, *Voenniye Idealogi Kapitalisticheskikh Stran o Kharaktere i Sposobakh Vedeniya Sovremennoi Voiny* (Znaniye, 1967). General Zavyalov's article in *Red Star* on 19 April 1973 says essentially the same thing. See also *BSE*, 3rd ed., vol. 5, p. 283.

202 See, for instance, David Lloyd George, *The Truth about the Peace Treaties* (Gollancz, 1938), p. 319.

203 For further details on 'counter-revolution' and 'the dictatorship of the proletariat', see my *Guide to Marxism*, pp. 148–9.

204 See, for instance, the articles entitled 'Pol'sha' and 'Pol'skii Revolyutsionnyi Komitet' in *BSE*, 2nd ed.

205 *BSE*, 3rd ed., vol. 7, p. 368.

206 *Ibid.*

207 *Ibid.*

208 Carr, *op. cit.*, vol. 1, p. 349.

209 I suspect that the detailed exposition of the need to 'sovietize' is to be found in his *The War of the Classes* (*Voina Klassov*), which was published in 1921. Modern Soviet sources insist that it is one of his major works; and it is therefore significant that, except for a few

snippets, it has been omitted from the two volumes of his *Selected Works*, which were published in Moscow in 1964. The few snippets are concerned exclusively with details of strategy and tactics; political matters are not discussed in any of them. Yet the very title of Tukhachevsky's book indicates clearly that political matters must have formed an important part of their content. I must warn the reader, however, that as I have never yet succeeded in finding a library with a copy of the first edition, I have only surmise to guide me as to its contents. If anyone knows where a copy is to be found, I would be very glad indeed of the information.

210    M. N. Tukhachevsky, *Izbranniye Proizvedeniya* (Voenizdat, 1964), vol. 1, p. 258. The modern editorial footnote is very amusing. It is also very revealing.

211    Triandafillov, *Kharakter Operatsii Sovremennykh Armii*, p. 167. All my references to this work are taken from the second edition (Voenizdat, 1932).

212    *Ibid.*, p. 167.

213    *Ibid.*, p. 168.

214    *A voevodstvo (województwo* in Polish) is a Polish province; *uezd* is the old Russian word for a district.

215    A valuable, but nowadays rather neglected source is the anonymous work *The Dark Side of the Moon* (Faber, 1946).

216    *Ibid.*, p. 51.

217    For a discussion on the exodus of the Finnish population, see A. F. Upton, *Finland in Crisis, 1940–1941* (Faber, 1964), pp. 64–7.

218    M. Djilas, *Conversations with Stalin* (Hart-Davis, 1962), p. 105.

219    For a more detailed explanation of why a Marxist can genuinely think that there is no difference of real importance between (say) the Persian and the Lydian social systems, see *Guide to Marxism*, pp. 31–3.

220    Djilas, *op. cit.*, pp. 99–105.

221    *BSE*, 3rd ed., vol. 5, p. 282.

222    *Military Strategy*, p. 182. The third Russian edition has the same passage.

223    Sokolovsky, *op. cit.*, 3rd ed., p. 221.

224    *Ibid.*, pp. 217–18.

225    *BSE*, 3rd ed., vol. 5, p. 284.

226    *Krasnaya Zvezda*, 28 March 1973.

227    *Krasnaya Zvezda*, 7 February 1974.

228    *Voennaya Istoriya: Uchebnik* (Voenizdat, 1971), p. 340.

229    Lenin, *War and Revolution* (1917).

230    *Marksizm-Leninizm o Voine i Armii* (Voenizdat, 1968), 5th ed., p. 94.

231    *Military Strategy*, p. 203. The third Russian edition has the same passage.

232    *Ibid.*, p. 169.

233    *Ibid.*, p. 198. The third Russian edition carries the same paragraph.

234    Colonel-General Professor N. A. Lomov, *Sovietskaya Voennaya Doktrina* (Znaniye, 1963), p .26. Notice how the writer distinguishes between 'armed struggle', which is a purely military gefuffle, and 'war', which is a political business carried on by using soldiers.

235    *Military Strategy*, pp. 170–1. The third Russian edition has the same passage.

236    See, for instance, pp. 223, 226, 278 and 281 of *Military Strategy*.

237 *Voennaya Strategiya*, 3rd ed., pp. 298-9. I have used the Russian version, because at this point the English translation is faulty. *Konechnyi*, when applied to *tsel'*, does not mean 'final', which might be interpreted as meaning 'the last of a series', but 'fundamental'. See *Slovar' Sovremennogo Russkogo Literaturnogo Yazyka*, vol. 5, p. 1290, where this very example is given.

238 *Ibid. Military Strategy* has the same passage.

239 Lieutenant-General I. Zavyalov, *Tvorcheskii Kharakter Sovietskoi Voennoi Doktriny* (*Krasnaya Zvezda*, 19 April 1973).

240 Blind mole that I am, I cannot find this passage, despite my clear recollection of having seen it in this book, and despite hours spent in trying to find it again. I would willingly confess that my memory had played me false, had I not just stumbled upon Professor Raymond Garthoff's citation of the phrase in his introduction to the English translation of the book.

241 I must make quite clear that, although throughout this section I have depicted the Russians as keen to sovietize the territory of a beaten enemy and, in particular, as keen to sovietize America and Western Europe after their victory in a third world war, I do not believe for one moment that, so long as the balance of mutual deterrence remains much as it is today, the Russians would start a war of this kind simply in order to sovietize the West. If, however, by some appalling mischance a third world war should somehow happen to break out (and by 'world war' I mean a war on a world-wide scale employing thermonuclear weapons), then it is indeed my contention that the sovietization of Western Europe and America would be the *political* aim for which the USSR would be fighting.

242 'Force' is used here in the fifth of the meanings given to it in the *O.E.D.* (corrected reissue, 1933).

243 *Marksizm-Leninizm o Voine i Armii* (Voenizdat, Moscow, 1958), p. 54.

244 *Capital*, book I, ch. 31. Marx's original text has *ein ökonomische Potenz*. The Russian version prepared in Moscow by the Institute of Marxism-Leninism translates this phrase as *ekonomicheskaya potentsia*. I know of no English translation which has yet managed to convey the full meaning of the original; and I have certainly been unsuccessful in thinking of one myself.

245 The assassins were caught, and tried before a West German court. An account of the case, based upon official German records, can be found in Karl Anders, *Murder to Order* (Ampersand, London, 1965).

246 *The Proletarian Revolution and the Renegade Kautsky*, paragraphs 14 and 15 of the section entitled 'What is Internationalism?' The version above is my own translation, taken from the fifth Russian edition.

247 I am here using 'exploitation' and 'exploited' in the Western, not in the Marxist, sense. For details, see, for instance, Professor Hugh Seton-Watson's *The East European Revolution* (Methuen, 1952).

248 Except in the case of Lithuania, where it was the Poles who were mainly responsible for expelling the Reds.

249 For Lenin, see, for instance, his remarks to the correspondent of the American journal, *The World*, 21 February 1920. Stalin's acknowledgment of Soviet weakness was made in his speech of 4 February 1931, at the First All-Union Conference of Leading

I*

Personnel of Socialist Industry. It was quoted by Deutscher in his *Stalin* in the chapter entitled 'The "Great Change" '. The whole speech can be found in J. Stalin, *Works*, vol. 13, pp. 31–44; but the reader should be aware that there are significant differences of translation between that version—the 1953 edition of the *Problems of Leninism*—and the edition of the *Problems of Leninism* which appears to have been used by Deutscher.

250 See, for instance, *Marxism-Leninism on War and Army* (Progress Publishers, 1972), pp. 324–34.

251 For the value of nuclear weapons as a means of winning the war quickly, see *Marxism-Leninism on War and Army*, pp. 392–3.

252 For a recent authoritative statement of the value of surprise, see V. E. Savkin, *Osnovniye Printsipy Operativnogo Iskusstva i Taktiki* (Voenizdat, 1972), pp. 302–15.

253 Both papers covered both exercises in detail. The relevant dates are 22–9 September 1967 and 9–15 March 1970.

254 See Judges, chapters 7 and 8.

255 In January 1970, I quoted these remarks of Deutscher in a lecture I was giving at the Royal United Service Institution (as it then was). I was speaking without notes, and I stated that Deutscher came to visit Sandhurst in 1951; and this date was published in the report of the lecture that appeared in the June 1970 number of the Institution's *Journal*. The correct date is 1958, as I have given it above.

256 Strobe Talbott (trans. and ed.), *Khrushchev Remembers* (Andre Deutsch, 1971).

257 'Coalition warfare' in the Soviet sense can be reduced to the proposition that, in a war between East and West, the NATO Alliance would disintegrate owing to mutual jealousy and suspicion, while the Warsaw Pact would hold firm. For further details see pp. 45–8.

258 See, for instance, *BSE*, 2nd ed., vol. 8, p. 258.

259 On page 5 of the 1958 edition, and on page 13 of the 1968 edition. The dictum is quoted in many other authoritative publications, and not only those of the Ministry of Defence.

260 *Pravda*, 31 March 1971. *Formirovaniye* is the Russian word which I have translated *moulding*. Those who say that the Russian-English dictionaries give 'forming' or 'formation' or (of an army) 'raising' as the sole meanings of that word should look at the original Russian text of *The Programme of the Communist Party of the Soviet Union*, and compare it with the official Soviet translation of it into English. The Russian has the precise phrase that Brezhnev used, *formirovaniye novogo chelovieka*, which the authorized translation renders as 'the moulding of the new man' (*The Programme of the Communist Party of the Soviet Union* (FLPH, Moscow, 1961), p. 106).

261 A résumé of the differences between socialism and communism, as Soviet Marxism-Leninism understands them, can be found in *A Guide to Marxism*, pp. 99–107.

262 *Pravda*, 31 March 1971. Brezhnev began by saying that this was also the formula adopted at the Twenty-third Party Congress of 1964. He was, of course, using the expression 'world war' in the Soviet, not in the Western, sense (see pp. 38–9).

263 A concise exposition of the *Soviet* understanding of the meaning of 'peaceful coexistence' can be found in *A Guide to Marxism*, pp. 164–6.

264   This ignores those wars which are begun by accident. But these are, by definition, irrational, and therefore not susceptible to rational analysis. I have consequently ignored them here.

265   I use the term 'propaganda statements' here, because that is how they would be regarded by the Westerners in question. The Russians, of course, would describe them as 'statements of policy'.

266   The West, of course, had; but the chief purpose of the midnight despatch of the Soviet ambassadors round the capitals of the Western world was to ensure that the missiles were not fired.

267   *The Military Balance, 1974-1975* (Institute of Strategic Studies, 1974), p. 7.

268   Captain S. W. Roskill, DSC, RN, *The War at Sea, 1939-1945* (HMSO, 1961), vol. 3, part 2, pp. 17-19.

269   *Jane's Fighting Ships, 1967-68* (David & Charles), pp. 456-9.

270   Andrei Amalrik, *Can Russia Survive Until 1984?* (Allen Lane, 1970).

271   See, for instance, *The Programme of the Communist Party of the Soviet Union*, p. 56.

272   For a Soviet acknowledgment of the strategic importance of the territory in question, see *BSE*, 2nd ed., vol. 45, p. 187.

273   For a Stalinist statement that the Finns began it, see *BSE*, 2nd ed., vol. 39, p. 511. For a more modern statement, see *Diplomaticheskii Slovar'*, 2nd ed., vol. 3, p. 276.

274   *BSE*, 3rd ed., vol. 5, p. 282.

275   14 February 1974.

276   *Red Star*, 19 April 1973.

277   *Marxism-Leninism on War and Army*, p. 392, where it says that the war in question 'may be' nuclear but goes on in the next sentence to say that nuclear weapons 'will' play the decisive role.

278   *Red Star* said so, clearly and unmistakably, on 19 April 1973.

## Chapter 3   The Soviet Concept of Peace

1   Although I account myself reasonably fluent in two Western European languages besides my own, it would be foolish for me to imagine that I have anything like the same depth of comprehension of the meanings of words in either one of them that I have of my mother tongue. So any analysis in this chapter of the meaning of what the West means by the word 'peace' should perhaps be taken as being confined to what I think that the English-speaking world understands by it.

2   Not 'communist'; because what the West usually terms 'the communist countries' have not yet achieved communism, nor do they claim to have done so. They do claim, however, to have reached the transitional stage of socialism; and they describe themselves as being socialist countries. For a succinct account of the essential differences between socialism and communism, as Marxism-Leninism understand these terms, see, for instance, P. J. Wiles, *The Political Economy of Communism* (Blackwell, 1964), pp. 331-66; or my own *A Guide to Marxism* (Faber, 1966), pp. 101-7.

3   *A Dictionary Of Philosophy* (Progress Publishers, Moscow, 1967), p. 122.

4   *The Fundamentals of Marxism-Leninism* (FLPH, Moscow, 1963), pp. 77–8.
5   *Ibid., passim.*
6   See, for instance, the entry under 'development' in *A Dictionary Of Philosophy* for a statement of this.
7   And once again it must be remembered that it is *authoritative* Soviet opinion with which this book is exclusively concerned.
8   From a Western point of view, that is. The latest edition of the encyclopaedia has not yet got far enough to enable us to know whether 'peace' in our present sense is going to be discussed in it.
9   *Entsiklopedicheskii Slovar'* (St Petersburg, 1896).
10  Speech at the Seventh Party Congress.
11  *Peredishka*, which is the Russian for 'breathing-space', was the very word that Lenin used to describe the Treaty of Brest-Litovsk. Among several instances, his speech at the Seventh Party Congress furnishes as good an example as any.
12  See, for instance, *Strange and Monstrous* (1918) and also his speech to the Seventh Party Congress.
13  N. S. Khrushchev, *Report to the Twenty-Second Congress of the Communist Party of the Soviet Union* (Soviet Booklet No. 80, London, 1961), p. 25.
14  *Observer*, 10 February 1974.
15  The original intention had been to hold it in Sheffield; but the Attlee Government refused entry visas for most of the communist delegates from abroad, whom the organizers wished to attend. Accordingly, they decided to shift the venue to Warsaw. The Congress opened in the latter city only five days after the decision to move was taken. The fact that this was possible when there were 1,756 delegates to be accommodated, and when, in addition, much of Warsaw was still in ruins, demonstrates the importance which the Soviet Government at that time attached to the 'Peace Campaign'.
16  The full text can be found in the *Daily Worker*, 23 November 1950.
17  It has since changed its name to the *Morning Star*.

## Chapter 4   The Soviet Concept of Neutrality

1   See, for instance, H. Lauchterpacht (ed.), *Oppenheim's International Law* (Longmans Green, 1955), 7th ed., vol. 2, pp. 663–4.
2   I am speaking here of popular Western usage. As I have said, many Western international lawyers take a much stricter view, which closely resembles the Russian.
3   When American support for Britain increased still further, though without reaching the stage of declaring war on Germany, the Americans themselves realized that they could no longer fairly describe themselves as 'neutral', and therefore adopted the appellation 'non-belligerent'.
4   *Oppenheim's International Law* gives both 'permanent neutrality' and 'perpetual neutrality'. The latter, however, is the term it clearly prefers; and I have therefore followed its example.
5   *Diplomaticheskii Slovar'* (1961), vol. 2, p. 396.
6   Article 42 of the Charter of the United Nations.
7   *Diplomaticheskii Slovar'* (1961), vol. 2, pp. 394–5.

8   See Article 5 of the Peace Treaty between Russia and Lithuania of
    12 July 1920 (*Dokumenty Vneshnei Politiki SSSR*—hereafter
    referred to as *DVP*—vol. 3, p. 32) and Article 5 of the Peace Treaty
    between Russia and Estonia of 2 February 1920 (*DVP*, vol. 2,
    p. 342). The Peace Treaty between Russia and Latvia of 11 August
    1920 (*DVP*, vol. 3, pp. 101–21) contains no such clause.
9   *Diplomaticheskii Slovar'* (1961), vol. 2, p. 396.
10  Recent events may well have caused the Russians to alter their
    opinion; but I have not so far come across an authoritative pro-
    nouncement on the matter.
11  Lenin agreed with this dictum. See his speech at the Seventh All-
    Russia Congress of Soviets.
12  *Ibid.*
13  These so-called 'non-aggression pacts' with Estonia, Latvia and
    Lithuania must not be confused with the Peace Treaties which the
    Soviet Union signed with each of them in 1920. The dates of the
    actual non-aggression pacts were 4 May 1932, 5 February 1932,
    and 28 September 1926, respectively. The texts can be found in
    *DVP*, vol. 15, documents nos 201 and 67, and *DVP*, vol. 9,
    document no. 271, respectively.
14  The date of the original treaty with Germany was 24 April 1926,
    and it was to last for five years. On 24 June 1931, a protocol was
    signed in Moscow, which extended the life of the treaty for an
    unspecified number of years.
15  Formally, this statement is incorrect. Estonia was not accused by
    the Russians of having violated her Treaty of Neutrality, but of
    being unable to maintain her neutrality against German pressure.
    With Estonian 'agreement', the Russians therefore moved in.
16  For details of the Soviet proposals, see *Soviet News*, 22 April 1959,
    and 6 May 1959.
17  In the case of Germany, when the Paris treaties were signed; in the
    case of Japan, when the revised treaty was finally ratified.
18  The 1971 edition of *Diplomaticheskii Slovar'* defines peacetime
    neutrality as consisting of 'not being a member of military blocs'.
    It is clear from the context that, in order to qualify as a peacetime
    neutral, one must refrain from belonging to communist military
    blocs as well as to imperialist ones.
19  Of course, in the period that immediately followed the break
    between Stalin and Tito, Yugoslavia ceased to be described as a
    'socialist' country; but instead she was declared to have become an
    'enemy of the USSR' (and therefore, incidentally, still not neutral).
    Since 1955, however, relations between the two countries have
    much improved; and, by Soviet reckoning, Yugoslavia is now a
    socialist country once more (and therefore still not neutral).
20  I hope to include a chapter on the National Liberation Movement
    in a future volume.
21  The best studies of 'neutralism' in English of which I am aware are:
    Peter Lyon, *Neutralism* (Leicester University Press, 1963) and
    Laurence W. Martin (ed.), *Neutralism and Non-Alignment* (Praeger,
    1962). There is also a brief, but illuminating, discussion of it in the
    RIIA's *Survey of International Affairs, 1954.*
22  Yugoslavia, 1945–8.
23  The countries attending the Belgrade Conference were: Afghanistan,
    Algeria, Burma, Cambodia, Ceylon, Congo, Cuba, Cyprus, Ethiopia,

Ghana, Guinea, India, Indonesia, Iraq, Lebanon, Mali, Morocco, Nepal, Saudi Arabia, Somalia, Sudan, Tunisia, UAR, Yemen, and Yugoslavia. This cannot claim to be a definitive list of the 'neutralist' countries of the world, but it is a fair sample.

24    L. Modjoryan, 'Neutrality' (*New Times*, February 1956).
25    E. A. Korovin, 'The Problem of Neutrality Today' (*International Affairs*, 1958, no. 3).
26    A recent example of the use of the adjective 'neutralist' can be found in *Kratkii Politicheskii Slovar'* (1971), p. 174. When it comes to the choice of nouns, this work prefers 'neutralism' to 'positive neutrality'.
27    In L. Modjoryan's speech at the Seventh Congress of the International Association of Democratic Lawyers in 1960, she frequently uses 'neutral' when she means 'neutralist', but never the other way round—cf. *Legal Aspects of Neutrality: Proceedings of the Third Commission* (Publications of the International Association of Democratic Lawyers, Brussels, n.d.), pp. 109–12.
28    *Kratkii Politicheskii Slovar'*, p. 174. Interestingly enough, the *Dictionary of Diplomacy* also states that it contains an entry which in fact is not to be found, this time for 'perpetual neutrality'. See vol. 2, p. 374, of the 1971 edition.
29    *Ibid.*

## Chapter 5    Theory and Practice

1    Sir Eric Teichman, *Affairs of China* (Methuen, 1938), pp. 65–6.
2    *Krasnoznamennyi Dal'nevostochnyi* (Voenizdat, 1971), pp. 110–15.
3    *Narodnoye Khozyaistvo SSSR 1961 gody* (Gosstatizdat, 1962), p. 8.
4    This version is taken from the second edition of the *BSE*, vol. 39, p. 511. This volume appeared in 1956, but subsequent Soviet writing has continued to tell essentially the same story. See, for instance, *Voennaya Istoriya: Uchebnik*, published in 1971 by the Soviet Ministry of Defence.
5    See K. Booth, *The Military Instrument in Soviet Foreign Policy, 1917–1971* (RUSI, 1974).
6    Colonel Repington, *After the War: A Diary* (Constable, 1922), p. 329.
7    *Ibid.*, p. 331.
8    *La Conférence de Moscou pour la limitation des armaments* (Commissariat du Peuple aux Affaires Etrangères, Moscow, 1923).
9    Repington, *op. cit.*, p. 331.
10    *BSE*, 1st ed., vol. 5, p. 463 (also quoted in Raphael Ambramovitch, *The Soviet Revolution*, London, 1963).
11    Carr, *The Bolshevik Revolution* (3 vols, London, 1950–3), vol. 2, p. 311.
12    *Krasnoznamennyi Zakavkazskii* (Voenizdat, 1969), p. 74.
13    For Lenin's attitude towards the 'bourgeois' at this time, see his speech of 6 December 1920, given to a meeting of activists.
14    *Ibid.*
15    See the article on the Red Army in the first edition of the *BSE*, vol. 47, pp. 775–803.
16    Malcolm Mackintosh, *Juggernaut: A History of the Soviet Armed Forces* (Secker & Warburg, 1967), p. 56.
17    Robert Herrick, *Soviet Naval Strategy* (United States Naval Institute, 1971), pp. 3–27.

18   *Voennaya Istoriya: Uchebnik*, p. 141.
19   *Ibid.*, p. 142.
20   *Ibid.*, p. 143.
21   Agesilaus' biographer was a Roman, Cornelius Nepos. Hence the phenomenon of Agesilaus, a Greek, being made to talk in Latin.
22   There are strong hints of this in the writings of both Frunze and Tukhachevsky. For the former, see his *Voenno-Politicheskoe Vospitaniye Krasnoi Armii* of 1922; for Tukhachevsky, see his article 'Voina' ('War') in the first edition of *BSE* and also his *Voprosy Sovremennoi Strategii*.
23   *Poslednii Shturm (Berlinskaya Operatsiya 1945 g.)* (Voenizdat, 1970), p. 435.
24   *Ibid.*
25   The Russians got from the West about 22,000 aeroplanes and just under 13,000 tanks. These figures are insignificant compared with the Russian output.
26   *Narodnoye Khozyaistvo SSSR v 1963 g.* (Statizdat, 1965), p. 167. This figure of 69,662 should be compared with the approximately 2,000,000 motor cars produced annually in Britain nowadays.
27   American official figures quoted in B. B. Schofield's *The Russian Convoys* (Batsford, 1964), p. 213.
28   *Istoriya Velikoi Otechestvennoi Voiny Sovietskogo Soyuza, 1941–1945* (Voenizdat, 1965), vol. 6, p. 72.
29   For a lengthier discussion of the Russians' difficulties, see Geoffrey Jukes, 'Russia: the Perils of Peace' in Parnell's *History of the Second World War*, vol. 7, pp. 2725–9.
30   Quoted in Alfred J. Rieber, *Stalin and the French Communist Party* (Columbia University Press, 1962), p. 114.
31   *Istoriya Voenno-Morskogo Iskusstva* (Voenizdat, 1969), p. 468.
32   *BSE*, 3rd ed., vol. 5, p. 488.
33   *BSE*, 2nd ed., vol. 9, p. 359.
34   *Istoriya Velikoi Otechestvennoi Voiny Sovietskogo Soyuza, 1941–1945*, vol. 4, pp. 513–16 and p. 553.
35   I. Deutscher, *Stalin* (Oxford University Press, 1967), p. 594.
36   Adam B. Ulam, *Expansion and Coexistence* (Secker & Warburg, 1968), p. 465.
37   In evaluating this argument, it should be borne in mind, though Stalin may have forgotten it when he gave vent to his outburst about his finger, that there were Soviet troops in Hungary, Bulgaria, Poland and Czechoslovakia, but none in Yugoslavia.
38   Deutscher, *op. cit.*, p. 594.
39   For the visits of the Soviet Ambassadors, see Robert Rhodes James (ed.), *The Czechoslovak Crisis 1968* (Weidenfeld & Nicolson, 1969), pp. 80, 142.
40   *Survey of International Affairs, 1952* (Oxford University Press, 1955), p. 47.
41   A succinct account of this aspect of affairs is to be found in Eleanor Lansing Dulles, *Berlin: The Wall is not Forever* (University of North Carolina Press, 1967), pp. 109–10.
42   For Lenin's declared intention to attack the 'bourgeois' so soon as he was strong enough, see his speech of 6 December 1920 to a meeting of Party activists.
43   *Observer*, 10 February 1974.

# Select
# Bibliography

## 1  The classics of Marxism-Leninism on the subject of war

MARX, K. No single work by Marx devoted to the subject of war exists. His
views must be learnt from a careful compilation of odd paragraphs or
sentences scattered throughout his writings. The nearest that comes to
a single opus on the subject is probably *The Civil War in France*,
together with Engels' 'Introduction'. Apart from this, the best means
for the ordinary reader of assessing Marx's views on the subject of war
is to consult the indexes to such extracts from his total opus as *Marx-
Engels: Selected Works* (FLPH, Moscow, 1962) or *Marx-Engels:
Selected Correspondence* (FLPH, Moscow, 1956).

ENGELS, F. Most of what Engels wrote on the subject of war was written
by him in English; but, apart from the selection contained in that
admirable little volume compiled by W. H. Chaloner and W. O.
Henderson, and entitled *Engels as a Military Critic* (Manchester
University Press, 1959), most of it nowadays is difficult of access.
Ironically, the selection translated into Russian and published by
Voenizdat in 1957 under the title *F. Engels: Izbranniye Voenniye
Proizvedeniya* is probably more readily available to those Englishmen
who happen to speak Russian. Apart from the above, there is an important work by Engels on the subject of war which is always easy to find
in an English translation, and that is *Anti-Dühring*. The work itself is
not a treatise on war; but the Appendix, entitled 'Infantry Tactics
Derived from Material Causes', and Part 2 of the work itself are
obligatory reading for anyone wanting to make a serious study of the
communist theory of war.

LENIN, V. I. The serious student will wish to pursue every reference to
military matters contained in the several indexes to the fifth Russian
edition of Lenin's works. The less serious student will find most of his
needs covered by the two-volume compendium *V. I. Lenin o Voine,
Armii i Voennoi Nauke* (Voenizdat, 1957), which contains the greater
part of what Lenin wrote on military subjects. There are, however,
serious omissions from both the above-mentioned works, of which by
far the most important is *Vypiski i Zamechaniya na Knigu Klauzevitsa
'O Voine i Vedenii Voin'*. This was first published in Moscow in 1928
as part of the *Leninskii Sbornik XII*, which itself has recently been
reprinted by Klaus Reprint Ltd, Nendeln, Leichtenstein, in 1966. The
*Vypiski* are fundamental for a proper understanding of the Soviet
theory of war; and it is highly significant that it has been omitted from
the fifth Russian edition of Lenin's *Works*, the so-called 'complete'
edition. It has also been omitted from the so-called *Collected Works* in

English. There is no doubt that the work is still being studied attentively by Soviet officers, because references to it are continually being found in Soviet military writing, even today.

CLAUSEWITZ, GENERAL CARL VON, *Vom Kriege*. There is no really satisfactory translation of this work in English: the best is that by Colonel J. J. Graham, of which a new edition in three volumes was published by Routledge & Kegan Paul in 1962. Though Clausewitz was not, of course, a Marxist, a great deal of his thought is inherently congenial to Marxism; and he is accepted by Marxism-Leninism as one of its prime authorities on war. Those wishing to study the Soviet view of war should therefore read the *whole* of Clausewitz, and not just the snippets actually quoted by Lenin. Still less should they read the condensed versions in English occasionally to be met with in paperback.

## 2   The Soviet view of war from 1917 to the death of Stalin

*BSE* (1st ed.). The numerous volumes of this encyclopaedia contain a large number of entries on the subject of war; though the reader must always remember that, though the first twenty-seven volumes were published in the seven years from 1926 to 1933, volume 28 did not appear until 1937, and the final volume not until 1947. The slightest acquaintance with Soviet history will indicate that a marked change of tone was likely to take place, and did in fact take place, between the first of the volumes and the last. Rothstein's splendid, lucid, scholarly analysis of war as seen from a Marxist viewpoint would never have appeared in print, if the volume containing the entry 'Voina' had not happened to be among those published in the 'twenties. Incidentally, Tukhachevsky's contribution, which forms part 2 of the 'Voina' article, is more famous than Rothstein's, but nowhere near so valuable.

*BSE* (2nd ed.). Although some of the later volumes appeared after the death of Stalin, the tone of the writing is markedly Stalinist in feeling. Indeed, the articles on war, military science and a number of related subjects were published while Stalin was still alive.

FRUNZE, M. V., *Izbranniye Proizvedeniya* (Voenizdat, 1951).

SHAPOSHNIKOV, MARSHAL B. M., *Mozg Armii* (Moscow, 1929). The famous work on the way that a General Staff functions by the Soviet Chief of the General Staff and Deputy People's Commissar for Defence.

STALIN, J. V., *Works* (Moscow, 1953). Stalin's views on war are scattered, like those of Marx, and have to be tracked down throughout the thirteen volumes of the Moscow edition, together with the three additional volumes, available only in Russian, published in 1967 by Stanford UP under the editorship of Robert H. McNeal.

TARANCHUK, M. V., *O Postoyanno Deistvuyushchikh Faktorakh Reshayushchikh Sud'bu Voiny* (Voenizdat, 1952). A work devoted entirely to an uncritical, but detailed exposition of Stalin's 'permanently operating factors deciding the outcome of a war'.

TRIANDAFILLOV, V. K., *Kharakter Operatsii Sovremennykh Armii* (Moscow, 1932). This work by the then Deputy Chief of Staff of the Red Army is useful for its views on the handling of troops in a possible war in the 'thirties, but is absolutely invaluable for its final chapter, which explains in detail how captured territory was to be 'sovietized'.

TUKHACHEVSKY, MARSHAL M. N., *Izbranniye Proizvedeniya* (Voenizdat, 1964).

ERICKSON, PROFESSOR J., *The Soviet High Command: A Military-Political History, 1918–1941* (Macmillan, 1962). The classic work on the subject.

GARTHOFF, R. L., *How Russia Makes War* (Allen & Unwin, 1954). This book, which was an epoch-making work in its day, is more concerned with strategy and tactics than with the socio-political aspects of war.

WOLLENBERG, E., *The Red Army: A Study of the Growth of Soviet Imperialism* (Secker & Warburg, 1940). The author was Commander-in-Chief of the short-lived Bavarian Soviet Republic, subsequently fled to Moscow, enlisted in the Red Army, and rose to high rank.

## 3    The Soviet view of war from the death of Stalin to 1968

KOZLOV, S. N. *et al.*, *O Sovietskoi Voennoi Nauke* (Voenizdat, 1964). A radical criticism of Stalin's views on war.

*Marksizm-Leninizm o Voine i Armii.* This important work, published by Voenizdat, ran through four editions between 1958 and 1968, when the fifth edition appeared. This last introduced some important forward-looking changes into the text, and is accordingly listed in the next section.

*Metologicheskiye Problemy Voennoi Teorii i Praktiki* (1st ed., Voenizdat, 1966). This is the most boring book I know, with the possible exception of the second edition, which is listed in the next section; but it is essential reading for anyone who wishes to keep up with the developments in the Soviet view of war.

SOKOLOVSKY, MARSHAL V. D. (ed.), *Voennaya Strategiya.* The three editions of this work were published by Voenizdat in 1962, 1963 and 1968 respectively. An English translation of the first edition was published by Praeger in 1963 under the title of *Military Strategy*.

KINTNER, W. R., and SCOTT, H. F., *The Nuclear Revolution in Soviet Military Affairs* (University of Oklahoma Press, 1968). The best study of this period available in English.

PARRISH, M., *The Soviet Armed Forces: Books in English, 1950–1967* (Stanford University Press, 1970). An invaluable bibliography for those wishing to study this period deeply.

## 4    The Soviet view of war from 1969 to 1972

*BSE* (3rd ed.). This edition of the encyclopaedia has not yet appeared in its entirety; but those volumes that have already been published shed a good deal of light on recent developments in the Soviet view of war. See especially the articles entitled 'Voina' and 'Voennaya Nauka' in volume 5.

LOMOV, COLONEL-GENERAL N. A., *Nauchno-Tekhnicheskii Progress i Revolyutsiya v Voennom Dele* (Voenizdat, 1973).

*Marksizm-Leninizm o Voine i Armii* (Voenizdat, 1968). This, the fifth edition of this famous work, contains some important changes in the text, as compared with previous editions.

*Marxism-Leninism on War and Army* (Progress Publishers, 1972). This English-language version must be a translation of a sixth edition, of which no Russian original has so far been seen in the West, since the text contains still further changes of importance.

*Metodologicheskiye Problemy Voennoi Teorii i Praktiki* (Voenizdat, 1969). The second edition of the work listed in the previous section. Those who feel strong enough to tackle it will have their reward, because it contains a great deal of value for the serious student of the subject.

SAVKIN, COLONEL V. E., *Osnovniye Printsipy Operativnogo Iskusstva i Taktiki* (Voenizdat, 1972). Contains an important section on the value of surprise in modern war.

SIDORENKO, COLONEL A. A., *Nastupleniye* (Voenizdat, 1970). Also in English, translated by US Air Force and on sale to the general public, under the title of *The Offensive*.

SKIRDO, COLONEL M. P., *Narod, Armiya, Polkovodets* (Voenizdat, 1970).

*Voennaya Istoriya: Uchebnik* (Voenizdat, 1971). Mostly a military history, whose chief interest therefore consists in the glimpse it gives into Soviet attitudes towards 'bourgeois' wars of the past. In its final pages it also contains some useful definitions of categories of wars of the present.

ERICKSON, PROFESSOR J., *Soviet Military Power* (RUSI, London, 1971). This study deals with the evolution of the Soviet command structures, and of its thinking and weapons, from 1965 to 1970.

HERRICK, R. W., *Soviet Naval Strategy* (US Naval Institute, 1971). An outline of Soviet naval strategy and of Soviet shipbuilding programmes from the birth of the Red Navy to recent times.

MCCGWIRE, PROFESSOR M. (ed.), *Soviet Naval Developments: Capability and Context* (Praeger, 1973). The papers contained in this compendium cover a wide range of Soviet naval affairs.

SCOTT, H. F., *Soviet Military Doctrine: Its Continuity, 1960–1970* (Stanford University Press, 1971).

THEBERGE, J. D. (ed.), *Soviet Seapower in the Caribbean: Political and Strategic Implications* (Praeger, 1973).

WOLFE, T. W., *Soviet Naval Interaction with the United States and its Influence on Soviet Naval Development* (Rand, 1972).

## 5  Soviet critiques of 'bourgeois' wars and 'bourgeois' military thinking

*BSE* (1st, 2nd and 3rd editions). Each contains a large number of articles on 'bourgeois' wars, 'bourgeois' battles and 'bourgeois' military thinking. The date of the relevant volume must of course be ascertained, in order to set the criticism in its proper context. The first edition's articles on naval matters, for instance, appeared at a time when the Red Navy hardly existed, and when the British and American navies' command of the seas was an obvious fact which was really not worth disputing. As Soviet naval pretensions grew, and with them the size of their navy, the tone of the subsequent editions changed considerably on matters concerned with the navies of Great Britain and America.

SKOPIN, V. I., *Militarizm* (Voenizdat, 1956). The classic Soviet critique of 'bourgeois' attitudes to war.

STROKOV, COLONEL A. A., *Istoriya Voennogo Iskusstva*. The two volumes of this massive history of warfare treat the subject from the earliest times to the First World War, and were published by Voenizdat in 1965 and 1967 respectively. They contain useful assessments from a Soviet point of view of many of the best-known Western military thinkers.

# Index

(Note: Since Marx's views on military matters were mostly identical with those of Engels, and since the latter is regarded by the Soviet Union as the founder of communist military science, only those views are listed under 'Marx' which were peculiarly his.)